TOEFL
토플 초보를 위한
기본독해

정연재

중앙대학교 영어영문학과와 같은 학교 대학원 영어영문학과를 졸업하였다.
고등학교 영어교사, 토플·토익 강사로 여러 해 영어를 가르쳤고,
도서출판 고려원 부설 「고려원어학연구원」 원장으로 재직하면서
많은 영어 교재들을 연구하고 개발하였다.
저서로는 《좋은 지문 다 모은 테마영문독해》(전7권)
《TOEFL에 자주 나오는 1000단어》《TOEFL 초보를 위한 기본독해》
《영미문화사전》 등이 있다.

TOEFL 초보를 위한 기본독해

편저자 정연재
2002년 9월 25일 초판 1쇄 발행
2005년 4월 1일 초판 7쇄 발행
발행처 영어포럼
발행인 정연재
편 집 이병일
디자인 김남주 정혜경
마케팅 김용구

(우) 121-883 서울시 마포구 합정동 91-11호 2층
(전화) 02-323-7901 (팩스) 02-323-7902
등록 1999년 2월 2일 제 11-169호
TOEFL Beginner's Reading Comprehension © Jung Yun Jae 2002 Printed in Korea
ISBN 89-88891-07-4 13740

값 11,000원

TOEFL

English forum

Beginner's
Reading Comprehension

토플 초보를 위한
기본독해

정연재 편저

영어포럼
ENGLISH·FORUM

영어로 된 정보를 빠르고 정확하게 습득할 수 있는가를 평가하는 것이 토플의 목적이다. 따라서 이 책은 영어 학습자들이 영어로 된 정보를 빠르고 정확하게 습득하는 능력을 구체적인 훈련을 통하여 키울 수 있도록 구성하였다.

토플을 준비하는 사람은 토플의 문제 유형에 익숙해지는 것이 중요하지만, 이것에 앞서 효과적인 영문독해를 위한 리딩스킬(reading skill)을 체계적으로 훈련해야 한다. 이 책은 리딩스킬에 대한 훈련을 바탕으로 토플에 접근하도록 구성하였다.

〈Part 1 효과적인 영문독해〉에서는 효과적인 영문독해를 위한 여섯 가지의 열쇠를 제시하였다. 이것은 학습자들이 영문을 읽을 때 항상 염두에 둬야 하는 것이고, 훈련을 통해서 익숙해져야 하는 것이다.

〈Part 2 독해기초연습 1〉은 좀더 구체적인 독해 훈련을 위한 part이다. 독해력 향상을 위해서는 좋은 글을 많이 읽어야 하지만, 무턱대고 많이 읽는 것이 방법은 아니다. 리딩스킬을 여러 가지 훈련을 통해서 익혀야 한다. Part 2에서 제시하고 있는 일곱 가지의 훈련은 영어 학습자들이 효과적으로 영문을 읽는 능력을 키워줄 것이다.

〈Part 3 독해기초연습 2〉에서는 토플의 리딩 파트를 분석하여 사실적 이해, 추론적 이해, 종합적 판단 등의 세 가지 유형으로 나누었고, 이를 토플 기출문제를 통하여 훈련할 수 있도록 하였다. 여러분은 이 part를 통해서 토플 리딩 파트의 문제 유형에 익숙해질 수 있고, 또한 영문 정보를 효과적으로 다루는 방법을 배울 수 있을 것이다.

〈Part 4 독해종합연습〉에서는 앞에서 배운 것을 토플 기출문제를 통하여 충분히 연습할 수 있도록 꾸몄다.

여러분은 앞으로 글읽기 훈련을 체계적으로 할 것이지만, 영문을 읽을 때 항상 염두에 둬야 할 것은, 번역을 하지 말아야 한다는 점이다. 우리말 단어를 떠올리지 말고, 우리말 문장을 만들지 말자. 영문을 읽어 가면서 뜻을 머릿속에 바로 그릴 수 있어야 한다. 이것이 이 책의 궁극적인 목적이다. 이것은 또한 영어를 학습하는 여러분의 목표가 되어야 할 것이다.

이 책의 특징

1. 토플 초보를 위한 책이다

토플의 리딩 파트는 대학에서의 학문활동과 관련된 다양하고 비교적 짧은 글의 이해를 묻는다. 토플에 처음 입문하는 사람은 무엇보다도 먼저 토플 지문에 익숙해지는 것이 필요하다. 이 책에서는 토플 초보가 토플에 나오는 지문에 쉽게 익숙해질 수 있도록 비교적 평이한 지문을 선정하였다.

2. 효과적인 영문독해를 위한 리딩스킬이 있다

토플의 주된 목적은 영어로 된 정보를 정확하고 빠르게 습득할 수 있는 능력에 대한 평가에 있다. 따라서 토플 R/C 문제는 영문에 대한 리딩스킬의 숙련이 반드시 필요하다. 이 책에서는 효과적인 영문독해를 위한 여섯 가지의 열쇠를 제시하고, 이를 충분히 익힐 수 있도록 다각도로 구성하였다.

3. 토플 문제의 유형을 완전 분석하였다

토플 문제에는 일정한 유형이 있다. 토플 문제 유형에 대한 분석과 여기에 적응하는 과정은 단순히 시험 요령만을 습득하는 과정은 아니다. 학습자들은 토플 문제에 적응하는 것을 통하여 영어로 된 정보를 효과적으로 얻을 수 있는 능력을 키울 수 있을 것이다. 이 책은 토플 R/C의 문제 유형을 완전 분석하여 체계적으로 정리하였다.

4. 정확한 해석과 해설이 있다

초보자들이 토플을 쉽게 익힐 수 있도록 정확한 해설과 해석을 붙였다. 특히 대부분의 지문에 주제문, 서술문, 결론문 등의 해설을 붙여 독자들이 자연스럽게 영문의 구조를 파악하는 능력을 습득할 수 있도록 하였다.

5. 리딩의 기본서다

토플은 영어에 대한 기본 능력을 묻는 시험이다. 이것은 토플이 어떤 특정 분야의 전문성을 평가하는 시험이 아니라는 것을 의미한다. 따라서 영어를 공부하는 사람들은 누구나 토플에서 제시하는 틀에 따름으로써 높은 학습 성과를 기대할 수 있다. 이 책은 토플 초보자를 위한 책이지만, 영문독해 기술을 익히고자 하는 모든 독자들에게 효과적인 학습서가 될 것이다.

Contents

TOEFL
초보를 위한 기본독해

TOEFL Beginner's Reading Comprehension

Part 1

효과적인 영문독해

번역을 하지 말아야 한다

영어 문장을 눈으로 읽고, 우리말을 머리에 떠올린 다음, 뜻을 새기는 태도를 고쳐야 한다. 우리는 뜻글자인 한자(또는 한문)를 공부하던 태도와 같이 외국어의 단어나 문장의 뜻을 우리 글로 옮기는 작업을 '읽기'라고 생각한다. 이것은 말이나 글의 뜻을 새기는 단계를 지나 번역 작업에 치우친 것이다. 우리가 흔히 '해석'이라고 하는 이 번역 작업은 읽기(reading comprehension, 독해)와 다르다.

영어 문장을 읽어 나갈 때, 대역되는 우리말 단어를 생각하며 번역 문장을 만들고 나서, 다시 그 의미를 새기는 과정은 '독해' 시간을 오래 걸리게 한다. 눈으로 영문을 보는 즉시 바로바로 의미를 떠올리도록 훈련해야 한다. '글'을 읽고 '그림'(의미)을 떠올리는 것이 읽기인데, 중간에 우리말을 끼워넣는 과정을 거치지 말자는 것이다.

다음 글을 읽으면서 머릿속에 그림을 떠올려 보자. 무슨 그림이 떠오르는가.

예문 1

It was a routine flight from Hilo on Hawaii to Kahului 110 miles away. Suddenly, there was a tremendous noise and the top of the plane was torn away! Ninety four passengers dared not move, wondering what would happen next. They need not have worried because Reben Schornsteimer, the pilot, was firmly in control. For 25 minutes they hardly dared to breathe, though there was plenty of unwelcome fresh air "I didn't dare to open my mouth." one of the passengers said later. "I hardly need to tell you how terrified I was." The passengers embraced the pilot who had brought the plane down safely. "I've heard of a plane flying off a roof." joked one of them later, "but never of a roof flying off a plane!"

routíne [ruːtíːn] *adj*. 일상적인, 판에 박힌 treméndous [triméndəs] *adj*. 무시무시한, 굉장한 tear [teər]-tore[tɔːr]-torn[tɔːrn] : 찢다 be in (firmly) contról : (굳건히) 관리하고 있는, 조종하고 있는 off [ɔːf] *prep*. 물체의 표면에서 떨어진 상태를 나타내는 전치사

위의 글을 읽고 비행중인 여객기의 동체 일부가 파손되어 날아간 상황에서 승객들이 겁에 질려 있는 장면, 그리고 침착한 조종사 덕분에 무사히 착륙한 후, 승객들이 기뻐서 기장을 얼싸안고 좋아하는 장면 등이 머릿속에 떠오르면 제대로 읽은 것이다.

해석 1　하와이 힐로에서 110마일 떨어진 카훌루이로 가는 일상적인 비행편이 한 편 있었다. 갑자기 무서운 굉음이 나더니 비행기의 천장이 떨어져 나갔다! 94명의 승객들은 이어서 무슨 일이 일어날지 두려워 감히 꼼짝을 못했다. 로버트 슨스타이머라는 조종사가 훌륭하게 조종하고 있었기 때문에 승객들은 걱정할 필요가 없었다. 반갑지 않은 외부의 신선한 공기가 많이 들어왔지만 승객들은 25분간 거의 숨도 쉴 수가 없었다. 나중에 한 승객이 말했다. "저는 입이 벌어지지 않았어요. 말씀드릴 필요도 없이 얼마나 무서웠는지 몰라요." 승객들이 비행기를 무사히 안착시킨 조종사를 껴안았다. 뒤에 한 승객이 이렇게 농담을 했다. "저는 비행기가 지붕에서 떨어져 날아가는 건 들어봤지만, 비행기에서 지붕이 떨어져 날아가는 것은 들어본 적이 없습니다!"

우리는 다음에서 여러 가지 방법으로 글 읽기 훈련을 하겠지만, 무엇보다도 중요한 것은 글을 읽고 의미를 바로바로 떠올리는 연습이다. 영문을 큰 소리로 읽는 것은 영문을 읽을 때 앞뒤로 왔다갔다 하면서 번역하는 것이 습관이 된 학습자들에게 좋은 학습법이다.

다음 글을 읽고 그림(의미)을 바로바로 떠올리는 연습을 더 해보자.

예문 2

It had been a particularly bad winter in Chicago. Nearly forty inches of snow had fallen in a week. Railway workers at Chicago station didn't know what to do with it. The foreman advised them to shovel it into huge mountains to keep the platforms clear. He told them not to leave any snow on the platforms because it was dangerous for passengers. But it was an impossible task! Suddenly, one of the workers had a bright idea. "I know how to get rid of it," he said. "Let's load it onto this freight train. We can send it south to Mississippi and New Orleans. It'll just melt away." The next day five tons of snow arrived in Memphis, Tennessee. "It's welcome gift," a railway worker said. "We know What to do with it here. We'll send what we can to the children's playground. Some of us have never seen snow before!"

shovel [ʃʌ́vəl]　*n.* 삽　*v.* 삽으로 푸다　freight train 화물열차

해석 2　시카고에서 어느 혹한의 겨울이었다. 1주일간 거의 40인치나 눈이 내렸다. 시카고 역의 철도 노동자들은 어쩔 줄을 몰랐다. 감독은 눈을 큰산으로 퍼내 플랫폼을 치우자고 충고를 했다. 감독은 눈이 플랫폼에 남아있으면 승객들이 위험하니까 깨끗이 치우라고 하였다. 하지만 그건 불가능한 일이었다. 그런데 노동자 한 사람에게 갑자기 좋은 생각이 떠올랐다. "눈을 치우는 방법이 있어요. 눈을 화물열차에 실읍시다. 그걸 미시시피나 뉴올리언즈 등 남부로 보내는 겁니다. 금방 녹을 겁니다." 다음날 눈 5톤이 테네시주 멤피스에 도착하였다. 한 철도 노동자가 말했다. "좋은 선물입니다. 이 눈을 이곳에서 처리할 방법이 있지요. 가능한 양을 아이들의 운동장에 보낼 겁니다. 우리들 중에도 일부는 아직 눈을 한 번도 보지 못했잖아요!"

문단의 구조를 습득한다

문단 내에서 문장들은 논리적·시간적으로 일정한 순서로 조합되는데, '문단의 구조를 습득한다' 는 것은 이 문장들의 순서(sentence order)를 습득하는 것이다. 하나의 주제 아래 통일된 의미를 전달하기 위해 여러 문장들이 일관성 있게 조합된 형식을 '문단'(paragraph)이라고 한다. 이 문단이 구성된 패턴 즉, 문단 구조을 미리 알면 독해를 빨리, 그리고 훨씬 효과적으로 할 수 있다. 대체로 한 문단의 주제문은 맨 앞에 오며, 이어서 주제문을 설명하는 서술문이 오며, 문단의 끝에 결론문이 온다.

어떤 글을 읽을 때 단지 한문장 한문장 읽어나가는 데에만 급급할 것이 아니라, 글의 전체적인 구조 등을 생각하면서 읽어야 독해 실력이 향상될 수 있다.

다음은 전형적인 문단 구조를 갖고 있는 예이다.

예문 3

    <u>Gold, a precious metal, is prized for two important characteristics.</u> <u>First of all</u>, gold has a lustrous beauty that is resistant to corrosion. <u>Therefore</u>, it is suitable for jewelry, coins, and ornamental purposes. Gold never needs to be polished and will remain beautiful forever. <u>For example</u>, a Macedonian coin remains as untarnished today as the day it was minted twenty-three centuries ago. <u>Another important characteristic of gold</u> is its usefulness to industry and science. <u>For many years</u>, it has been used in hundreds of industrial applications. <u>The most recent use of gold</u> is in astronauts' suits. Astronauts wear gold-plated heat shields for protection outside the spaceship. <u>In conclusion, gold is treasured not only for its beauty, but also for its utility.</u>

주제문 (subject sentence)

서술문 (supporting sentences)

결론문 (concluding sentence)

prize *v.* 높이 평가하다 be prized for - ~로 높이 평가되다 lustrous [lʌ́strəs] *adj.* 번쩍이는, 광채나는 be resistant to - ~에 강한, 저항하는 corrosion *n.* 부식, 침식 be súitable for - ~에 어울리는 ornamental [ɔːrnəméntl] *adj.* 장식용의, 장식의 Macedonia *n.* 옛 그리스 북부지방 마케도니아 untarnished [ʌntɑ́ːrniʃt] *adj.* 변색되지 않은, 녹슬지 않은 mint *v.* 화폐를 주조하다(= coin) applicátion *n.* 적용, 사용 ástronaut [ǽstrənɔːt] *n.* 우주비행사 gold-plated heat shields 도금된 열 차단복 be tréasured for - ~이유로 귀하게 소장되다.

해석 3   귀금속인 황금은 두 가지 중요한 특징에서 높이 평가된다. 첫째, 황금은 부식되지 않는 빛나는 아름다움을 가지고 있다. 그러므로 보석이나 동전, 장식용으로 적당하다. 황금은 결코 광택을 내려고 닦을 필요가 없고, 영원히 아름다움을 유지한다. 예를 들면, 마케도니아의 동전은 23세기 전 주조될 당시처럼 오늘날도 녹슬지 않은 채 남아 있다. 황금의 또 다른 중요 특징은 산업과 과학에 활용되는 점이다. 오랜 세월 수백 가지의 산업용에 사용되었다. 가장 최근에 황금이 사용된 것은 우주인들의 복장이다. 우주인들은 우주선 외부로부터 보호하기 위해 도금한 열 보호장비를 입는다. 결론적으로, 황금은 아름다움과 활용도 때문에 소중히 여겨진다.

문단(단락)의 구성요소를 정리하면 다음과 같다.

(1) 주제어/핵심어(topic, main idea, key words, subject word)
- 흔히 첫 문장에 있으며, 그 문단에서 가장 자주 등장하는 말이다.

(2) 주제문(topic sentence, subject sentence)
- 하나의 문단은 반드시 하나의 주제를 갖춘다.
- 일반적으로 문단의 첫 문장인 경우가 대부분이다.
- 문단에서 설명하게 될 주제를 정의하거나 논지의 방향을 제시한다.

(3) 서술문(supporting sentence)
- 서술문은 주제문을 발전시킨다.
- 사실을 열거하거나 예를 들고, 통계, 인용 또는 이유를 제시하면서 주제문을 설명한다.

(4) 결론문(cuncluding sentence)
- 문단을 끝맺으며, 요점을 정리해 준다. 흔히 주제와 같다.

하나의 문단은 '하나의 주제' 만을 논의하며, 문장들이 주제를 벗어나 우왕좌왕하지 않는다 (통일성, unity). 또 한 문단을 구성하는 문장들은 한 주제를 중심으로 논리정연한 순서(logical order)로 전개된다 (일관성, coherence).

Key 3 | 습득한 문단 구조를 바탕으로, 의미어 중심으로 훑어 읽는다 (skimming)

각 단락의 첫 문장과 마지막 문장을 먼저 읽는다. 대체로 각 단락의 첫 문장은 그 단락의 주제를 내포하고, 첫 단락의 첫 문장은 글 전체의 주제를, 마지막 단락의 마지막 문장은 결론을 내포한다. 이때, 자주 등장하는 어구들(대체로 명사)은 보통 글의 핵심어(key world)이므로 기억해 둔다.

초점을 단어 하나하나에 집중하지 않고, 구(phrase) 단위 또는 절(clause) 단위로 훑어 내려가며 시선을 매끄럽게 옮긴다. 중요한 것은 눈에 띄는 어휘를 발견할 때, 되도록 우리말 단어를 찾지 말고 곧바로 '뜻' (의미)을 연상해야 한다. 머릿속에 떠오르는 그림(내용, 의미)을 붙잡도록 해야 한다. 처음에는 영어 문장들이 무슨 뜻인지 모르지만, 몇 문장을 차분히 그렇게 시선을 옮겨가다 보면 '무엇' (주제 또는 핵심어)에 대해 서술하고 있는지 감이 잡힌다. 즉, 전달받은 어떤 내용이 머릿속에 그림으로 잡힌다.

연결어들을 살펴가면서 읽으면 좀더 정확히 그리고 효과적으로 문맥을 파악할 수 있다.

모르는 단어가 나올 경우, 문장과 문단의 전후 맥락을 통해 그 단어의 뜻을 추측하여 읽는다.

다음 글에서 먼저 주제문을 파악한 후에, 볼드체를 중심으로 훑어 읽어 보면서 머릿속에 떠오르는 그림을 붙잡아 보자.

예문 4

In very cold parts of the world, scientists study the past. They find animals frozen in the ice. The animals look alive, **but they are not. They were frozen many years ago.**

Russian scientists found a large animal called a mastodon in the ice. It looked like an elephant. **But** it was larger, and it had lots of hair. **In fact, the elephant is the mastodon's younger cousin.**

In 1984, American scientists were working near the North Pole. They found the body of a man frozen in the ice. This man went to the North Pole **in 1846**. He died, and his friends buried him in the ice. **Today**, his body looks the same. **It did not change at all in the ice.**

These facts interest doctors. They have some patients who are very sick. No one can help these patients. **But** some day there may be a new medicine for them. These doctors want to save people for the future. **Maybe patients can be frozen until there is medicine to help them.**

alíke [əláik] *adj.* 똑같은 mástodon [mǽstədàn] *n.* 마스토돈(거대한 코끼리 종류) North Pole : 북극

해석 4

지구의 아주 추운 지방에서 과학자들은 과거를 연구한다. 그들은 얼음 속에 냉동되어 있는 동물들을 찾는다. 동물들은 똑같아 보이지만 그러나 다르다. 그것들은 여러 해 전에 냉동되었다.

러시아 과학자들은 얼음 속에서 마스토돈이라고 하는 큰 동물을 발견하였다. 코끼리 같았다. 그러나 좀더 크고, 털이 더 많았다. 사실, 코끼리는 마스토돈의 사촌동생뻘이다.

1984년에 미국 과학자들이 북극 근처에서 작업을 하고 있었다. 그들은 얼음 속에 냉동되어 있는 한 남자의 시체를 발견하였다. 이 남자는 1946년에 북극에 갔다. 그가 죽자 동료들이 얼음 속에 그를 묻었다. 오늘 그의 시체는 그대로이다. 얼음 속에서 전혀 변하지 않았다.

이 사실들이 의사들의 흥미를 끈다. 그들에겐 심하게 아픈 환자들이 있다. 아무도 이 환자들을 도울 수 없다. 그러나 언젠가 그들을 위한 새로운 약품이 나올 것이다. 이 의사들은 미래를 위해 사람들을 보존해 두려 한다. 이들을 도울 수 있는 약품이 있을 때까지 환자들이 냉동될 수도 있을 것이다.

구와 절 단위로 끊어 읽는다

구나 절 단위로 문장을 끊어 읽는 것이 빨리 읽는 데 크게 도움을 준다.
구·절 단위로 끊어서 내리 해석해 나가면 내용이해나 해석 역시 크게 도움이 된다.
'직독 직해'라고 하는 속독방식이 바로 이것이다.
구·절의 핵심인 의미어에 초점을 주면서 읽는다. 이 의미어들은 말할 때도 강세가 주어지므로 내용이해에 결정적인 역할을 하는 핵심어이다.

(1) 구 단위로 끊어 읽는다.

예문 5

The very great advances / in science / just before and after the midpoint / of the twentieth century / have caused / educators / in the United States / to realize / that science teaching / in the future / must differ / from science teaching / in the past. //

advánce [ædvǽns] *n*. 진보 mídpoint [mídpɔint] *n*. 중간점 díffer from ~ : ~와 구별하다

해석 5

매우 위대한 진보 / 과학에서 / 중엽을 바로 전후하여 / 20세기의 / 원인이 되었다 / 교육자들에게 / 미국의 / 깨닫게 / 과학교육이 / 미래에 / 달라야 한다 / 과학교육과 / 과거에 //

(2) 접속사, 관계사, 의문사 등의 앞에서 끊어 읽는다. 즉, 절은 반드시 끊어 읽는다.

예문 6

Generally they fly away or hide, / because they know / that most people want to throw stones at them. //

해석 6

흔히 그들은 날아가서 숨는다 / 그들이 알고 있기 때문에 / 대부분의 사람들이 자기들에게 돌을 던지고 싶어한다는 것을 //

예문 7

How nice it would be / if all the creatures / we met out of doors / tame, / and would play with us / as they do in the fairy stories. //

créature [krí:tʃər] *n.* 피조물, 동물 tame [teim] *adj.* 길들여진, 순한

해석 7　얼마나 좋을까 / 만일 모든 동물들이 / 우리가 야외에서 만나는 / 길들여져 / 우리와 함께 논다면 / 동화에서 그들이 하는 것처럼 //

(3) 구두점(. : ; ! ?) 등이 있는 곳에서 끊어 읽는다.

예문 8

There are four seasons in a year: / spring, / summer, / fall and winter. //

해석 8　1년에는 4계절이 있다 : / 봄, / 여름, / 가을, / 겨울. //

예문 9

There are three qualities which distinguish perfect concentration: / it should be intense, / prolonged, / and voluntary. //

distínguish [distíŋgwiʃ] *v.* 구별짓다, 뛰어나다 concentrátion [kɑnsəntréiʃən] *n.* 집중 inténse [inténs] *adj.* 강렬한
prolónged [prəlɔ́:ŋd] *adj.* 연장된, 늘어난 vóluntary [vɑ́lənteri] *adj.* 자발적인

해석 9　완전한 집중을 알수 있는 3가지 특징이 있다 : / 그것은 강도이다, / 지속성, / 그리고 자발성. //

＊단어의 분류

1. 의미어(meaningful words)
   명사, 동사, 형용사, 부사, 의문사, 지시사 등
   의미를 가지고 있어서 글이 내용을 알 수 있다.
   문장의 핵심어가 된다.
   강세가 있고, 고음, 장음으로 발음되는 경향이 있어, 뚜렷하게 들린다.

2. 기능어(functional words)
   관사, 전치사, 접속사, 관계사, 대명사, 조동사, be동사 등
   스스로는 의미가 없다.
   단어나 문장들을 서로 연결해주거나, 의미어를 보조하는 기능적인 단어들이다.
   강세가 없고, 저음, 단음으로 발음되는 경향이 있어, 뚜렷하게 들리지 않는다.

다음 글을 구 · 절 단위로 읽어보자.

예문 10

For breakfast, / my family and I / usually eat / as we did / in South Vietnam; / in Asia, / breakfast / is the principal meal / of the day. // We begin / with steamed or fried rice / served with a fried egg. // For the main dishes / we have meat / boiled with soy sauce / and soup / which is cooked / with chicken, / pork, / and vegetables. // After eating, / we usually have hot tea / and sometimes coffee as well. // After a long night, / breakfast gives us / much energy / so that we can work all day / until the evening. //

príncipal [prínsəpəl] *adj.* 주요한, 주된 steam [sti:m] *v.* 찌다, 증기를 내다 fry [frai] *v.* (기름으로) 튀기다 steamed or fried rice : 밥 main dish : 주식 boil [bɔil] *v.* 삶다 soy sauce : 간장 soup [su:p] *n.* 국, 수프 pork [pɔːrk] *n.* 돼지고기 végetable [védʒətəbəl] *n.* 채소

해석 10

아침식사로 / 가족과 나는 / 늘 먹는다 / 우리가 하던대로 / 베트남에서; / 아시아에서 / 아침식사는 / 중요한 식사이다 / 그날의. // 우리는 시작한다 / 솥에 삶고 튀긴 밥으로 / 달걀 후라이가 같이 나오는. // 주식으로는 / 우리는 고기를 먹는다 / 간장을 넣어 삶은 / 국과 / 요리된 / 닭고기, / 돼지고기, / 그리고 채소. // 식사 후에는 / 우리는 늘 뜨거운 차를 마신다 / 그리고 가끔은 커피도. // 긴 밤이 지난 뒤에, / 아침식사는 우리에게 준다 / 많은 에너지를 / 우리가 종일 일할 수 있도록 / 저녁까지. //

예문 11

On hot days / I feel very lazy / and would prefer to sit quietly / under a tree, / listening / to the birds singing. // The classroom seems / hot and stuffy. // The time / seems to go by / very slowly / when I am in class, / and my thoughts / always drift away / from what the teacher / is saying. // In the evening, / it is difficult / for me / to concentrate / on my homework. // I would rather be enjoying / a picnic / in the mountains. // For all these reasons, / I will be glad / when summer school / is over. //

stuffy [stʌfi] *adj.* 숨막히는, 답답한 drift away : 정처 없이 떠나다, 떠돌다

해석 11

더운 날에 / 나는 매우 나른함을 느낀다 / 그리고 차라리 조용히 앉아 / 나무 밑에 / 듣고 싶다 / 새가 노래하는 것을. // 교실은 같다 / 덥고 숨이 막히는. // 시간은 / 가는 것 같다 / 아주 천천히 / 내가 수업중일 때는, / 그리고 내 생각은 / 언제나 정처없이 떠돈다 / 선생님이 / 말씀하시는 것. // 저녁에는 / 그것이 어렵다 / 내가 / 집중하기가 / 내 숙제에. // 나는 차라리 즐기리라 / 소풍을 / 산에서.// 이런 모든 이유들 때문에 / 나는 좋을 것이다 / 여름학기가 / 끝날 때. //

Key 5 | 6하원칙을 중심으로 읽는다
(when, where, who, what, how, why)

> 글을 읽을 때는 늘 6하원칙을 파악한다. 글은 대부분 6하원칙에 따라서 의사를 전달하므로, 이 6하원칙을 파악하는 것이 곧, 독해의 목적이라 할 수 있다. 독해 문제는 결국 이 여섯 가지 사항을 묻는 문제이다.
> 고유명사, 지명, 연도를 포함하여 각종 숫자들을 눈여겨보며 읽는다.

다음 글은 피카소의 그림을 통하여 화가로서 피카소의 인생을 시간의 순서에 따라 보여주고 있다.
글에는 언제, 어디서, 누가, 무엇을, 어떻게, 왜 등의 정보가 담겨있다. 이를 염두에 두고 볼드체로 표시된 부분에 좀더 집중해서 읽는다면 글의 정보를 빠르고 정확하게 얻을 수 있다.

예문 12

Picasso's art shows his growth as an artist and his life story. **In 1900, Picasso left Spain for Paris.** Then he painted in the academic style, the orderly manner of **seventeenth-century French artists. Within a year,** he had begun what is called his **Blue Period. By 1906, Picasso** was starting a new phase, the Pink or Rose Period. He used the warmer, softer color, but a harder, more definite line. He became **a Cubist. For about ten years (until around 1917)** he painted the geometric designs of Cubism with his subjects. **Then, in 1917, Picasso** returned to realism, but he did not continue in any one style. **All his work from about 1928 until his death in 1973 was certainly the work of an expressionist, but Picasso's art was always distinctly his own.**

the académic stýle : 학구적인 형식 the órderly mánner : 질서정연한 양식 what is called : 소위 the Blue Period : 푸른 시기 the Pink or Rose Period : 핑크 또는 장미 시기 phase [feiz] *n.* 단계 définite [défənit] *adj.* 한정된, 제한된 Cúbist [kjú:bist] *n.* 입체파 예술가 Cúbism : 입체파 expréssionist [ikspréʃənist] *n.* 표현주의자(*cf.* expréssionism : 표현주의) distínctly [distíŋktli] *adv.* 뚜렷하게, 분명하게

해석 12　피카소의 그림은 화가로서의 성장과 그의 인생을 보여준다. 1900년에 피카소는 스페인을 떠나 파리로 갔다. 그때 그는 17세기 프랑스 화가들의 질서정연한 양식인 학구적인 스타일로 그렸다. 1년 안에 그는 소위 그의 '푸른 시기'를 시작하였다. 1906년까지 피카소는 새로운 단계인 핑크 혹은 장미시기를 시작하였다. 그는 좀더 따뜻하고 부드러운 색과 더 딱딱하고 제한된 선을 사용하였다. 그는 입체파 화가가 된 것이다. 약 10년 동안 (1917년경까지) 그는 입체파의 기하학적 디자인을 자신의 주제로 삼아 그렸다. 그러나 1917년에 피카소는 사실주의로 돌아온다. 하지만 그는 어떤 하나의 스타일로 계속하지 않았다. 1928년부터 1973년 죽을 때까지 그의 모든 작품은 분명히 표현주의자의 작품이었다. 그러나 피카소의 예술은 언제나 뚜렷이 자신만의 것이었다.

예문 13

　　In industry, especially on assembly lines, robots are better workers than human beings. Unlike men, robots work in boring, dirty or unpleasant jobs without complaint or absence. Robots also work in jobs too dangerous over a long period of time for men, jobs which cause disease, or jobs in which frequent accidents occur with fumes or radiation. In addition, robots on the assembly line are more effective than men; they can work 24 hours a day, and their "up time" (that is, the time they are operable) is nearly 95%, as opposed to 75% for the average human worker. Furthermore, they are accurate; human error is responsible for a 10% rejection rate, but the robots' rejection rate is zero. For all these reasons, industries are moving from human to robot employees.

assémbly line : 조립공정 bóring [bɔ́:riŋ] *adj.* 지겨운 without compláint or ábsence : 불평이나 결근 없이 fume [fju:m] *n.* (유독)가스 radiátion [reidiéiʃən] *n.* 방사능 up time : 작동시간 óperable [ápərəbəl] *adj.* 작동하는 as oppósed to ~ : ~와는 대조적으로, 달리 áccurate [ǽkjərit] *adj.* 정확한 be respónsible for ~ : ~에 책임이 있는 rejéction rate : 불량률

해석 13　산업에서, 특히 조립공정에서 로봇은 인간보다 더 나은 일꾼이다. 인간과는 달리, 로봇은 지겹고, 더럽고, 유쾌하지 않은 일을 불평이나 결근도 없이 수행한다. 또한 로봇은 인간을 대신해서 아주 장기간 매우 위험한 일들이나 질병을 유발하는 일들, 유독가스나 방사능으로 흔히 사고가 생기는 일들을 수행한다. 게다가 조립공정에 있는 로봇은 인간보다 더 효율적인 것이, 하루 24시간 일할 수 있는 데다, 그들의 작동시간은 평균적인 인간 작업자의 75%와는 대조적으로 거의 95%이다. 게다가, 그들은 정확하다. 인간의 실수는 불량률이 10%인데, 로봇의 불량률은 제로이다. 이 모든 이유들 때문에 산업이 인간에서 로봇 일꾼에게로 이동하고 있다.

필요한 부분만 읽는다(scanning)

우리는 여러 가지 이유로 글을 읽는다. 영문을 읽을 때도 마찬가지다. 전체를 꼼꼼하게 읽어야 할 필요도 있지만, 필요한 부분만 읽어야 할 경우도 있다. 시험을 준비하는 학습자라면, 문제가 요구하는 답을 찾기 위해 필요한 부분만 읽는 훈련을 많이 해야 한다. 물론 이런 훈련은 시험을 준비하는 학습자에게만 유용한 것은 아니다. 영어 정보를 습득하려는 학습자에게도 필요한 훈련이다.

이상에서 우리는 효과적인 영문독해를 위해 꼭 필요한 사항을 검토해 보았다. 좋은 글을 많이 읽는 것이 독해력 향상에 필요하지만 무턱대고 읽는 것은 효과적인 방법이 아니다. 우리는 다음 장에서 좀더 구체적인 방법으로 글 읽기 훈련을 할 것이다.

그러면 효과적인 영문독해를 위한 여섯 가지 사항을 다시 한번 검토해 보고 다음 글을 읽어보자.

예문 14

Some people believe that if they read too fast their comprehension will suffer. However, research shows that as you learn to read rapidly, comprehension may even better than it was before. Such improvement generally is attributed to the fact that the more rapidly you read, the more you must concentrate on what is being read. Therefore, you comprehend more.

rápidly = fast impróvement [imprúːvment] *n*. 향상 be attríbuted to ~ : ~때문이다, 탓이다 The more A, the more B : A하면 할수록 더욱 B하다 cóncentrate [kánsəntreit] *v*. 집중하다

예문 14

어떤 사람들은 글을 너무 빨리 읽게 되면 이해하기가 힘들 것이라고 믿고 있다. 그러나 빨리 읽을 때 전보다 이해가 훨씬 더 쉬울 것이라는 연구가 있다. 그런 향상은 일반적으로 빨리 읽으면 빨리 읽을수록, 읽는 내용에 더욱 더 집중을 하게 된다는 사실 때문이다. 그러므로 더 많이 이해하게 된다.

예문 15

The Indians walk to the city with many colorful things to sell. There are beautiful baskets, colorful clothes, and hand-made dolls to be sold or traded. The market is always crowded, and the air is filled with the aroma of roasting corn, peanuts, and many strange foods. The tourist may join in the spirited bargaining or merely sit and watch the colorful market place.

sell－sold－sold (팔다) trade [treid] v. 교환, 교역하다 be filled with ~ : ~로 채워지다 aróma [əróumə] n. 향기 roast [roust] v. 굽다 the spírited bárgaining : 활기찬 거래

해석 15

인디언들은 시내를 걸어다니며 여러 가지 형형색색의 물건들을 판다. 예쁜 바구니, 화려한 색상의 옷가지, 수공인형들을 팔거나 교환한다. 시장은 언제나 붐비고, 옥수수나 땅콩, 여러 가지 낯선 음식을 굽는 향기가 대기를 가득 채운다. 여행객들은 이 활기찬 거래에 참가하거나, 그냥 앉아서 화려한 시장을 구경할 수 있다.

예문 16

Recycling aluminum cans conserves energy. In fact, recycling saves 95 percent of the energy needed to make new aluminum from ore. Last year, the aluminum industry saved enough energy through recycling to meet the residential electrical needs of a city the size of Pittsburgh for about six years. Since 1970, aluminum can recycling has created over 40,000 new jobs at recycling centers. Do you part to help recycle cans and save energy.

recýcle [ri:sáikəl] v. 재활용하다 consérve [kənsə́:rv] v. 보존하다 save [seiv] v. 절약하다 ore [ɔːr] n. 광석, 원광 residéntial eléctrical néeds : 주거용 전기수요 part [pɑːrt] v. 나누다

해석 16

알루미늄 깡통 재활용은 에너지를 보존한다. 사실, 재활용은 원광에서 새로운 알루미늄을 만들어내는 데 드는 에너지의 95%를 절약한다. 작년에 알루미늄 산업은 재활용을 통해서 약 6년 동안 피츠버그 만한 도시의 주거용 전기수요를 충족시킬 만한 충분한 에너지를 절약하였다. 1970년부터 알루미늄 깡통 재활용은 재활용센터에 4만종이 넘는 새로운 일자리를 창출하였다. 깡통을 재활용하고 에너지를 절약하는 데 도움이 되도록 자신을 나누어주어라.

예문 17

If flying saucers do exist, they might be dangerous to our society. Thus, we should be afraid of flying saucers, if there are such things, because they could do a good deal of harm to the people of earth. Peter, my next door neighbor, claims that he doesn't consider flying saucers dangerous. In fact, he says that he would enjoy riding in a flying saucer from another planet because he loves to ride in airplanes. Personally, I do not think that flying saucers are a danger because I do not think they even exist; after all, I have never seen one.

flýing sáucer : 비행접시 be áfraid of ~:~을 두려워하다 do harm to ~:~에게 해를 끼치다 claim [kleim] v. 주장하다

해석 17

비행접시가 존재한다면, 그들은 우리 사회에 위험할지도 모른다. 만일 그런 것이 있다면, 그들은 지구인들에게 많은 해를 끼칠 수 있기 때문에, 우리는 비행접시를 두려워해야 할 것이다. 우리 이웃인 피터는 비행접시가 위험하지 않다고 주장한다. 사실, 그는 비행기 타기를 좋아하기 때문에 다른 혹성에서 온 비행접시를 타보고 싶다고 말한다. 개인적으로 나는 비행접시가 위험한 존재라고 생각하지 않는다. 왜냐하면, 나는 그것들이 존재한다고도 생각하지 않기 때문이다. 결국 나는 한 번도 보지 못했다.

예문 18

Despite its reputation, stress itself is neither bad nor good. It's a state of heightened function that allows you to cope with or adapt to change–change that, for whatever reason, you deem as different from that to which you are accustomed. The stress reaction is physiologically identical to your responses to fear or excitement your heart pounds, your breathing quickens, your body pumps out adrenaline. In short, stress is energy and, channeled constructively, it can help you achieve far more that you ever dreamt possible. The key is channeling this energy release.

despite [dispáit] prep. ~임에도 불구하고 reputátion [repjətéiʃən] n. 명성 stress [stres] n. 스트레스 héightened fúnction : 고양된(향상된) 기능 cópe with ~ : ~와 대항하다 adápt to ~ : ~에 적응하다 for what reason : 이유야 어떻든 deem [di:m] v. 생각하다(= think) be accústomed to ~ : ~에 익숙해지다 stréss reáction : 스트레스 반응 physológically [fiziəládʒikəli] adv. 생리적으로 idéntical to ~ : ~와 꼭 같은 respónse [rispáns] n. 반응(= reáction) excítement [iksáitmənt] n. 흥분 pound [paund] v. 쿵쾅거리다 quícken [kwíkən] v. 빨라지다 pump out : 뿜어내다, 펌프질해내다 adrénalin [ədrénəlin] n. 아드레날린 in shórt : 간단히 말해서 chánnel [tʃǽnl] v. 통로를 내다, 흐르다 costrúctively [kənstrʌ́ktivli] adv. 건설적으로 achíeve [ətʃí:v] v. 성취하다 chánnel (this energy) reléase : (이 에너지)를 방류하다

해석 18

그 명성에도 불구하고, 스트레스 그 자체는 나쁜 것도 좋은 것도 아니다. 그것은 이유야 어떻든, 여러분이 익숙한 것과는 다르다고 여기는 변화, 그 변화에 적응하거나 대항하도록 해주는 고양된 기능의 한 형태이다. 스트레스 반응은 심장이 쿵쾅거리고, 호흡이 가빠지고, 신체에서 아드레날린을 뿜어내는 공포나 흥분상태에서 여러분이 나타내는 반응과 꼭같다. 간단히 말해서, 스트레스는 에너지이고, 건설적으로 흐르게 한다면, 그것은 여러분이 지금까지 가능하다고 꿈꾸었던 것을 훨씬 더 많이 성취하도록 도와줄 수 있다. 해답은 이 에너지를 방류하는 일이다.

예문 19

The cockroaches that inhabit many city apartments and homes are parasites that are al-most impossible to exterminate completely. One hundred seventy million years older than the dinosaur, the cockroach, with its five eyes and six legs, can hide in the dark for weeks without food or water. Whenever a new roach poison is created, some of the insects become immune. And in one year a female can have 35,000 offspring. This, coupled with the fact that there are, at last count, 55 kinds of roaches in the United States, makes us hope only to control the pest but probably never to kill him completely.

cóckroach [kákroutʃ] *n.* 바퀴벌레 inhábit [inhǽbit] *v.* 서식하다 párasite [pǽrəsait] *n.* 기생동물 extérminate [ikstə́ːrməneit] *v.* 박멸하다 dínosaur [dáinəsɔːr] *n.* 공룡 róach póison : 바퀴약 become immúne : 면역이 되다 óffspring [ɔ́fspriŋ] *n.* 새끼 cóupled with ~ : ~을 연관지어 생각한다면 pest [pest] *n.* 해충

해석 19

도시의 많은 아파트나 주택에 서식하는 바퀴벌레는 완전히 박멸하기가 거의 불가능한 기생동물이다. 공룡보다도 1억7천만 년이나 더 오래된 바퀴벌레는 눈이 다섯 개, 다리가 여섯 개로 음식이나 물 없이도 몇 주일을 어둠 속에 숨어 지낼 수 있다. 새로운 바퀴 약이 개발될 때마다, 이 곤충의 일부가 면역이 된다. 그리고 1년이 지나면 암컷은 35,000마리의 새끼를 낳는다. 이것은, 최근의 계산으로 미국에 55종의 바퀴가 있다는 사실과 관련지어 생각해 볼 때, 우리에게 이 해충을 통제할 수는 있겠으나 결코 완전히 죽이지는 못한다는 희망밖에 줄 수 없게 한다.

예문 20

I never drink Coke because it is really bad for your health. I discovered this when I worked with some biologists last summer; we did two simple experiments. In the first, we measured the pH (that is, the grade of acidity) of the Coke. We found that Coke has a pH of 3.2. That is extremely acidic, and so it is bad for your body. In the second experiment, we decided to examine the effects of high acidity in Coke. We put a shark's tooth in a glass of Coke. In just seven days, the tooth had completely disappeared; the Coke had dissolved it. If the Coke can do that to a tooth, what can it do to human teeth or to a human stomach or intestine? For these reasons, I never drink Coke, and I advise my friends not to drink it either.

bíologist [baiálədʒist] *n.* 생물학자 méasure [méʒər] *v.* 측정하다 ácid(ic) [ǽsid] *adj.* 산성이 많은 gráde of acídity : 산성도 dissólve [dizálv] *v.* 녹이다, 용해하다 intéstine [intéstin] *n.* 장(소장, 대장)

해석 20

나는 절대로 콜라를 먹지 않는다. 콜라가 실제로 건강에 나쁘기 때문이다. 나는 지난 여름에 어떤 생물학자들과 함께 두 가지 간단한 실험을 했을 때 이 사실을 발견하였다. 첫째, 우리는 콜라의 pH(산성도)를 측정하였다. 콜라의 산성도가 3.2라는 것을 알았다. 그것은 극도로 산성이 많은 것이고, 인체에

나쁘다. 두번째 실험에서, 우리는 콜라의 높은 산성도가 미치는 영향력을 검사하기로 작정하였다. 우리는 콜라가 들어 있는 잔 속에 상어의 이빨을 집어넣었다. 7일이 지난 뒤에 그 이빨은 완전히 없어졌다. 콜라가 녹여버린 것이었다. 만일 콜라가 이빨에 그렇게 할 수 있다면, 인간의 이빨 혹은 인간의 위나 장은 어떻게 할까? 이런 이유들 때문에, 나는 절대로 콜라를 마시지 않고, 친구들에게도 마시지 말라고 권한다.

예문 21

Water supply systems for farmsteads and rural homes may be developed from either ground water or surface water sources. Ground water sources are wells and springs. Surface water sources include streams, lakes, ponds, and cisterns. A properly located and constructed well is the preferred source of water for domestic use. Well water is less likely to be con-taminated than water from other sources. It is, however, apt to contain more dissolved minerals such as iron and manganese. Surface water sources should be used only as a last resort because of the cost and difficulty of making the water safe to drink. However, surface water may be suitable for irrigating, firefighting, livestock, and other non-domestic purposes.

wáter supplý sýstem : 급수체계 fármstead [fáːrmsted] *n.* 농장 rúral hómes : 시골가정 gróund water : 지하수 súrface wáter sóurce : 지표수원 well [wel] *n.* 우물 spring [spriŋ] *n.* 샘 stream [striːm] *n.* 강, 시내 cístern [sístərn] *n.* 유수지 doméstic [douméstik] *adj.* 가정의, 국내의 contáminate [kəntǽməneit] *v.* 오염시키다 be apt to do : ~하기 쉽다 dissólve [dizálv] *v.* 녹이다, 용해시키다 resórt [rizɔ́ːrt] *n.* 유원지 be súitable for ~:~로 적당한 irrigate [írəgeit] *v.* 물을 대다, 관개하다 fírefighting : 소화, 소방 lívestock [láivstak] *n.* 가축 non-doméstic púrpose : 비가정용

해석 21

농장이나 시골가정에 대한 급수체계는 지하수나 지표수원으로부터 개발될 수도 있다. 지하수원은 우물과 샘이다. 지표수원은 강이나 호수, 연못, 유수지를 포함한다. 적당한 곳에 자리잡고 건설된 우물은 가정용으로 선호하는 수원이다. 우물물은 다른 수원에서 나오는 물보다 오염될 확률이 적다. 그렇지만, 철분이나 망간 같은 광물이 더 많이 용해되어 있을 수 있다. 지표수원은 마시기에 안전한 물로 만들기 어렵고 비용도 비싸서, 최후의 유원지로나 이용되어야 한다. 그러나 지표수는 관개나 소방, 가축, 기타 비가정용수로 적당할 수 있다.

예문 22

Synonyms, words that have the same basic meaning, do not always have the same emotional meaning. For example, the words "stingy" and "frugal" both mean "careful with money." However, to call a person stingy is an insult, while the word frugal has a much more positive connotation. Similarly, a person wants to be slender but not skinny, and aggressive, but not pushy. Therefore, you should be careful in choosing words because many so-called synonyms are not really synonymous at all.

sýnonym [sínənim] *n.* 동의어(*opp.* ántonym [ǽntənim] *n.* 반의어) sýnonymous [sinánəməs] *adj.* 동의어의, 비슷한 뜻의 stíngy [stíndʒi] *adj.* 인색한 frúgal [frú:gəl] *adj.* 검약한 ínsult [ínsʌlt] *n.* 모욕, 무례 pósitive [pázətiv] *adj.* 긍정적인(*opp.* négative [négətiv] *adj.* 부정적인) connotátion [kànoutéiʃən] *n.* 함축, 내포(*opp.* denotátion [dì:noutéiʃən] *n.* 외연(外延)) slénder [sléndər] *adj.* 홀쭉한, 날씬한 skínny [skíni] *adj.* 바싹마른 aggréssive [əgrésiv] *adj.* 호전적인, 공격적인 púshy [púʃi] *adj.* 적극적인, 추진력이 강한 so-called : 소위 not ~ at all : 전혀 ~ 아닌

해석 22 비슷한 기본의미를 가진 단어인, '비슷한 말'이라는 것이 언제나 감정상의 비슷한 의미를 가지는 것은 아니다. 예를 들어, 'stingy'(인색한)와 'frugal'(검소한)이라는 말은 둘 다 '돈을 주의하다'는 뜻이다. 그러나 어떤 사람을 'stingy'(인색하다)라고 하면 모욕이 되지만, 반면에 'frugal'(검소하다)이라는 단어는 훨씬 긍정적인 뜻을 함축한다. 비슷하게, 사람들은 날씬하기를 바라지만, 여위기를 바라지는 않으며, 적극적인 것은 바라지만 공격적인 것은 원하지 않는다. 그러므로, 어휘를 선택할 때는 주의해야 한다. 왜냐하면, 소위 많은 '비슷한 말'이라는 것들이 결코 실제로 비슷하지 않기 때문이다.

예문 23

The government in Indonesia has a three-step program to decrease population. The first and most important step is the education of the people about the problems of overpopulation and about the processes of controlling population. Next, the goverment tells the people about the availability of birth prevention techniques and methods like birth control pills and instrauterine devices. In addition, the people are able to learn the facts about sterilization for both men and women. Finally, the government is making laws to control the birth rate in Indonesia. The first step has been to eliminate the financial allowance for all third children of government employees. Eventually the government intends to make that law applicable to the entire populace. The ultimate result of this program will be to limit the growth to approximately 2%, thereby making the income per capita in Indonesia significantly higher.

a three-step program : 3단계 프로그램 decréase [dikrí:s] *n.* 감소시키다 overpopulátion [ouvərpapjuléiʃən] : 인구과잉 prócess [práses] *n.* 과정 availabílity [əvèiləbíləti] *n.* 활용, 이용 bírth prevéntion techníques and méthods : 출생방지 기술과 방법 birth contról pills : 피임약 intraúterine devíces : 자궁내용 기구 sterilizátion [stèrəlizéiʃən] *n.* 불임화 elíminate [ilímineit] *v.* 제거하다, 없애다 fináncial allówance : 수당, 부조금 góvernment employée : 공무원 inténd to do : ~하려고 의도하다 ápplicable [ǽplikəbəl] *adj.* 적용가능한, 적절한 pópulace [pápjələs] *n.* 주민, 대중 entíre pópulace : 전 주민 últimate [ʌ́ltəmit] *adj.* 최종적인, 궁극적인 therebý [ðèərbái] *adv.* 그래서 íncome per cápita : 1인당 평균소득(per capita : 균등할)

해석 23 인도네시아 정부는 인구를 감소시키는 3단계 프로그램을 가지고 있다. 첫번째 가장 중요한 단계는 인구과잉 문제와 인구통제 과정에 대한 국민교육이다. 다음으로, 정부는 피임약과 자궁내용 기구 같은 출생방지 기술과 방법의 활용을 국민들에게 알린다. 더불어, 국민들은 남녀 모두를 위한 불임화에 관한 사실을 배울 수 있다. 마지막으로, 정부는 인도네시아의 출생률을 조절하는 법률을 제정하는 것이다. 그 첫 단계는 공무원들의 세번째 출산아들에게 주는 수당을 없애는 것이었다. 궁극적으로 정부는 그 법률이 전 주민에게 적용되도록 하려는 의도이다. 이 프로그램의 최종결과는 약 2%까지 성장을 억제하게 될 것이다. 그래서 인도네시아의 1인당 평균소득을 상당히 높이게 될 것이다.

TOEFL Beginner's Reading Comprehension

Part 2

독해기초연습 1

Focus 1

| 문단의 주제 찾기 |

주제문은 전체의 글이나 문단을 요약하고 전반적인 진술을 하는 문장이다.

너무 포괄적인 표현이나 너무 자세한 표현은 주제문이 될 수 없다.

일반적으로 주제문은 문단의 첫 문장인 경우가 대부분이다.

주제어는 흔히 첫 문장에 있으며, 그 문단에서 가장 자주 등장하는 말이다.

결론문은 주로 문장의 끝에 오며, 요점을 정리해 준다. 흔히 주제와 같다.

Question Type 1

다음 각 문단을 읽고 가장 알맞은 주제를 고르시오.

1

All around the world large cities have the same problem. That problem is air pollution. Mexico City has very bad air. The air there is dirty and very unhealthy. Cars are one reason for the dirty air. Many Mexicans now own their own cars and drive in the city. The factories in the area also cause air pollution. These factories put a lot of smoke into the air. It is not easy to clean up the air in a large city. The government has to make new laws and everyone has to help.

(A) Air pollution
(B) Mexico City's air pollution
(C) How factories cause air pollution

2

In the United States there are two kinds of television stations. One kind is commercial. About 841 of the television stations in the United States are commercial stations. These stations are businesses. They show ads to make money. The other kind of television station is public. These stations do not show any ads. They get some money from the government. They also get money from the people who watch public stations.

télevision státion : 텔레비전 방송국 ad : 광고, advertisement의 약어

(A) The two kinds of television stations in the U.S.
(B) Public television stations
(C) Television in the United States

3

Large forests are important to us in many ways. They give us wood for building and heating. They are a home for many kinds of plants and animals. And for many city people, forests are a place to go for a vacation. People can learn about nature there. They can breathe fresh air and sleep in a quiet place. But there is one more reason why forests are important for everyone. The leaves on the trees in a forest help clean the air. Dirty air is a problem in many parts of the world. Without our forests this problem might be much worse.

go for a vacation : 휴가를 떠나다 breathe [briːð] *v.* 호흡하다, 숨쉬다(*cf.* breath [breθ] *n.* 호흡) help (to) clean the air : 공기정화를 돕다

(A) The importance of forests
(B) Taking vacations in forests
(C) Large forests

4

It is easy to make a good cup of tea. Just follow these steps. First, boil some water. Next put some hot water in the tea pot to warm it. Pour the water out of the pot and put in some tea leaves. You will need one teaspoon of tea leaves for each cup of tea you want. Then pour the boiling water into the tea pot. Cover the pot and wait for a few minutes. Now the tea is ready to drink.

boil [bɔil] v. 끓이다 warm [wɔːrm] v. 덥히다, 따뜻하게 하다 pour [pɔːr] v. 붓다, 따르다

(A) Good tea
(B) How much tea to use
(C) How to make a good tea

Question Type 2

다음 각 문단을 읽고 가장 알맞은 주제어를 고르시오.

5

The people in the United States speak the same language as the people in Great Britain. However, American English is different from British English in many ways. First, the sounds of American English are different from the sounds of British English. For example, most Americans pronounce the "r" in the word "car" but most Britons do not. Most Americans pronounce the word "dictionary" like this: "dik-shun-ar-y," but the British pronounce it like this "dik-shun-ry." Some spellings are also different. People in Britain write "colour" and "centre," but people in the United States write "color" and "center."

Finally, some words are different. People in the United States use "gasoline" in their cars, but people in Britain use "petrol." Gasoline and petrol are the same thing, but the Americans and the British use different words for it.

American English : 미국영어 British English : 영국영어 pronóunce [prənáuns] v. 발음하다

(A) American English
(B) The English language
(C) The different sounds of American and British English
(D) The differences between American and British English

주제문 : However, … ways
서술문 : 3행(First …), 7~8행(some spellings are also different …), 10행(Finally …)

6

Do you have trouble remembering new words in English? Many people have this problem. This method may help you to remember new words. (1) Look at the new word. Look at the letters and the shape of the word. Close your eyes. Can you see the word? (2) Listen to the word. Listen to the sounds in the word. Look at the word as you listen. (3) Say the word aloud. Close your book. Do not look at the word. Can you say it? (4) Write the word. Write it three or four times. Say the word as you write it. (5) Use the new word. Use it in class today, and use it at home tonight. Use it tomorrow and next week. Look for the new word in the newspaper and listen for it on the radio or on television. To remember a new word, you must use it.

have trouble (in) remémbering : 외우기 어렵다 listen to ~ vs. listen for ~ : ~을 (막연히) 듣다, 청취하다 vs. ~을 귀 기울여 듣다, 주의깊게 듣다

(A) A method for remembering new words
(B) New words in English
(C) Looking at new words
(D) The uses of new words in English

주제문 : 1행 핵심어 : remembering, new words, method 결론문 : 마지막 문장

7

Computer chips have changed our way of life. With computer chips we can make very small computers. Space scientists use these small computers in satellites and space ships. Large companies use these small computers for business. We can make very small calculators with computer chips. Some calculators are as small as a credit card, and these calculators are not very expensive. Computer chips are also used for making digital watches. A normal watch has a spring and moving hands, but a digital watch has no moving parts. A digital watch shows the time and the date with numbers, and some digital watches even have an alarm and a stop-watch. The computer chip makes all of this possible.

sátellite [sǽtəlait] *n.* 위성 space ship : 우주선 cáculator [kǽlkjəleitər] *n.* 계산기

(A) Small computers
(B) Uses of computer chips
(C) Digital watches
(D) Uses of computers

주제문 : 첫 두 문장 핵심어 : computer chips 서술문 : 이하 모두 결론문 : 마지막 문장

8

Today most cars use gasoline, but in the future many people may drive electric cars. Electric cars do not pollute the air. Electricity from a battery powers the motor of an electric car. Drivers of electric cars do not fill their cars with gasoline; they connect their cars to an electrical outlet to charge the battery with electricity. The driver of an electric car connects the car to an electrical outlet at night. In the morning, the battery is charged with enough electricity to drive all day. Electric cars are not as fast as gasoline-powered cars, and they cannot travel more than 150 miles (270 kilometers). After 150 miles, the driver must charge the battery again. However, electric cars may be one answer to the problems of pollution and high gasoline prices.

pollúte [pəlúːt] *v.* 오염시키다(*cf.* pollútion [pəlúːʃən] *n.* 오염) pówer [páuər] *v.* 동력을 공급하다 connéct [kənékt] *v.* 연결하다 óutlet [áutlet] *n.* (전기) 콘센트, 출구, 판로(매장) charge [tʃɑːrdʒ] *v.* 충전시키다

(A) Pollution and expensive gasoline
(B) The batteries of electric cars
(C) Gasoline cars
(D) Electric cars

주제문 : 첫 두 문장 핵심어 : Electric cars 서술문 : 2~10행 전부 결론문 : 마지막 문장

9

    John and Marsha live in a solar house in New Mexico, a state in the Southwest of the United States. There are fifteen windows on the south wall of the house, and there are four solar collectors on the roof. Two of the solar collectors heat water for washing, and two collectors help to heat the house. In the winter, John and Marsha open the curtains on the south side of the house every morning, and they close them every evening. The rays of the sun heat the house during the day, and the curtains hold the heat in the house during the night. In the hot summer season, John and Marsha close the curtains during the day, and they turn off two of their solar collectors.

sólar house : 태양열 주택 sólar colléctors : 집광판, 햇빛을 모으는 장치 turn off : 끄다

(A) John and Marsha
(B) New Mexico
(C) A solar house
(D) Solar collectors

주제문 : 첫 문장 핵심어 : a solar house 서술문 : 나머지 문장 전체

다음 각 문단을 읽고 가장 알맞은 주제문을 고르시오.

10

Most Americans think of cats as pets. But not all cats are pets. Some cats help people and others are a problem. For example, on farms and in old houses, cats can help. They kill small animals such as rats or mice. But sometimes, people do not want cats around. Some people like to watch birds in their yards. Cats may kill the birds or scare them away. Cats are also a problem in cities. In Rome, for example, thousands of cats live in the streets and old buildings. They make a lot of noise, and they are dirty and dangerous.

---

pet [pet] *n.* 애완동물　scare (them) away : (그들)을 쫓아내다　make a noise : 소리를 내다

(A) Cats can be a problem.
(B) Most Americans think of cats as pets.
(C) Cats are not just pets.
(D) Cats always help people.

주제문 : 1~2행　서술문 : 이하 전체문장. 첫 문장을 읽고 뒤에 But로 역접이 되는 것에 유의할 것.

11

The earth is always changing. One way it changes is by erosion. Some erosion is caused by the weather. For example, the wind causes erosion. In a desert, the wind blows the sand around. Rain also causes erosion. It washes away earth and even changes the shape of some rocks. Another kind of erosion is caused by rivers. When a river goes through a mountain, it cuts into the mountain. After a long time, the mountain is lower and the land is flatter.

---

erósion [iróuʒən] *n.* 침식　wash away ~ : ~을 씻어내다　flat [flæt] *adj.* 평평한

(A) Rain causes erosion.

(B) Mountains change after a long time.

(C) Erosion changes the earth.

(D) Erosion is caused by rivers.

주제문 : 1~2행
서술문 : 이하 전체문장. 2행(For example, …), 3행(Rain also …), 5행(Another kind of erosion …)

12

There are many ways to improve your vocabulary in English. One way is to read fiction (novels and stories) in English. Novels and stories often contain new words. It is not difficult to understand these new words because you can usually guess their meanings. The other words in the sentences will help you, and the story will also help you. An interesting story will help you understand the new words because the meanings of the new words are part of the meaning of the story.

impróve [imprúːv] v. 향상시키다 fíction [fíkʃən] n. 허구, 소설 contáin [kəntéin] v. 담다, 내포하다

(A) There are many ways to improve your vocabulary.

(B) One way to improve your vocabulary is to read fiction.

(C) New words will help you to improve your vocabulary.

(D) An interesting story will help you understand new words.

주제문 : 첫 두 문장   서술문 : 이하 전체문장

13

Do you want to know more about your family history? Maybe a genealogist can help you. A genealogist is specially trained to find information about family histories from many different sources. Some of this information comes from old records, such as birth certificates, marriage certificates, and death certificates. Often the genealogist finds information in old newspapers, tax records, or immigration records. It may even be necessary to visit distant towns and villages to collect information from the people who live there. Once the information is complete, the genealogist writes a genealogy which describes the family's history.

geneálogist [dʒiːniǽlədʒist] *n.* 족보학자 geneálogy [dʒiːniǽlədʒi] *n.* 족보학, 계통학 certíficate [sərtífəkit] *n.* 증명서 immigrátion [iməgréiʃən] *n.* 이민(입국) (*opp.* emigrátion [eməgréiʃən] *n.* 이민(출국))

(A) A genealogy describes a family's history.
(B) Genealogists look for information in different places.
(C) Genealogists can find information about family histories.
(D) Information about family histories comes from many different sources.

주제문 : 첫 두 문장 핵심어 : genealogist 서술문 : 2행 이하 전체문장

14

Most children are excellent language learners. They can learn a second language quickly and easily. Most adults, on the other hand, find learning a second language difficult. They must study hard, and it usually takes them a long time to master the language. Adults usually try to learn a second language the same way they learn mathematics, science, history, or other subjects; but children learn a second Language the same way they learned their first language. The child language learner has all the necessary skills to learn another language, but the adult language learner often has to relearn these skills in order to learn a second language.

(A) Children are excellent language learners.
(B) Adults find language learning difficult.
(C) Children are better language learners than adults.
(D) Children can learn more quickly and easily than adults.

주제문 : 첫 세 문장(1~3행) 서술문 : children과 adult의 대비. 2행(most adults … on the other hand), 6행(but children …), 9~10행(but the adult …)

15

PLATO is my favorite teacher. He is very patient with me. He never gets tired or angry when I make too many mistakes. He always explains everything very carefully and makes sure that I answer every question correctly. When I need extra help after class, he is always in his "office"—even late at night. Not only does he teach me English, but he is also teaching me to type. But PLATO is not as friendly as my human teachers. He never smiles or laughs, and he doesn't ask about my family or what I plan to do next weekend. In fact, he doesn't talk at all. You see, PLATO is a computer, a special computer that teaches me English.

Pláto [pléitou] : n. 플라톤 be pátient with ~ : ~을 참다, 인내하다 get tíred : 지치다 not as friendly as ~ : ~만큼 친근하지 않다

(A) PLATO is my favorite teacher.
(B) Computers are better than human teachers.
(C) PLATO is a special computer that teaches English.
(D) Human teachers are more friendly than computers.

주제문(결론문) : 마지막 문장 서술문 : 1행에서부터 9행까지 계속 PLATO의 기능에 대해 은유적으로 설명하고 있다. 연결어 : but, in fact, you see

16

The government of India encourages married men and women to be sterilized so they cannot have more children. In China, families can be punished for having more than one child. Both of these countries have very large populations, and if the number of people continues to increase, there will not be enough food, houses, or jobs for the people. As a result, India, China, and other populous countries are following a family-planning policy—they want families to limit the number of children they will have. Teachers, doctors, and social workers are explaining to the people why they should have fewer children by using birth control methods such as contraception and sterilization.

encóurage [enkɔ́:ridʒ] v. 격려하다 stérilize [stérəlaiz] v. 불임시키다 sterilizátion [sterəlizéiʃən] n. 불임(cf. stérile [stéril] adj. 불임의, 불모의, 메마른 opp. fértile [fɔ́:rtl] adj. 비옥한) pópulous [pápjələs] adj. 인구가 많은(cf. pópular [pápjələr] adj. 대중적인, 통속적인, 인기있는, 유행하는) contracéption [kàntrəsépʃən] n. 피임

(A) Some populous countries are following a family-planning policy.

(B) India and China have very large populations.

(C) The government of India encourages sterilization.

(D) In China, families can be punished for having more than one child.

주제문 : 6~8행(흔치 않게도 주제문이 문단의 한가운데에 있는 경우)
서술문 : 1~5행(India와 China의 상황서술), 8~10행(가족계획 수행의 서술)

17

Before the introduction of the computer search, library research was a long and tedious task. Now, instead of spending long hours looking through the card catalog and periodical indexes for books and articles on your subject, you can have a computer do the looking for you. All you need to do is to give your subject to the computer. This is not as easy as it sounds, however, because you must know exactly what your subject is, and you must express it in words the computer can understand. The computer then searches its memory for books and articles about your subject. It takes less than a second for the computer to complete its search. Finally, it prints a bibliography—a list of the authors and titles of the books and articles it has found—for your subject.

computer search : 컴퓨터 검색 tedious task : 지루한 작업 periodical [piəriádikəl] *adj.* 정기적인, 주기적인 index [índeks] *n.* 찾아보기, 색인표 article [á:rtikl] *n.* 기사, 짧은 평논문 bibliography [bibliágrəfi] *n.* 참고문헌

(A) Library research is a long and tedious task.

(B) A bibliography is a list of authors and titles of book and articles.

(C) A computer can find books and articles for you.

(D) A computer search can save time in library research.

주제문 : 2~5행 서술문 : 주제문 이하 전체문장이 computer search의 작업과정이 설명되어 있다. 5행(All you need to do is …), 8행(… then searches …), 10행(Finally …)

다음 각 문단을 읽고 주제문을 찾아 쓰시오.

18

Population growth is a serious problem around the world. At the beginning of the 20th century there were about 1.5 billion people in the world. In 1984 the world population was 4.8 billion people. By the year 2000, it will be about 6.1 billion.

bíllion [bíliən] *n.* 10억

주제문 : 첫 문장   서술문은 시대순으로 배열되어 있다. (All the beginning of the 20th century ····1.5 billion people / In 1984 ··· 4.8 billion people / By the year 2000 ··· 6.1 billion)

19

Cities began to have many serious problems. The rich people and the businesses did not pay city taxes anymore. The poor people could not pay much money in taxes. So cities had less money for schools and housing. Sometimes they could not pay their police officers or firefighters. And they could not take good care of their streets and parks.

pay city taxes : 시(市) 세금을 내다 hóusing [háuziŋ] *n.* 주택 fírefighter [fáiərfaiter] *n.* 소방관

주제문 : 첫 문장   서술문은 주제문의 problems를 구체적인 예를 들면서 설명하고 있다. (The rich people ··· / The poor people ··· / So cities ··· / Sometimes ··· / And ···)

20

Changes in the prices of goods can cause changes in production and consumption. Production increases when the prices are high. As the prices of goods go up, producers make more goods because they can make more money when they sell the goods. On the other hand, consumption increases when the prices are low. As the prices of goods go down, consumers buy more goods because of the low prices.

consúmption [kənsʌ́mpʃən] *n.* 소비 consúmer [kənsúːmər] : *n.* 소비자(*cf.* consúme [kənsúːm] *v.* 소비하다) goods [gudz] *n.* 상품

주제문 : 첫 문장
서술문의 구조 : 대비구문 (As the prices of goods go up, producers make more goods … On the other hands, … / As the prices of goods go down, consumers buy more goods …)

21

Clothes can tell a lot about a person. Some people like very colorful clothes. They want everyone to look at them. They want to be the center of things. Other people like to wear nice clothes. But their clothes are not colorful or fancy. They do not like people to look at them. There are also some people who wear the same thing all the time. They do not care if anyone looks at them. They do not care what anyone thinks about them.

주제문 : 첫 문장
서술문 전개 : 1행(Some people …), 3행(Other people …), 5행(There are also some people …)

22

Scientists know a lot about the earth. For example, they understand how mountains are made and what a volcano is. But they do not know when a volcano will send hot rock into the air. They may know about the outside of the earth. But they still are not sure about the inside. And scientists are not sure about how the earth was made. They have many different ideas about this. There are still many difficult questions for scientists who study the earth.

volcáno [vɑlkéinou] *n.* 화산 hot rock : 용암

주제문 : 첫 문장
서술문의 전개 : 1행(For example, …), 2행(But …), 4행(But …), 5행(And …) But과 And등을 주의하면서 보자. 앞 문장과 역접관계에 있다.
결론문 : 마지막 문장 (주제와 다른 견해의 결론)

23

When you rent an apartment, it is important to have an apartment lease. A lease is an agreement between the owner of the apartment and you, the renter. It tells you the amount of rent for the apartment, and it gives you information about when and where you must pay the rent. It also tells you how long you can live in the apartment. A lease helps the owner of the apartment, but it also helps the renter. If you sign a lease, the owner cannot increase the rent or tell you to leave the apartment without a good reason.

lease [liːs] *n.* 임대계약, 차용계약 rent [rent] *v.* 세를 얻다, 임대하다 rénter [réntər] *n.* 세입자(*opp.* ówner [óunər] *n.* 소유주)

주제문 : 첫 문장
결론문 : 마지막 문장(주제와 다른 견해의 결론) 이하 설명문은 a lease의 개념과 효력에 대해 설명하고 있다.

24

The Great Depression of the early 1930s surprised many people. They did not think American business could have such terrible problems. For a long time, they did not believe the problems were serious. Many businessmen hoped for better times soon. Even President Hoover did not think the Depression was serious. He told Americans in 1930 that the problems were already going away. But this was not true.

Millions of Americans did not have jobs. Many of these people did not have homes or food. Life was hard for many Americans. And it did not get easier for many years.

The Great Depréssion : 1930년대 미국의 경제대공황 surpríse [sərpráiz] *v.* 놀라게 하다 térrible [térəbəl] *adj.* 무서운(*cf.* terrífic [tərífik] *adj.* 굉장한, 훌륭한)

주제문 : The Great Depression of the early 1930s   서술문 : 주제문 이하 전체문장으로 당시 상황을 묘사

25

We can learn a lot about a country from the "personal" ads. These ads tell us about people and their problems. One example of this is from Spain. In a small town in Spain there were forty-two men. But there were not many women there. The men wanted to find wives. So they put a personal ad in a city newspaper. Some women in the city were not happy living alone. So they answered the ad by telephone. They wanted to find out more about the town and the men. But the women did not go to live in the town. They did not really want to work on farms. They did not really want to marry small-town men. So the men did not find wives. And the women are still alone. Not all men and women in Spain are like these people. But this ad may tell us something about larger problems in Spain.

주제문 : 첫 두 문장   서술문 : 2행 One example …부터 10행까지   결론문 : 마지막 두 문장

다음 각 문단을 읽고 결론(Conclusion)이 되는 문장을 찾아 쓰시오.

26

Protectionists argue that an excess of exports over imports is essential to maintaining a favorable balance of trade. The excess can then be "cashed in" as precious metals. This means, however, that the most favorable of all trade balances will occur when a country exports its entire national product and, in turn, imports only gold and silver. Since one cannot eat gold and silver, the protectionists must surely be wrong.

---

protéctionist [prətékʃənist] *n.* 보호무역주의자(*cf.* protéct [prətékt] *v.* 보호하다 protéction [prətékʃən] *n.* 보호) árgue [á:rgju:] *v.* 주장하다 excéss [iksés] *n.* 초과 éxport [ékspɔ:rt] *n.* 수출(*opp.* ímport [ímpɔ:rt] *n.* 수입) maintáin [meintéin] *v.* 유지하다 fávorable [féivərəbəl] *adj.* 유리한(= advantageous) cash in : 입금하다 précious [préʃəs] *adj.* 귀한 entíre nátional próduct : 국민총생산 in túrn : 차례로

핵심어 : 첫 문장　결론문 : 마지막 문장 (Since …)

27

Administration officials say to scrap oil taxes, import fees, and subsidies for alternative fuels. The free market, they say, will produce the right amount of oil at the right price. That has always been a glib analysis. Now, in light of the administration's willingness to risk lives and dollars in the defense of oil from the Persian Gulf, it seems totally absurd. The real cost of oil should include the cost of military forces protecting supplies.

---

administrátion offícials : 행정부 관료들 scrap [skræp] *v.* 폐지하다(= junk, discard) *n.* 스크랩, 조각 súbsidy [sʌ́bsidi] *n.* (민간에 대한 정부의) 보조(장려)금 altérnative fúel : 대체연료 glib [glib] *adj.* 그럴듯한 análysis [ənǽləsis] *n.* 분석(*cf.* ánalyze [ǽnəlaiz] *v.* 분석하다) in light of ~ : ~을 비추어 보건대 in the défense of ~ : ~을 방어(보호)하는 데에 Pérsian Gulf : 페르시아만 absúrd [æbsə́:rd] *adj.* 불합리한, 부조리한, 앞뒤가 맞지 않은

주제문 : 1~3행 (주제도입)　서술문 : 3~6행 (이의제기)　결론문 : 마지막 문장

28

It is easy to find out the prices of goods, but what are the costs of the goods? Many consumers think that "price" and "cost" are the same, but they are mistaken. The price is the amount of money the consumer must pay in order to buy the goods, but the cost is the amount of money the producer must pay in order to make the goods. If a producer is making shoes, for example, the producer must buy leather, thread, glue, and sewing machines in order to make the shoes. The producer must also pay the workers who make the shoes. The money for leather, thread, glue, sewing machines, and workers is the cost of making the shoes. Then the producer decides the price of the shoe. The price is always higher than the cost because some money must go to the producer for making the shoes.

---

leather [léðər] *n.* 가죽 thread [θred] *n.* 실 glue [gluː] *n.* 풀 sew [sou] *v.* 바느질하다 séwing machíne : 재봉틀

결론문 : 11~12행(마지막 문장) 서술문 : 3~10행(핵심어인 price 와 cost의 개념과 차이를 설명하고 있다.)
도입(introduction) : 1~3행

29

The 1814, George Rapp started a utopian community in Harmony, Indiana. In 1824, Rapp sold the community to Robert Owen, who started a new utopian community there. He named the new community "New Harmony." New Harmony lasted only two years. In 1825, Francis Wright started the community of Nashoba near Memphis, Tennessee. The Nashoba community ended in 1830. Brook farm, a utopian farming community, lasted from 1841 to 1847. Modern Times, an anarchist community near New York City, was started by Josiah Warren in 1851. It ended in 1857. We can see that these utopian communities that started in the 1800s lasted only a short time.

---

a utópian commúnity : 이상 공동체 ánarchist [ǽnərkist] *n.* 무정부주의자

결론문 : 마지막 문장 서술문 : 시대순으로 나열 (① 1814~1824 George Rapp. / ② 1824~1825 Robert Owen. "New Harmony." / ③ 1825~1830 Francis Wright. "The Nashoba community" / ④ 1841~1847 "Book farm." / ⑤ 1851~1857 "Modern Times")

30

The tuition and other costs of getting a college education continue to soar, and recent cutbacks in government aid for students have made it even more difficult for the ordinary families to finance their children's education. We may soon see the day when a college education is once again the privilege of only the very rich.

tuition [tju:íʃən] *n.* 수업료 soar [sɔːr] *v.* 치솟다, 날아오르다 cútback [kʌ́tbæk] *n.* 삭감 finánce [finǽns] *v.* 자금을 조달하다, 재정을 대다 prívilege [prívəlidʒ] *n.* 특권

주제문 & 결론문 : 마지막 문장(4~5행) 서술문 : 1~4행

31

A band saw is more efficient than a reciprocating saw. The blade of a band saw travels at the rate of from 8,000 to 10,000 feet per minute, whereas a reciprocating saw making 200 strokes of 18 inches each minute would have a cutting speed of only 300 feet per minute.

a band saw : 띠톱 a recíprocating saw : 왕복운동을 하는 일반 톱 blade [bleid] *n.* 날, 꽃잎 at the ráte of ~ : ~의 비율로 whereás [hwɛərǽz] *conj.* ~임에 반하여 stroke [strouk] *n.* 타격, 치기

결론문 : 첫 문장 서술문 : 2~4행의 문장으로 첫 문장의 결론에 대해 이유를 제시하고 있다.

32

Nicholas Nickleby, the second novel of Charles Dickens, has been referred to by some commentators as romantic, but the novel is actually highly realistic. Dickens collected material for his novel on a journey to Yorkshire during which he investigated for himself the deplorable conditions of the cheap boarding schools which produced broken bones and deformed minds in the name of education.

refér [rifə́:r] *v.* 언급하다 cómmentator [kámənteitər] *n.* 평론가(*cf.* cómment [kámənt] *v.* 논평하다, 의견을 말하다 *n.* 논평, 주석) No comment. : 할 말이 없음 realístic [ri:əlístik] *adj.* 사실적인, 사실주의적인 deplórable [diplɔ́:rəbl] *adj.* 개탄할, 통탄할 defórmed [difɔ́:rmd] *adj.* 일그러진 bróken bónes and defórmed mínds : 부서진 뼈대와 일그러진 마음. 부서지고 상처받은 학생들을 가리킨다 bones and minds : 학생들

결론문 : 첫 문장 핵심어 : romantic, realistic
서술문 : 둘째 문장은 첫 문장의 결론에 대한 근거를 제시하여 보충하고 있다.

33

The Federal Reserve Board must have moved last month to slow the growth of the money supply. Following a month in which prices rose more than the month before, interest rates rose noticeably, and in similar situations in the past the Board has moved to counteract inflation.

The Féderal Resérve Bóard : 미 연방 지불준비위원회 move [muːv] v. 동의하다 rise-rose-risen (향상되다, 인상되다) ínterest rátes : 이자율 nóticeably [nóutisəbəli] adv. 뚜렷하게, 눈에 띄게 counteráct [kauntərǽkt] v. 저지하다, 반작용하다 infláction [infléiʃən] n. 인플레이션, 통화팽창(opp. defláction [difléiʃən] n. 디플레이션, 통화수축)

결론문 : 첫 문장 서술문 : 둘째 문장은 이유를 설명하고 있다.

34

Producers make more goods when prices are high, and consumers buy more goods when prices are low. As prices go up, producers make more goods because they can make more money for their goods. As prices go down, consumers buy more goods because of the low prices. This shows us how changes in the prices of goods can cause changes in production and consumption.

주제문 : 첫 문장 서술문 : 2행(As … because), 3행(As … because)
결론문 : 마지막 문장 (This show us how …)

35

When prices are high, producers can get more money for their goods. When prices are low, consumers can get more goods for their money. These changes in the prices of goods can cause changes in production and consumption. As the prices of good go up, producers will make more goods in order to make more money. As the prices go down, consumers will buy more goods because of the low prices.

주제문 : 첫 두 문장 결론문 : 셋째 문장
서술문 : 4~6행(As the prices of goods go up … / As … go down.)

Focus 2 |제목 고르기|

흔히 주제문에서 뽑는다.

주제문을 찾아 읽고, 글 전체의 핵심어를 찾는다.

문장을 제목으로 하는 경우는 드물고, 단어나 구로 구성된다.

Question Type 1

다음 각 문단을 읽고 가장 알맞은 제목(Title)을 고르시오.

1

Computers are very useful. However, they also can cause problems. One kind of problem is with the computer's memory. It is not perfect, so sometimes computers lose important information. Another problem is with the machinery. Computers are machines, and machines can break down. When computers break down they may erase all the information, like chalk on a blackboard.

pérfect [pə́:rfikt] *adj.* 완벽한 machíne [məʃí:n] *n.* 기계 (보통명사로 복수형이 있음) machínery [məʃí:nəri] *n.* 기계류 (추상명사) break down : 부서지다 eráse [iréis] *v.* 지우다(*cf.* eráser [iréisər] *n.* 지우개)

(A) Usefulness of Computers

(B) Some Troubles with Computers

(C) Information Given by Computers

(D) Uses and Abuses of Computers

주제문 : However, they(=computers) also can cause problems.(1~2행)
서술문 : One kind of problem … (2행) / Another problem … (4행)

2

Chemistry, as a science or field of knowledge, is concerned with ideas and concepts relating to the behavior of matter. Although these concepts are abstract, their application has had a concrete impact on human culture. This impact is due to modern technology, which may be said to have begun about 200 years ago and which has grown rapidly ever since.

be concérned with ~ : ~와 관련이 있다 cóncept [kánsept] *n.* 개념 reláting to ~ : ~과 관련이 있는 behávior [bihéivjər] *n.* 행동 ábstract [ǽbstrækt] *adj.* 추상적인(*opp.* cóncrete [kánkriːt] *adj.* 구체적인(= réal, práctical, áctual)) applicátion [ǽplikéiʃən] *n.* 적용, 응용 ímpact [ímpækt] *n.* 영향 be due to ~ : ~에 기인하다 begin-began-begun rápidly [rǽpidli] *adv.* 신속하게(= prómptly, quíckly)

(A) Chemical Elements

(B) The Behavior of Matter

(C) Chemistry and Modern Technology

(D) Culture and Society

핵심어 : Chemistry (1행), technology (4행)

3

Nicky is taking part in a sponsored climb at the beginning of September to raise money for an extention to the children's section at her hospital. She and nine others will spend a month climbing up and down Mt. Everest. This is the final attempt to raise funds they need to build facilities for the families of children ill in hospital. They have been trying to raise the money for five years.

take part in ~ : ~에 참석, 참가하다 a spónsored climb : 후원등반 raise [reiz] *vt.* ~을 올리다, 향상시키다(*cf.* rise [raiz] *vi.* 오르다, 성장하다) exténsion [ikstén∫ən] *n.* 확대, 연장 attémpt [ətémpt] *n.* 시도, 도전 raise fund : 모금하다

(A) Sports for Nurses

(B) Hospitals for Children

(C) Parents of Sick Children

(D) A Climb for Fund Raising

주제문 : 첫 문장(1~3행)   서술문 : 주제문 이하 전체문장   핵심어 : climb, raise the money

4

Britain consists of four countries: England, Scotland, Wales and Northern Ireland. London, the capital, is the center of government for Britain, but local authorities are partly responsible for education, health care, roads, etc. Laws are made by Parliament. Members of Parliament are elected by the people from a particular area.

consíst of ~ : ~로 구성되다 lócal authórities : 지방정부 be respónsible for ~ : ~에 책임이 있는 Párliament [pá:rləmənt] *n.* 영국의회

(A) The Geography of Britain

(B) The Political System of Britain

(C) How Laws Are Made in Britain

(D) The Responsibility of Local Authorities

이 글은 어떤 주제를 설명하는 부분이다. 이런 경우, 여러 개의 핵심어(Britain, London, local authorities, law, Parliament)를 종합하여 주제를 파악해야 한다.

5

The lowest temperature on earth was recorded in Antarctica at the Soviet scientific station Vostok on August 26, 1960. Vostok, however, is a place where people stay for a short time. The coldest place where people choose to live year-round is a village of six hundred souls in a mountain valley 700 meters above sea level. It is Oymyakon.

Antárctica [æntá:rktikə] *n.* 남극대륙(= the Antárctic cóntinent) soul [soul] *n.* 영혼. 여기서는 '사람'을 가리킴 above sea lével : 해발

(A) Human Life in Antarctica
(B) Recording of the Temperature
(C) The Village Called Vostok
(D) The Coldest Place in the World.

핵심어 : The lowest temperature, The coldest place   결론문 : 마지막 문장

6

According to Margaret Mead, the younger generation is essentially different from the older generation. The world of the older people has vanished, and they do not understand all of the problems of the modern world. On the other hand, the younger people have grown up with these problems, and they are deeply concerned about them. The older generation still controls the power in business organizations, government, and education. The young people want to make changes in these areas to fit the needs of modern society. In order to reconcile their differences, both generations must realize that the world has changed, and that new responses are necessary for many of the problems of society.

be dífferent from ~ : ~와 다른 vánish [vǽniʃ] *v.* 사라지다 be concérned about ~ : ~을 염려하다 réconcile [rékənsail] *v.* 화해하다, 조화시키다 respónse [rispáns] *n.* 반응

(A) Power Control
(B) Generation Gap
(C) Problems of Society
(D) History of Society

핵심어 : the younger generation, the young people / the older generation, the old people, both generations   연결어 : on the other hand

7

First of all, list your fixed expenses, the money you must spend each month for rent, food, and so on. If you have to guess at some of your expenses, you should guess higher, rather than lower. Then list large expenses, such as insurance, and figure out their monthly costs. Now list expenses for emergencies, such as medical care. The rest is your "spending money" for entertainment, travel, and so on. By making the list and following it, you won't have to worry about being short of cash each month.

fixed expénses : 고정비용 and so on : 등등 insúrance [inʃúərəns] *n.* 보험 fígure out : 추산하다, 예산하다 emérgency [imə́:rdʒənsi] *n.* 비상사태, 위급상황 entertáinment [entərtéinmənt] *n.* 오락 be shórt of ~ : ~가 부족한, 떨어진

(A) How to Plan a Monthly Budget
(B) How to Make Money More Easily
(C) How to Save Money for the Future
(D) How to Invest Monthly Income

핵심어 : list expenses, spend money, each month (= monthly)   연결어 : First of all (1행), Then (3행)

8

James wrote a play for television, about an immigrant fam-ily who came to England from Pakistan, and the problems it had setting down in England. The play was surprisingly successful, and it was bought by an American TV company.

James was invited to go to New York to help with the production. He lived in Dulwich, which is an hour's journey from the airport. The flight was due to leave at 8:30 a.m., so he had to be at the airport about 7:30 in the morning. He ordered a taxi for 6:30, set his alarm for 5:45, and went to sleep. Unfortunately he forgot to wind the clock, and it stopped shortly after midnight. Also the taxi driver had to work very late that night and overslept.

an ímmigrant fámily : 이민자 가족 set down : 정착하다 surprísingly [sərpráiziŋli] *adv.* 놀랍게도 an hour's jóurney : (자동차로) 한 시간 거리 be due to ~ : ~하기로 되어 있는 wind [waind] *v.* 감다(*cf.* wind [wind] *n.* 바람)

(A) The Man Who Missed the Plane

(B) Journey to London

(C) A Happening in the Airport

(D) Opportunity in Life

9

The situation comedies (sitcoms) we see on television have a very long history. The first sitcoms go back to the fourth century B.C. In that period, people had active social lives, and they liked entertainment. Much of this came in the form of plays. A man named Menander wrote many light plays or sitcoms. His best play is about a grouch who has lots of money. Many people don't like him and like to play tricks on him. The tricks make him mad, but they made the audiences laugh. That's what the situation comedies of today do for us.

play [plei] *n.* 연극 grouch [grautʃ] *n.* 항상 불평을 늘어놓는 사람 play a trick on ~ : ~에게 장난을 치다, ~를 속이다

(A) Menander's Tricks

(B) Tricks of TV

(C) The Origin of Sitcoms

(D) The Audiences of Sitcoms

10

Last fall, the city of Philadelphia put 11 tons of garbage on a plane to Switzerland. Two weeks later the shipment came home. It was dry, chemically stable, and separated into reusable products such as plastics, paper fiber, metals, and organic material for fuel. The trash flight was undertaken to test out a Swiss-designed recycling system, which turns garbage into raw materials in just 17 minutes. The plant is one of several systems designed to bring as much automation as possible into waste recycling. Increasingly, waste is being seen as a resource. We have no choice but to recycle if we are to preserve natural resources that are being depleted at geometrically increasing rates.

gárbage [gá:rbidʒ] *n.* 쓰레기(= trash, waste) stáble [stéibl] *adj.* ① 안정된, 견실한 (= firm, permanent, steady) ② 화학적으로 분해하기 어려운 séparate [sépəreit] *v.* 분리하다 such as ~ : ~같은(= like) reúsable [ri:jú:zəbəl] *adj.* 재생할 수 있는 páper fíber : 종이섬유 recýcle [ri:sáikəl] *v.* 재생하다, 재활용하다 plant [plænt] *n.* 공장, 식물 incréasingly [inkrí:siŋli] *adv.* 점점 resóurce [ri:sɔ́:rs] *n.* 자원 have no chóice but to do : ~할 수밖에 없다 presérve [prizɔ́:rv] *v.* 보존하다 depléte [diplí:t] *v.* 고갈시키다, 소모하다 at geométrically incréasing rátes : 기하학적으로 증가하는 비율로

(A) Waste Recycling

(B) Trash and Trade

(C) Organic Material for Fuel

(D) The Use of Natural Resources

핵심어 : garbage, reusable products, recycling system, waste recycling

문장의 전개 순서 찾기

문장 전개 순서는 대개 시간적 순서가 근거가 된다.

먼저 주제문과 결론문을 찾는 것이 중요하다.

연결어들을 참고하여 문장 전개 순서를 찾는다.

Question Type 1

다음 각 문항의 글을 읽고 그 흐름에 따라 문장의 전개 순서를 찾으시오.

1

(A) Rent control began fairly recently in the United States.

(B) During World War II, the U.S. government imposed rent control on all the cities in the U.S.

(C) At the beginning of the 1980s nearly one fifth of the people in the U.S. lived in cities with rent control.

(D) Few American cities had rent control before World War II.

(E) After World War II, only one city—New York—continued rent control.

rent contról : 임대관리 impóse [impóuz] v. 강요하다, 부과하다

주제에 대한 서술을 시대별로 나누어놓았다.

시간을 나타내는 연결어 During World War II, As the beginning of the 1980s, before World War II, After World War II를 참고. 주제문은 A.

2

(A) Next, add antifreeze to your windshield washer fluid; otherwise, the fluid will freeze and possibly break the container.

(B) First, put on snow tires if you plan to drive on snowy, icy roads very often.

(C) Driving in winter, especially on snowy, icy roads, can be less troublesome if you take a few simple precautions.

(D) Finally, it is also a good idea to carry tire chains, a can of spray to unfreeze door locks and a windshield scraper in your car when driving in winter weather.

(E) Second, check the amount of antifreeze in your radiator and add more if necessary.

ántifreeze [ǽntifriːz] *n.* 부동액 wíndshield flúid : 유리창 세척액 fréeze [friz] *v.* 얼다 contáiner [kəntéinər] *n.* 용기, 그릇 put on : 입다, 장착하다 tróublesome [trʌ́blsəm] *adj.* 골치 아픈 precáution [prikɔ́ːʃən] *n.* 주의사항, 예방책 unfréeze [ʌnfríːz] *v.* (언 것을)녹이다 a wíndshield scráper : 창유리 긁개 rádiator [réidieitər] *n.* 냉각장치, 라디에이터

각 문장의 첫 머리에 있는 연결어 Next, First, Finally, Second를 참고한다. 몇 가지 주의사항(precautions)을 순서대로 나열했다. 주제문은 C.

3

(A) However, the consumers did not buy more shoes because of the high price.

(B) As a result, the shoe producers reduced the price of the shoes so that the consumers could buy more shoes.

(C) The prices of shoes are related to the number of shoes the producers make.

(D) At the same time, the shoe producers reduced their products of shoes because the prices went down.

(E) For example, the price of shoes was high last month, so the shoe producers made more shoes.

---

redúce [ridjúːs] *v.* 감소하다, 줄이다

각 문장의 첫머리에 있는 연결어 However, As a result, At the same time, For example를 참고할 것.

4

(A) In most cities, the rent for a one-bedroom apartment is more than $250 per month.

(B) For example, if you live in Los Angeles, you must pay $400 or more to rent a one-bedroom apartment, and the same apartment rents for $625 and up in chicago.

(C) In some smaller cities such as Louisville, Kentucky or Jacksonville, Florida, the rent is less, but in larger cities the rent is more.

(D) The most expensive rents in the U.S. are in New York, where you must pay at least $700 a month to rent a one-bedroom apartment in most parts of the city.

(E) The cost of renting an apartment varies from one American city to another.

핵심어 : cost of renting, American city 주제문 : E
전개순서 : broad → specific
① most cities …$250
② smaller cities … the rent is less, larger cities … the rent is more.
③ For example, Los Angeles. $400 chicago … $625 and up
④ most expensive … New York … $700.

5

(A) Later on, people began to write on pieces of leather, which were rolled into scrolls.

(B) In the earliest times, people carved or painted messages on rocks.

(C) In the Middle Ages, heavy paper called parchment was used for writing; books were laboriously copied by hand.

(D) With the invention of the printing press in the middle of the fifteenth century, the modern printing industry was born.

(E) Some form of written communication has been used throughout the centuries.

later on : 나중에 roll [roul] *v.* 구르다, 감다 scroll [skroul] *n.* 두루말이 carve [ka:rv] *v.* 새기다, 조각하다 párchment [páːrtʃmənt] *n.* 양피지 labóriously [ləbɔ́ːriəsli] *adv.* 힘들여, 수고스럽게 invéntion [invénʃən] *n.* 발명 the prínting préss : 인쇄기

주제문은 E이며, 시대순으로 전개되어야 하는 글이다.
각 문장의 연결어 Later on, In the earliest times, In the Middle Ages, …in the middle of the fifteenth century 등을 참고한다.

6

(A) If there had been a big storm on the day of a baby's birth, the baby might have been named Thunder Cloud.

(B) American Indian names are very descriptive, for Indians were usually named for a physical attribute, for an occurrence in nature, or for an animal.

(C) Grey Eagle, Red Dog, Big Bear, and Spotted Wolf are examples of Indians named after animals.

(D) Indians with distinctive physical characteristics might be given such names as Big Foot or Crooked Leg.

---

the day of a baby's birth : 아기탄생일 descríptive [diskríptiv] *adj.* 설명적인, 묘사적인 name for/after ~ : ~의 이름을 따서 이름짓다 attríbute [ətríbjuːt] *n.* 속성, 특질 occúrrence [əkɔ́ːrəns] *n.* 사건발생(*cf.* occúr [əkɔ́ːr] *v.* (어떤 일이) 발생하다) distínctive [distíŋktiv] *adj.* 특징적인, 뚜렷한 characterístic [kæriktərístik] *n.* 특징 cróoked [krúkid] *adj.* 꼬부라진, 비뚤어진

> 주제문은 B이다. 주제문의 자료가 제시된 순서를 참고한다.
> …named for a physical attribute, for an occurrence in nature, or for an animal

7

(A) For one thing, individual I.Q. scores vary considerably.

(B) Many experts also question whether I.Q. scores are related to intelligence.

(C) Furthermore, most psychologists agree that intelligence tests are biased in favor of middle-class children.

(D) The validity of standardized intelligence tests is being seriously questioned by educators and psychologists.

(E) In fact, motivation seems to be just as important as intelligence in determining a person's ability to learn.

I.Q. : 지능지수(Intélligence Quótient) váry [vέəri] *v.* 변하다(= change) consíderably [kənsídərəbli] *adv.* 상당히 be reláted to ~ : ~와 관련이 있는 intélligence [intélədʒəns] *n.* 지능 psychólogist [saikálədʒist] *n.* 심리학자 bíased [báiəsid] *adj.* 치우친, 편견을 가진 in fávor of ~ : ~을 위하여, ~에게 유리한 valídity [vəlídəti] *n.* 타당성, 정당성 éducator [édʒukeitər] *n.* 교육자 motivátion [moutəvéiʃən] *n.* 성취동기 detérmine [ditɔ́ːrmin] *v.* 결정하다 detérmining [ditɔ́ːrminiŋ] *adj.* 결정짓는

> 각 문장에 있는 연결어 For one thing, also, Furthermore, In fact를 참고한다.
> 주제문은 D이다.

8

(A) Furthermore, researchers are continuing to work on the development of an efficient, electrically powered automobile.

(B) Researchers in the automobile industry are experimenting with different types of engines and fuels as alternatives to the conventional gasoline engines.

(C) One new type of engine, which burns diesel oil instead of gasoline, has been available for several years.

(D) Finally, several automobile manufacturers are experimenting with methanol, which is a mixture of gasoline and methyl alcohol, as an automobile fuel.

(E) A second type is the gas turbine engine, which can use fuels made from gasoline, diesel oil, kerosene, other petroleum distillates, or methanol.

---

reséarcher [risə́ːrtʃər] *n.* 연구원 contínue to *do* : ~을 계속하다 efficíent [ifíʃənt] *adj.* 효율적인 áutomobile [ɔ́ːtəməbìːl] *n.* 자동차 expériment [ikspérəmənt] *v.* 실험하다 altérnative [ɔːltə́ːrnətiv] *n.* 대체물, 대안 convéntional [kənvénʃənəl] *adj.* 전통적인, 관습적인 méthanol [méθənɔ̀ːl] *n.* 메탄올 gas túrbine : 가스터빈 kérosene [kérəsìːn] *n.* 등유 dístillate [dístəlit] *n.* 추출물, 증류액 petróleum dístillates : 석유추출물

각 문장의 첫 머리에 있는 연결어 Furthermore, One new typer of …, Finally, A second type을 참고한다. 주제문은 B이다.

글은 하나의 주제를 설명하면서 다양한 연결어를 사용한다.

연결어가 들어갈 자리의 앞뒤 문맥의 관계를 파악한다.

연결어가 주어져 있다면 먼저 보고 문장을 읽는다.

Question Type 1

다음 각 문장을 읽고 빈칸에 들어갈 가장 적당한 연결어를 고르시오.

1

_____ the many hardships they had to face, the balloonists managed to reach their destination.

hárdship [háːrdʃip] *n.* 고난 face [feis] *v.* 만나다 mánage to do : 가까스로 ~하다 destinátion [destənéiʃən] *n.* 목적지

(A) Despite
(B) Because of
(C) In accordance with
(D) In addition to

face the many hardships – reach their destination : 종속절과 주절의 내용이 서로 역접관계이다.

2

The candidate has complied with all the requirements set by the university; this institution, _____, awards her the degree of Master of Arts.

cándidate [kǽndədeit] *n.* 후보자 complý with ~ : ~에 따르다, ~에 부합하다 requírement [rikwáiərmənt] *n.* 요구조건, 자격요건 awárd[əwɔ́ːrd] *v.* 상을 주다, 수여하다 degrée [digrí:] *n.* 학위, 등급 Master of Arts : (문학)석사학위(*cf.* Master's degree : (문학/이학) 석사학위) Doctor's degree : 박사학위, 대학원에서 수여하는 법학, 의학, 신학을 제외한 학문의 최고학위 (= dóctorate), Ph. D.(= Philosophy Doctor, Doctor of Philosophy) báchelorship : 학사자격

(A) moreover
(B) however
(C) therefore
(D) nevertheless

The candidate has complied with all the requirements ⋯ awards her the degree. : 두 문장의 내용이 원인－결과의 순접관계이다.

3

At first glance the idea appears to be attractive; _____ there are a lot of details to be cleared up.

glance [glæns] *n.* 일견, 한 번 봄 attráctive [ətrǽktiv] *adj.* 매력적인 détail [díːteil] *n.* 세부사항, 자세한 것 clear up : 깨끗이 치우다, 정돈하다, 해결하다

(A) and
(B) however
(C) furthermore ·
(D) in addition

appears to be attractive와 a lot of details to be cleared up는 내용이 상치되는 역접관계이다.

4

The problem is that, _____ children who are given cow's milk from birth benefit greatly from it, those who have never drunk it by a certain age are not able to tolerate it.

bénefit [bénəfit] *v.* 이익을 받다, 혜택을 받다 tólerate [táləreit] *v.* 견디다, 내성이 있다

(A) because

(B) in view of the fact that

(C) whereas

(D) since

5

It is true that other Europeans visited the new world before the fifteenth century, _____ Columbus is rightly credited with its discovery because of the ultimate consequences of his voyages.

discóvery [diskʌ́əri] *n.* 발견 the últimate cónsequence : 최종결과 vóyage [vɔ́iidʒ] *n.* 항해

(A) so

(B) therefore

(C) but

(D) and

6

_____ it must be admitted that the NASA space program has been extremely costly, there has been a considerable advantage in terms of new commercial applications of space technology.

admít [ædmít] *v.* 인정하다 NASA : 미국항공우주국 (Nátional Aeronáutics and Spáce Administrátion) NASA space program : NASA의 우주계획 cóstly [kɔ́ːstli] *adj.* 비용이 많이 드는 in terms of : ~의 측면에서 볼 때

(A) Because

(B) Since

(C) In addition

(D) Although

7

_____ the extraordinarily good results, it was decided to try the same approach next year.

extraordinárily [ikstrɔ:rdənérəli] *adv.* 특별히 (extra+órdinary+ly) appróach [əpróutʃ] *n.* 접근

(A) In spite of
(B) In view of
(C) However
(D) Despite

good results라는 긍정적인 말로 볼 때, 이 전치사구의 내용이 decided to try the same approach처럼 주절에 긍정적인(좋은) 영향을 주었다고 유추해 볼 수 있다.

8

_____ no mutually acceptable agenda could be arrived at, the talks were eventually called off.

mútually [mjú:tʃuəli] *adv.* 서로, 상호 agénda [ədʒéndə] *n.* 안건, 의제 mútually accéptable agénda : 서로 받아들일 수 있는 안건 the talks : 회담 evéntually [ivéntʃuəli] *adv.* 궁극적으로 call off : 취소하다, 중지하다 (= cáncel)

(A) Because
(B) Although
(C) So
(D) Instead

종속절의 상황이 주절 내용의 원인이 되었다.
no mutually acceptable agenda the talks ⋯ called off.

9

Sleep researchers have been looking for over a decade for a specific enzyme that needs to be restored at night following daily exhaustion, _____ it is surprising that no signs of such a substance have been discovered, if one actually exists.

* enzyme [énzaim] : (화학) 효소

sleep reséarcher : 수면연구가 look for ~ : ~을 찾다 restóre [ristɔ́:r] v. 회복하다 exháustion [igzɔ́:stʃ∂n] n. 소모, 고갈 súbstance [sʌ́bst∂ns] n. 물질

(A) so
(B) but
(C) moreover
(D) in addition

it is surprising의 원인이 되는 앞 문장의 내용과 뒤의 종속절('if절')이 단서가 된다. 결과를 나타낸다.

10

The evidence includes the fact that the narwhal's tusk bears a striking resemblance to the unicorn's mythical horn and _____ the fact that northern European fishermen sold narwhal tusks known to have magical properties to pharmacies in the fifteenth century.

* nárwhal [nɑ́:rhwal] 고래의 일종 únicorn [júːnəkɔːrn] 유니콘

tusk [tʌsk] n. 엄니, 빼드렁니 stríking [stráikiŋ] adj. 놀랄 정도로(= remárkable) resémblance [rizémbl∂ns] n. 닮음(cf. resémble [rizémb∂l] v. 닮다) bear a striking resémblance to ~ : ~을 놀랄 만큼 닮다 únicorn [júːnəkɔːrn] n. 이마에 뿔이 하나 있는 말과 비슷한 전설적인 동물, 유니콘 the únicorn's mýthical hórn : 유니콘의 신화적인 뿔 próperty [prɑ́pərti] n. (약의) 효력, 성질 known to have mágical próperties : 신비한 효험을 가진 것으로 알려진 phármacy [fɑ́:rməsi] n. 약국, 약재상

(A) in view of
(B) thus
(C) therefore
(D) in addition

첫 행의 includes the fact that …와 같은 문장구조가 이어지며, 또 다른 사실이 첨가된다.

11

Cancer of the pancreas has spread with deadly results: U.S. cases have doubled in two decades and the disease now kills 20,000 Americans annually. It is also one of the hardest cancers to treat: _____ of its victims survive more than three years.

* páncreas [pǽŋkriəs] 췌장

déadly [dédli] *adj.* 치명적인 case [keis] *n.* 환자 treat [triːt] *v.* 치료하다 víctim [víktim] *n.* 희생자, 환자 survíve [sərváiv] *v.* 생존하다, 살아남다(*cf.* survíval [sərváivəl] *n.* 생존)

(A) almost all
(B) hardly any
(C) none
(D) not all

one of the hardest cancers to treat 이므로 완전부정 none은 곤란하다.

12

Vincent van Gogh's early pictures were dark, but after moving in 1886 to Paris, where he met Pissaro, Degas, and Gauguin, he began to paint the brilliantly colored and dynamic pictures that later made him famous. _____ periodic fits of insanity he succeeded in producing numerous, now-popular works.

* fit [fit] : 발작증세

brílliantly [bríljəntli] *adv.* 화려하게 fit [fit] *n.* 발작 insánity [insǽnəti] *n.* 광기(*opp.* sánity [sǽnəti] *n.* 온전함, *cf.* insáne [inséin] *adj.* 미친, 광기의 *opp.* sane [sein] *adj.* 온전한, 정상적인) periódic fíts of insánity : 정기적인 광기의 발작 succéed in ~ : ~에 성공하다 númerous [njúːmərəs] *adj.* 수많은

(A) Despite
(B) Because
(C) Though
(D) Instead

Periodic fits of insanity는 문맥상 다른 단어들과 상반되는 의미의 말이다.

13

The city tends to become the new country's major point of contact with the "outside" world. The new nation attracts political representatives from other countries. _____ , the city that stands at the head of the emerging country plays a very important role in providing a proper image of the new country to the outsider.

tend to *do* : ~하기 쉽다, ~하는 경향이 있다 attráct [ətrǽkt] *v.* 끌어 당기다, 마음을 끌다 represéntative [reprizéntətiv] *n.* 대표자, 대의원 emérging [imɔ́:rdʒiŋ] *adj.* 떠오르는, 나타나는(= appéaring) the city that stands at the head of the emerging country : 신생국의 수도 play a róle in : ~에 어떤 역할을 하다 próper [prápər] *adj.* 적절한

(A) Correspondingly
(B) Nevertheless
(C) Surprisingly enough
(D) Ultimately

앞의 두 문장은 뒷 문장의 결론을 위한 전제조건이 된다.

14

Every man lives in two realms, the internal and the ex-ternal. The internal is that realm of spiritual ends expressed in art, literature, morals and religion. The external is that com-plex of devices, techniques, mechanisms and instrumentalities by means of _____ we live.

realm [relm] *n.* 영역, 권역 intérnal [intɔ́:rnl] *adj.* 내부의, 내면적인(*opp.* extérnal [ikstɔ́:rnəl] *adj.* 외부의, 외면적인) spíritual [spírit͡ʃuəl] *adj.* 정신적인 end [end] *n.* 목적 expréss [iksprés] *v.* 표현하다 móral [mɔ́(:)rəl] *n.* 도덕(*cf.* morále [mourǽl] *n.* (군대의) 사기) compléx [kəmpléks] *n.* 복합 devíce [diváis] *n.* 장치, 고안물 techníque [tekní:k] *n.* 기능 méchanism [mékənizm] *n.* 기계론적 구조 instrumentálity [instrəmentǽləti] *n.* 수단, 도구 by méans of ~ : ~에 의하여, ~을 방편으로

(A) how
(B) what
(C) where
(D) which

전치사 by means of 와 결합이 가능한 관계대명사를 찾는다.

15

One of the greatest advances in modern technology has been the invention of computers. They are already widely used in industry and in universities and the time may come when it will be possible for ordinary people to use them _____.

---

advánce [ædvǽns] *n.* 진보 invéntion [invénʃən] *n.* 발명

(A) so well
(B) as well
(C) completely
(D) possibly

흔히 문장의 끝에 붙이며 첨언할 때 쓰는 부사

Focus 5

| 핵심어 넣기 |

영문을 읽을 때 모르는 단어를 앞뒤의 문맥을 살펴서 뜻을 유추하는 것은 중요하다.

따라서 핵심어를 넣는 연습은 독해력 향상을 위한 좋은 방법이다.

핵심어 넣기는 문장이나 글의 핵심을 빠르게 파악하는 능력을 높여준다.

Question Type 1

다음 각 문항의 문장을 읽고 빈칸에 들어갈 가장 적절한 말을 고르시오.

1

Hockey is a game played on a level field _____ 50 to 60yd. by 90 to 100yd. by two teams of 11 players.

a lével field : 평지 méasure [méʒər] v. 길이나 폭이 ~이 된다(ex. measuring 20 feet by 15 : 세로 20피트, 가로 15피트 되는)

(A) measuring
(B) sized
(C) spacing
(D) widened

50 to 60yd., 90 to 100yd.는 거리의 측정단위이다.

2

The introduction of fabrics made from rayon, nylon, and other _____ fibers has made many changes in our civilization.

fábric [fǽbrik] *n.* 직물 ráyon [réiɑn] *n.* 레이온 fíber [fáibər] *n.* 섬유 make a chánge : 변화시키다

(A) artificial
(B) manufactured
(C) new
(D) synthetic

rayon, nylon 등은 합성섬유(synthetic fibers)이다.

3

Davos, Switzerland, was pretty well-known to many tubercular patients. They went there to take advantage of the high mountain air. It was a good _____.

＊ tubércular [tjuːbə́ːrkjələr] 결핵환자

well-knówn to ~ : ~에게 잘 알려진 tubércular [tjubə́ːrkjələr] *adj.* 결핵의 *n.* 결핵환자 take advántage of ~ : ~을 이용(활용)하다

(A) dwelling place
(B) health resort
(C) place for retired persons
(D) institute for medical care

핵심어인 tubercular patients, high mountain air 등의 어휘로 유추한다. It = Davos, Switzerland

4

We do not make men automatically good and virtuous by making them rich and powerful; indeed the truth frequently seems to be _____.

automátically [ɔːtəmǽtikəli] *adv.* 자동적으로 vírtuous [və́ːrtʃuəs] *adj.* 덕망 있는 indéed [indíːd] *adv.* 참으로, 진실로

(A) the same

(B) the opposite

(C) unclear

(D) unknown

문장부호 ; (semicolon)은 but의 뜻이 포함된 것으로, 역접관계의 설명문이 따라온다.
핵심어 rich, power와 truth는 서로 반대되는 의미의 단어이다.

5

From an international perspective the achievements of the Korean War were very substantial, but its impact on the American public was overwhelmingly _____.

perspéctive [pəːrspéktiv] *n.* 전망, 시각 achíevement [ətʃíːvmənt] *n.* 성취, 성과 substántial [səbstǽnʃəl] *adj.* 실질적인, 중요한 ímpact [ímpækt] *n.* 충격, 영향 overwhélmingly [ouvərʰwélmiŋli] *adv.* 압도적으로

(A) remarkable

(B) informative

(C) negative

(D) positive

the achievements ⋯ substantial, but its impact ⋯ 등의 핵심어들이 but을 가운데 두고 서로 반대된다.
부정적인 개념의 어휘를 찾아야 한다.

6

No man should be praised for his goodness if he lacks the strength to be bad; in such cases goodness is usually only the effect of laziness or _____.

praise [preiz] *v.* 칭찬하다 lack [læk] *v.* 결핍하다 strength [streŋkθ] *n.* 힘 láziness [léizinis] *n.* 게으름, 나태

(A) desire for praises

(B) rudeness

(C) impotence of will

(D) a sense of public disgrace

lacks the strength, laziness 등과 같은 맥락의 표현을 찾는다.

7

The present rise of the Negro people of the United States grows out of a deep and passionate determination to make freedom and equality a _____ "here" and "now".

> pássionate [pǽʃənit] *adj.* 열렬한, 열정적인 determinátion [ditə:rmənéiʃən] *n.* 결의, 결정 make fréedom and equálity a réality : 자유와 평등을 실현하다

(A) reality
(B) revolution
(C) possibility
(D) significance

"here" and "now"와 같은 개념의 말을 찾는다.

8

Most histories in totalitarian countries are nationalistic, sentimental, and filled with the national ego and the delusion of the particular country's complete _____.

> hístory [hístəri] *n.* 역사책 totalitárian [toutælətɛ́əriən] *adj.* 전체주의의 nationalístic [næʃənəlístik] *adj.* 민족주의적인 be filled with ~ : ~로 채워지다 nátional égo : 민족적 자부심 delúsion [dilú:ʒən] *n.* 망상, 환상

(A) peacefulness
(B) superiority
(C) prosperity
(D) dependence

전체주의 국가의 특징을 서술하고 있다.

9

In the 1940's Korea was not only at the extreme outskirt of the United States foreign policy but, like most countries of Asia, it was _____ to the American public.

> extréme [ikstrí:m] *adj.* 극도의, 극단의 óutskirt [áutskə:rt] *n.* 변방, 교외, 변두리

(A) almost completely unknown

(B) very well known

(C) very much interesting

(D) of great importance

not only~but (also) 구문은 양쪽 문장이 같은 맥락의 의미여야 한다.

10

Just why sleep is necessary still baffles researchers. It doesn't seem to be essential for health. Long periods of lack of sleep may cause transient disorientation, but the effects aren't _____.

* disorientátion [disɔ:riəntéiʃən] : 시간 · 공간 · 관계 · 성질 · 인물판별 등의 감각이 상실된 상태

báffle [bǽfəl] v. 당황하게 하다, 좌절시키다 reséarcher [risə́:rtʃər] n. 연구가 esséntial [isénʃəl] adj. 필수적인 cause [kɔ:z] v. 일으키다, 원인이 되다 tránsient [trǽnʃənt] adj. 일시적인

(A) permanent

(B) mysterious

(C) apparent

(D) abnormal

역접관계 연결사 but을 단서로 답을 찾을 수 있다. transient의 반대되는 단어를 고른다.

11

Most homeowners realize that a dead tree standing near a house or a garage should be removed. They know that decaying branches or even the entire tree may fall and cause severe damage to the _____.

garáge [gərá:ʒ] n. 차고 remóve [rimú:v] v. 옮기다, 제거하다 decáy [dikéi] v. 썩다 dámage [dǽmidʒ] n. 손상, 피해

(A) roots

(B) buildings

(C) driveway

(D) tree

핵심어 homeowners(= They), a house or a garage 등을 포괄적으로 지칭하는 말을 찾는다.

12

The discoveries of science often are a mixed blessing; on the one hand they give us valuable pesticides that enable the farmer to grow much more crops and on the other hand they _____ the benefits by destroying the balance of nature.

discóvery [diskʌ́vəri] *n.* 발견 a mixed bléssing : 복합적인 은총 pésticide [péstəsaid] *n.* 살충제 crop [krɑp] *n.* 농작물, 수확 bénefit [bénəfit] *n.* 혜택 destróy [distrɔ́i] *v.* 파괴하다

(A) help
(B) misplace
(C) promote
(D) counteract

핵심어인 on the one hand와 on the other hand를 단서로 하여 앞 문장에 대한 반작용의 단어를 찾는다.

13

Man is one of the most formidable of all animals and the only one who continually chooses to attack his own species. Throughout history, he has never, except for short periods of time, dispensed with _____.

fórmidable [fɔ́ːrmidəbəl] *adj.* 무서운(= fearful) attáck [ətǽk] *v.* 공격하다 spécies [spíːʃiz] *n.* (생물학적인) 종(種), 종족 dispénse with ~ : ~없이 지내다

(A) community living
(B) vital outdoor sports
(C) biological preservation
(D) fierce warfare

핵심어인 Man, the most formidable, attack his own species 등의 단어들과 관련되는 말을 찾는다.

14

Thanks to the natural resources of the country, every American, until quite recently, could reasonably look forward to making more money than his father, so that, if he made less money, the _____ must be his, because he was either lazy or inefficient.

natural resóurce : 천연자원 réasonably [ríːzənəbli] *adv.* 이성적으로, 당연히 look forwárd to -ing : ~을 기대하다 his father : 자신들의 조상. 문장 머리의 every American의 every가 단수로 받으므로 every American은 단수 he/she/one (his/her/one's)로 받는다 so that : 그래서 inefficient [inifíʃənt] *adj.* 비효율적인, 무능한

(A) wealth

(B) possession

(C) expense

(D) fault

핵심어인 so that, he made less, lazy or inefficient 등과 관련지어 연상되는 단어를 찾는다.

15

Fears of massive unemployment have greeted technological changes ever since the Industrial Revolution. Far from destroying jobs, however, rapid technological advance has generally been accompanied by high rates of job _____.

mássive [mǽsiv] *adj.* 대량의, 큰 greet [griːt] *v.* 맞이하다 technológical [teknəládʒikəl] *adj.* 공학적인 Indústrial Revolútion : 산업혁명 far from -ing : ~하기는커녕 rápid [rǽpid] *adj.* 신속한(= prompt) accómpany [əkʌ́mpəni] *v.* 수반하다, 동반하다

(A) deprivation

(B) creation

(C) interview

(D) loss

핵심어 however, destroying job 과 반대되는 말을 찾는다.

16

The 19th century saw the completion of the modern symphony orchestra—often extremely raised by composers such as Richard Strauss and Mahler. Instruments most often found in the modern orchestra are _____ : violin, viola, cello. bass, harp.

complétion [kəmplíːʃən] *n.* 완성 (*cf.* compléte [kəmplíːt] *v.* 완성하다) extrémely [ikstríːmli] *adv.* 극도로, 매우 compóser [kəmpóuzər] *n.* 작곡가 (*cf.* compóse [kəmpóuz] *v.* 작곡하다) composítion [kampəzíʃən] *n.* 작곡 such as ~ : ~와 같은, ~등등의 ínstrument [ínstrəmənt] *n.* 도구, 악기 bass [beis] *n.* (악기) 콘트라베이스

(A) winds

(B) keyboards

(C) vocal

(D) strings

서양악기의 분류
- Strings(현악기) : 바이올린, 비올라, 첼로, 콘트라베이스, 하프 등
- Keyboard(건반악기) : 피아노, 오르간 등
- Winds(관악기/취주악기) : 입으로 불어서 소리를 내는 악기
  Brass(금관악기) : 트럼펫, 트럼본, 프렌치호른, 튜바, 수자폰 등
  Reeds : 클라리넷, 오보에, 색소폰 등 마우스피스에 reed(갈대)를 끼워 물고서 소리를 내는 악기
- Percussions(타악기) : 트라이앵글, 심벌, 실로폰, 드럼류 등

17

Changes in a developing science are not to be compared to the destruction of old buildings to make way for new ones, but rather to the gradual evolution of a zoological type. We must not believe that old theories have been _____.

be not to be : should not be be compared to ~ : ~에 비교되다 make way for ~ : ~를 위하여 길을 만들어주다 grádual [grǽdʒuəl] *adj.* 점진적인 evolútion [evəlúːʃən] *n.* 진화 zoológical [zouəládʒikəl] *adj.* 동물의, 동물학적인

(A) effectively adapted

(B) seriously considered

(C) used in molding new ideas

(D) either sterile or in vain

앞 문장 not to be compared to …but rather to …구문과 뒷 문장 We must not believe that …이 서로 같은 내용을 반복하고 있다.
두 구문 tearing down of old build-ings, sterile or in vain이 서로 연관이 있다.

18

You cannot judge by appearances. Because of their clumsy appearance and slow, heavy movements, bears have earned a reputation of stupidity. Among zoo keepers, however, it is agreed that, of all the animals they handle, bears are among the most _____.

judge [dʒʌdʒ] *v.* 판단하다, 심판하다 appéarance [əpíərəns] *n.* 외모, 겉모양 clumsy [klʌ́mzi] *adj.* 볼품없는, 흉한 earn [əːrn] *v.* ~을 얻다, 받다, 벌다 reputátion [repjətéiʃən] *n.* 명성, 평판 stupídity [stjuːpídəti] *n.* 어리석음, 우둔함 zoo keeper : 동물원 사육사

(A) dangerous

(B) stupid

(C) peaceful

(D) intelligent

however를 중심으로 앞뒤 문장이 서로 반대의미를 전달한다.
핵심어인 appearance, clumsy, slow, heavy movements, stupidity 등과 반대의미를 가진 단어를 찾는다.

19

A community may be as small as a family or as large as the human race. Each small community is a part of a larger community and each large community is made up of smaller communities. The single important element in determining a community is _____.

as ···as ~ : ~처럼 ···한 human race : 인류 be made up of ~ : ~로 구성되어 있는 determine [ditə́ːrmin] *v.* 결정하다, 결심하다

(A) People

(B) location

(C) size

(D) type

community를 구성하는 요소는 사람이다.

20

The different races of mankind have _____ sexual attraction for each other so that in the absence of any geographical or cultural obstacles to genetic mixture it is highly probable that in the course of a few thousand years the human race would become racially uniform.

séxual attráction : 성적매력 so that : 그래서 in the ábsence of ~ : ~가 없으면, 없는 경우에 geográphical [dʒiːəgrǽfikəl] *adj.* 지리학적인 óbstacle [ábstəkəl] *n.* 장애물 genétic míxture : 유전적인 혼합 in the course of ~ : ~의 과정에, ~의 시간이 지나면서 rácially [réiʃəli] *adv.* 인종적으로(*cf.* race [reis] *n.* 종족) úniform [júːnəfɔːrm] *adj.* 단일한, 균일한

(A) no

(B) no much

(C) a sufficient

(D) an insufficient

21

A certain historian has said of history that "it devours the present." I do not quite understand what he means, but in science it is surely the other way about: The _____ devours the past. This shows a scientist's misguided indifference to the history of ideas.

say of ~ : ~을 말하다 devóur [diváuər] v. 삼키다 mean [miːn] v. 의미하다 the other way about : 정반대 misgúide [misgáid] v. 오도하다, 잘못 인도하다 indífference [indífərəns] n. 무관심 the history of idea : 사상의 역사, 사상사

(A) future

(B) present

(C) past

(D) history

22

Humans, computers and animals could be said in some sense to think. Yet the thought processes of each of these would be _____: each would have its own strengths and its own weaknesses. The merit of a particular combination of strengths and weaknesses would depend on the job to be done.

in some sense : 어떤 의미에서 the thought prócesses : 사고과정 strength [streŋkθ] n. 강점 wéakness [wíːknis] n. 약점 mérit [mérit] n. 이점 depénd on ~ : ~에 의지하다, 달려 있다

(A) complex

(B) different

(C) mysterious

(D) similar

Question Type 2

다음 각 문항의 문장을 읽고 빈칸에 들어갈 가장 적절한 말을 고르시오.

23

Many foods can be successfully preserved by drying. The bacteria and molds that cause decay in food cannot thrive without _____.

presérve [prizə́:rv] v. 보존하다 mold [mould] n. 곰팡이 decáy [dikéi] v. 썩다, 부패하다 thrive [θraiv] v. 번성하다, 무성하게 자라다

(A) moisture

(B) drying

(C) heat

(D) powder

foods … drying과 The bacteria and molds … cannot thrive without 두 문장은 서로 대립되는 뜻이다. drying의 대립되는 뜻의 단어를 찾는다.

24

A hobby is anything to which a person chooses to give time and energy regularly as a matter of _____ rather than as means of earning a living.

régularly [régjulərli] *adv.* 규칙적으로 as means of earning a living : 생계를 벌기 위한 수단으로

(A) successful life

(B) spending one's time

(C) spending one's money

(D) personal interest

rather than(역접)을 단서로 생각하고 earning a living과 대립되는 개념의 표현을 찾는다.

25

An ancient religion taught that man should observe the good in the world without ignoring the evil. In other words, look for the good, but remember that _____.

áncient [éinʃənt] *adj.* 고대의 obsérve [əbzə́:rv] *v.* 준수하다, 따르다, 관찰하다 the good : 선(善) ignóre [ignɔ́:r] *v.* 무시하다 the évil : 악(惡) in other words : 다른 말로 하면, 다시 말해서 look for ~ : ~을 찾다

(A) evil is also there

(B) all is good

(C) all is evil

(D) it does not exist

In other words는 앞 문장을 다시 설명한다는 뜻의 연결어이다.
without ignoring the evil과 비슷한 표현을 찾는다.

26

Two basic aims of Western civilization are to preserve human life and to provide economic security. There is a concurrent striving for health and for _____.

aim [eim] *n.* 목표 civilizátion [sivəlizéiʃən] *n.* 문명 províde [prəváid] *v.* 제공하다 secúrity[sikjúəriti] *n.* 안전, 안정 concúrrent [kənkə́:rənt] *adj.* 동시적인, 공동의 strive [straiv] *v.* 노력하다, 분투하다 striving [stráiviŋ] *n.* 노력, 분투

(A) art

(B) freedom

(C) wisdom

(D) wealth

핵심어 : Two aims(to preserve human life (health) / to provide economic security (wealth))

27

The animal's mouth is too large in comparison with his narrow throat. When he fills his mouth with food, he must chew for a very long time before he can _____.

in compárison with ~ : ~와 비교할 때 nárrow [nǽrou] *adj.* 좁은 (*opp.* broad, wide) throat [θrout] *n.* 목구멍

(A) gnaw

(B) breathe

(C) eat

(D) swallow

핵심어 animal's mouth, large, with food, chew for a long time before 중에 chew ⋯ before를 단서로 유추한다.

28

Drama thrived in India a long time ago. Since the plays presented there always had happy endings, Hindu theatergoers were strangers to _____.

thrive [θraiv] *v.* 번성하다 presént [prizént] *v.* 상연(상영)하다 théatergoer [θí:ətərgouər] *n.* 관객(theater+go+er) stránger [stréindʒər] *n.* 이방인, 낯선 사람

(A) actors

(B) money

(C) costumes

(D) tragedies

29

The United Nations was created to solve problems, not to create them; to promote peace, not to deepen conflict; to encourage development, not to create obstacles to it; to nurture freedom, not to serve _____.

promóte [prəmóut] v. 증진시키다 déepen [díːpn] v. 심화하다(cf. deep [diːp] adj. 깊은) cónflict [kánflikt] n. 투쟁, 갈등 encóurage [enkə́ːridʒ] v. 북돋우다, 격려하다 devélopment [divéləpmənt] n. 발전, 개발 óbstacle [ábstəkəl] n. 장애 núrture [nə́ːrtʃər] v. 양육하다

(A) boundary

(B) bandage

(C) bondage

(D) band

30

In times of crisis there is a tendency to regard wistfully the "good old days," so that the virtues of the past seem greater and its faults are _____.

crísis [kráisis] n. 위기 téndency [téndənsi] n. 경향 regárd [rigáːrd] v. 생각하다 wístfully [wístfəli] adv. 그리워하듯이, 추억하듯이 vírtue [və́ːrtʃuː] n. 장점

(A) reduced

(B) new

(C) critical

(D) apparent

31

Since language is a form _____, we react to a person's speech patterns as we would react to any of his action.

reáct (~to) : (어떤 자극에 대하여) 반응하다 speech páttern : 언어양식

(A) of community class
(B) of different dialects
(C) of speech community
(D) of social behaviour

react to a person's speech patterns, react to any of his action 등의 문장이 behaviour라는 단어와 관련이 많다

32

A thief wished to divert the attention of the watchdog so that he could rob a house. He threw a piece of meat to the dog, hoping that the dog would eat the meat instead of barking to warn the household. But the dog refused the offer of food and alerted the household. Taking a lesson from the dog, a wise man should beware of _____.

divért [divə́:rt] v. ~을 딴 데로 돌리다 (= turn aside) throw [θrou] v. 던지다 (throw－threw－thrown) bark [bɑːrk] v. (개가) 짖다 warn [wɔːrn] v. 경고하다 hóusehold [háushould] n. 집주인 refúse [rifjúːz] v. 거절하다 alért [əlɔ́ːrt] v. 경보를 하다 take a lésson : 교훈을 얻다 bewáre of ~ : ~을 조심하다

(A) genuine friendship
(B) barking dogs
(C) gifts
(D) bribes

a piece of meat to the dog, the offer of food 등의 어휘가 상징하는 것은 무엇인가?

33

Since our democratic system of government is based on representation, and effective representation in turn depends on communication between candidate and voter, it is clear that the success of our form of government depends to great extent upon _____.

be based on ~ : ~에 바탕을 두다 representátion [reprizentéiʃən] n. 대의(대표)제도 in turn : 차례로, 교대로 depénds on/upon ~ : ~에 의존하다 cándidate [kǽndədeit] n. 후보 vóter [vóutər] n. 유권자 to great extént : 대단한 정도로, 크게

(A) the use of language

(B) ample funds

(C) the use of social activities

(D) the execution of power

34

Poverty and misfortune are coming, but _____ can be overcome by _____.

póverty [pávərti] *n.* 가난 misfórtune [misfɔ́:rtʃ ən] *n.* 불행 overcóme [ouvərkʌ́m] *v.* 극복하다 (overcome-overcame-overcome)

(A) knowledge—emotion

(B) religion—superstition

(C) knowledge—intelligence

(D) superstition—knowledge

35

People may be divided, according to their attitude towards money, into two classes: one wants to _____ money; the other wants to _____ it.

divíde [diváid] *v.* 나누다 accórding to ~ : ~에 따라 áttitude [ǽtitju:d] *n.* 태도 one ~ the other ~ : (둘 중에) 하나는 ~ 다른 하나는 ~

(A) save—spare

(B) have—spend

(C) spend—waste

(D) make—save

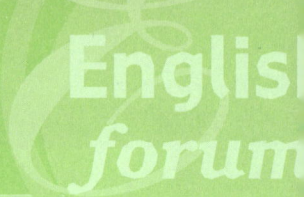
| 문장 완성하기 |

영문 독해에서 앞으로 전개될 내용을 미리 예측하는 능력은 중요하다.
문장 완성하기는 앞에 전개된 글을 통해서 뒤에 이어질 글을 찾는 연습이다.
문장 완성하기 연습을 통해서 글의 전체적인 흐름을 파악하는 능력을 높일
수 있다.

Question Type 1

다음 각 문항의 문장을 읽고 빈칸에 들어갈 가장 적절한 말을 고르시오.

1

Despite your imagined freedom, you are chained always by the laws of cause and effect. You may be free to leap from a skyscraper or to refrain from eating for a week, but you are not free to _____.

> despíte [dispáit] *prep.* ~에도 불구하고 (= in spite of) chain [tʃein] *v.* 구속하다, 묶다 the laws of cause and efféct : 인과의 법칙 be free to do : 자유로이/마음대로 ~하다 leap [liːp] *v.* 뛰어내리다 skýscraper [skáiskreipər] *n.* 고층건물 refráin from -ing : ~하는 것을 회피하다

(A) commit murder
(B) go abroad
(C) escape the consequence
(D) commit suicide

chained by the laws of cause and effect = you are <u>not</u> free to escape the results

2

Every day we use many things made in our own country from raw materials that are imported. Other countries have mineral and vegetable products that we do not have, and we have some that they cannot supply for themselves. Some of our factories would have to close if we were not able to _____.

raw matérial : 원료 carry on trade : 교역을 하다 míneral [mínərəl] *n.* 광물 végetable products : 채소제품, 농산물 supplý for oneself : 자급하다

(A) import food

(B) carry on international trade

(C) collect high tariffs

(D) invest in foreign factories

앞의 두 문장은 결국 국제교역(무역)의 개념을 설명한 글이다.

3

During the American Revolution the people of Canada remained loyal to England although the rebelling colonies tried to persuade them to _____.

the Américan Revolútion : 미국혁명, 영국의 식민지에서 벗어나려던 미국의 독립전쟁을 일컬음 remáin *v.* ~한 상태로 남다 loyal to ~ : ~에 충성하는 rebél [ribél] *v.* 봉기하다, 날뛰다 the rebélling cólonies : 독립을 원하여 봉기한 영국의 식민지들 persuade ~to *do* : ~하도록 ~를 설득하다.

(A) state exactly how they stood on the issue

(B) surrender to the English troops

(C) help England fight the rebelling colonies

(D) join the war for independence

양보의 연결어 although를 단서로 remained loyal의 대립되는 말을 찾는다.

4

People with fixed incomes are fortunate in time of falling prices. Their real incomes increase because their dollars will buy more goods and services than they did _____.

fíxed íncomes : 고정수입 fórtunate [fɔ́ːrtʃənit] *adj.* 다행인 in time of ~ : ~할 때 réal íncomes : 실질수입

(A) after war
(B) when goods and services were plentiful
(C) during inflation
(D) when prices were higher

연결어 more ~ than을 참고로 in time of falling prices의 반대되는 표현을 찾는다.

5

When you first come to college you are intellectually very young and have not yet learned to proceed safely under your own intellectual power. Your ideas are not yet your own. Therefore the first thing you must learn at college is _____.

intelléctually [intəléktʃuəli] *adv.* 지적으로 procéed [prousíːd] *v.* 나아가다, 진출하다

(A) to stand on your own ideas
(B) to know what safety is
(C) to proceed safely
(D) to know what intellectual power is

결과를 나타내는 연결어 Therefore가 단서로서, 바로 앞에 있는 문장이 문제해결의 열쇠가 된다.

6

The Korean economic system does not exist in isolation but is a part of the worldwide economic system. Thus, the economic life of the Korean people is greatly affected by _____.

isolation [aisəléiʃən] *n.* 고립, 소외 afféct [əfékt] *v.* 영향을 미치다

(A) prices which the farmers get for their products

(B) the daily rise and fall of the stock markets

(C) which political party is in control of the government

(D) the economic life of all other peoples

연결어 Thus를 힌트로 한다. 앞뒤 문장이 같은 맥락으로 한국경제 대 세계경제의 대비구문이다.

7

Many people go through life committing partial suicide—destroying their talents, energies, and creative qualities. To learn how to be good to oneself is often more difficult than to learn how to be good to others.

According to this passage, we should _____.

go through life : 인생을 살아가다 commít pártial súicide : 부분적인 자살을 하다 destróy [distrɔ́i] *v.* 파괴하다(*cf.* destrúction [distrʎkʃən] *n.* 파괴) creátive quálities : 창조적인 능력들

(A) be more selfish than we usually are

(B) know that human beings are self-seeking

(C) not commit suicide

(D) take care not to neglect our own abilities

결론을 묻는 문제이다. 둘째 문장은 good to oneself와 good to others의 대비구조다. 비교의 연결어 more~than을 참고할 것.

8

The ability to use good English is enhanced by careful observation of distinctions between uses of synonyms. A man who can not tell a mule from a horse would likely blunder in choosing a mount. If we are to avoid blunders in the choice of words, it is necessary to _____.

enhánce [enhǽns] *v.* 고양하다, 향상시키다 observátion [àbzərvéiʃən] *n.* 관찰 distínction [distíŋkʃən] *n.* 차이 sýnonym [sínənim] *n.* 비슷한 말 mule [mju:l] *n.* 노새 blúnder [blʎndər] *v.* 실수하다 (= make a mistake) mount [maunt] *n.* 탈 것 (말이나 낙타, 노새 등 짐승류)(*cf.* véhicle [víːikəl] *n.* 탈 것 (자동차 류))

(A) learn spelling along with pronunciation

(B) study differences in meanings of closely related words

(C) know the people to whom we are talking

(D) observe subtle differences in pronunciation

핵심어 careful observation of distinctions between uses of synonyms, tell a mule from a horse, blunder in choosing a mount, avoid blunders in the choice of words 등과 같은 의미의 표현을 찾는다.

9

When we hate our enemies, we give them power over us—power over our sleep, our appetites and our happiness. They would dance with joy if they knew how much they were worrying us. Our hate is not hurting them at all, but it is turning our own days and nights into hellish turmoil. The moral suggested by this passage is _____.

énemy [énəmi] *n.* 적(敵) áppetite [ǽpitait] *n.* 식욕 wórry [wɔ́ːri] *v.* 걱정 끼치다, 근심하게 하다, 괴롭히다 turn A into B : A를 B속으로 넣다 héllish [héliʃ] *adj.* 지옥 같은 túrmoil [tɔ́ːrmɔil] *n.* 소동, 소란 héllish túrmoil : 지옥 같은 혼란

(A) love your enemies

(B) don't let your hate make yourself unhappy

(C) you should not let your enemies have power over you

(D) your happy life depends on love, not hate

결국 이 글의 주제를 묻는 문제로서, 세 번째 문장(Our hate …)이 바로 주제문이다.

10

When a group of persons has been conquered by a nation and has been forced to learn the language and customs of the conquering nation, there is much resistance on the part of the conquered people to doing so. When, however, people voluntarily leave their home country and go to a new country, they should not hesitate to _____.

cónquer [kάŋkər] *v.* 정복하다 be force to *do* : ~하도록 강요받다 resístance [rizístəns] *n.* 저항 on the part of ~ : ~의 쪽에서는 vóluntarily [vάlənterili] *adv.* 자발적으로(*cf.* volúnteer [valəntíər] *n.* 지원자, 자원봉사자) hésitate [hézəteit] *v.* 주저하다

(A) learn the customs and language of their new home

(B) retain the customs and feelings of their old home

(C) discover ways in which their new home can be improved

(D) speak their own language

대조를 나타내는 however를 유의할 것.

Question Type 2

다음 각 문제 글의 다음에 이어질 글의 요지로 가장 적당한 표현을 고르시오.

11

Since the bamboo plants on which the Giant Panda in China depends for survival flower only once every eighty to one hundred years, it is remarkable that the creature continues to exist.

bambóo (plants) : 대나무 survíval [sərváivəl] n. 생존 flówer [fláuər] v. 꽃피다 remárkable [rimá:rkəbəl] adj. 놀라운 créature [krí:tʃər] n. 피조물, 생물 contínue (to do) : ~을 계속하다 exíst [igzíst] v. 존재하다, 생존하다

(A) Something more about the survival of the Giant Panda.

(B) Something more about the flowering cycle of the bamboo.

(C) Something about other animals native to China.

(D) Something about the way some other species are finding it difficult to survive.

12

Although several producers have been interested in backing a movie based on Hitler's last days, the necessary documentation to make such a film has not been found.

prodúcer [prədjúːsər] *n.* 제작자. 흔히 우리가 프로듀서(PD)라고 부르는 방송국의 프로그램 연출자는 director 또는 program director라고 한다. 그러므로 director란 영화를 만들 때 직접 연출을 지휘하는 감독을 말하고, producer는 영화를 제작하는 회사의 사주, 즉 제작자(제작업자)를 말한다. back [bæk] *v.* 지원하다 based on ~ : ~에 바탕을 둔 documentátion [dɑkjəmentéiʃən] *n.* 기록 film : 영화(= movie)

(A) A list of the interested producers.

(B) An account of Hitler's last days.

(C) More about film-making.

(D) More about the necessary documentation.

뒷 문장 the necessary documentation … has not been found. 가 이어질 글의 내용을 암시하는 단서가 된다.

13

The invention of the cotton gin meant more than just a way to get the green seeds of the cotton without damaging the fiber.

invéntion [invénʃən] *n.* 발명(*cf.* invént [invént] *v.* 발명하다) cótton gin : 조면기 mean [miːn] *v.* 의미하다, 뜻하다 (mean−meant−meant) seed [siːd] *n.* 씨, 씨앗 dámage [dǽmidʒ] *v.* 손상시키다, 파괴하다 fíber [fáibər] *n.* 섬유

(A) An account of how the cotton gin worked.

(B) An account of other effects the invention gave rise to.

(C) An account of how cotton was processed before the cotton gin was invented.

(D) An account of the importance of cotton to the world economy.

핵심어인 … meant more than just a way to get … 를 단서로 한다.

14

Something happens to men and women who are accepted in the astronaut program, something beyond mere improved physical fitness and increased technical competence.

accépt [æksépt] v. 받아들이다, 수용하다 ástronaut prógram : 우주비행사 프로그램 mere [miər] *adj.* 단지 ~에 불과한, 단순한
impróved phýsical fítness : 향상된 신체조건 incréased téchnical cómpetence : 향상된 기술적 능력

(A) An explanation of the qualities required for acceptance into the astronaut program.

(B) An explanation of why improved physical fitness and increased technical competence occur.

(C) An explanation of other ways in which those accepted change.

(D) An explanation of the significance of the astronaut program in improving physical fitness and technical competence.

주어 Something이란 바로 … something beyond mere improved … technical program. 이다

15

Thirty years before, it had taken him four days to make the trip from Seattle to Cleveland.

it takes (someone) (some time) to *do* ~ : (누가) ~하는데 (시간)이 걸리다 make a trip : 여행하다 from A to B : A에서 B
까지

(A) A description of Munich thirty years later.

(B) An explanation of the number of times he had made the trip over a thirty-year period.

(C) A description of modern Kaufbeuren.

(D) A contrast involving the time taken for the trip thirty years later.

Thirty years before, take him four days 등이 단서가 된다

16

The student was confused, not because of the content of the lecture, but because of the teacher's style of delivery.

confúse [kənfjúːz] v. 혼동시키다 not A but B : A가 아니고 B이다 cóntent [kántent] *n.* 내용 lécture [léktʃər] *n.* 강의
style [stail] *n.* 양식, 방법 (= manner) delívery [dilívəri] *n.* 전달(*cf.* delíver [dilívər] v. 전달하다)

(A) A description of the teacher's way of speaking.

(B) A summary of what the teacher said.

(C) A description of the course.

(D) An explanation of why the content was confusing.

not ··· but because of the teacher's style of delivery가 핵심어로서 이어질 글을 유추하는 단서가 된다

17

The study of function, rather than form, produces a different scheme.

fúnction [fʌ́ŋkʃən] *n*. 기능 schéme [ski:m] *n*. 체제, 구조 rather than : ~보다는 오히려

(A) How the new from is produced.

(B) How the study of function is different from that of form.

(C) Something about the study of function.

(D) Something about the study of form.

rather than form이 단서가 되는 말이다.

18

So fixed was the idea of the earth's being the center of the universe for people in the Middle Ages that they were reluctant to reconsider it in light of new discoveries and theories.

úniverse [júːnəvəːrs] *n*. 우주 Middle Ages : 중세 be relúctant to *do* : ~하기를 꺼리다 in light of ~ : ~의 측면에서 discóvery [diskʌ́vəri] *n*. 발견 théory [θíːəri] *n*. 이론

(A) Something about people in the Middle Ages.

(B) Something about the nature of fixed ideas.

(C) Something about the new discoveries and theories.

(D) Something about the earth's being the center of the universe.

consider it in light of new discoveries and theories라는 표현으로 볼 때, 구체적으로 new discoveries and theories가 무엇인지 제시될 것이다.
도치된 문장을 바로 적어보면, The idea of the earth's being the center of the universe for people in the Middle Ages was so fixed that they were reluctant to reconsider it in light of new discoveries and theories.

19

Until recently, the only way different segments of a population could come to know about each other was through direct contact.

ségment [ségmənt] *n.* 부분, 계층 populátion [pɑpjəléiʃən] *n.* 인구 diréct cóntact : 직접접촉

(A) Why direct contact is significant today.

(B) The difference in the situation today.

(C) Other ways in which different segments of a population could know about each other in the past.

(D) More about different segments of the population.

Until recently로 보아 시대에 따라 다른 접촉방식을 설명할 것으로 유추된다.

20

For this auto manufacturer however, there is a lot more at stake than next year's model.

áuto [ɔ́ːtou] *n.* 자동차 (automobile의 줄임말) áuto manufácturer : 자동차메이커, 자동차회사 be at stake : 돈이 걸려 있는

(A) What is at stake for other auto manufacturers.

(B) The characteristics of next year's model.

(C) The position of this auto manufacturer in relation to the others.

(D) What else is at stake for this auto manufacturer.

… a lot more at stake than에는 어떤 것이 있는지 부연설명이 요구된다.

21

Even at Westlake High School, where there are fully-equipped classrooms and a competent staff, there are many students who fail to pass the college entrance exams.

fúlly-equípped clássroom : 완벽한 시설의 교실 cómpetent [kámpətənt] *adj.* 능력 있는, 유능한(*cf.* cómpetence [kámpətəns] *n.* 능력) staff [stæf] *n.* 간부, 직원, 대학이나 학교 등의 교수나 교직원

(A) A explanation of the kind of equipment in the school's classrooms.

(B) More details about the staff of Westlake High School.

(C) A comparison of results at Westlake High School and those at other schools.

(D) An account of how Westlake High School students do at college.

Even at Westlake high school에서 이미 다른 학교와 비교하는 내용이 전개됨을 예상할 수 있다.

22

Perhaps we have to think in terms of bringing down unemployment levels rather than in terms of combating inflation at all costs.

in terms of ~ : ~의 관점에서, ~의 측면에서 bring down ~ : ~을 끌어내리다 unemployment level : 실업률 rather than ~ : ~ 보다는 차라리 combat [kámbæt] v. ~와 싸우다 at all costs : 어떤 대가(희생)를 치르고서라도, 무슨 수를 써서라도 (= at any cost)

(A) The importance of combating inflation.

(B) The importance of terms.

(C) The importance of costs.

(D) The importance of bringing down unemployment levels.

핵심어 : bringing down unemployment levels.   연결어 rather than도 핵심어를 강조한다.

23

The chairman of the company had wanted to say, in his speech to the shareholders in Chicago, that future pay increases should be kept to under 5 percent.

Cháirman [tʃέərmən] n. 회장 <기업의 직위 명칭> chairman 회장 président 사장 exécutive diréctor 전무 mánaging diréctor 상무 diréctor 이사 mánager 부장 députy mánager 차장 chief 과장 sháreholder [ʃέərhouldər] n. 투자자, 주주 (= stóckholder) pay [pei] n. 임금 <임금(pay)의 종류> salary:연봉과 같이 비교적 장기간에 걸쳐 정기적으로 지불되는 임금 wage:시간급, 일급, 주급 등으로 계산되어 지불되는 급료 fee:변호사료(lawyer's fee), 진료비(doctor's fee) 따위

(A) The reasons why earlier pay increases had been above 5 percent.

(B) The reasons for keeping future pay increases under 5 percent.

(C) An account of what the chairman actually said.

(D) An explanation of why the meeting had been held in Chicago.

24

So fixed is the equation of tourism with escape and holiday-making that we are reluctant to consider it in the same light as a pilgrimage.

equátion [ikwéiʒən] n. 등식화, 동일시 같은 것으로 여김(cf. équal [í:kwəl] adj. 동등한 équalize [í:kwəlaiz] v. 평등하게 하다, 같게 하다 equátor [ikwéitər] n. 적도) escápe [iskéip] n. 탈출 v. 탈출하다 holiday-making : 휴일행락, 휴일 즐기기(cf. holiday-maker : 휴일행락객) be relúctant to do ~ : ~하기를 꺼리다 in the same light as ~ : ~와 같은 측면(관점)에서

(A) Considerations before beginning a pilgrimage.

(B) Suggestions for unusual vacations.

(C) Distinctions between tourism and a pilgrimage.

(D) Similarities between tourism and a pilgrimage.

the equation of A with B : A를 B와 동일시 함
주어인 the equation of tourism with escape and holiday-making이 핵심어이다. equation과 similarities는 같은 내용을 달리 표현한 것뿐이다.
도치된 문장을 바로 써보면, The equation of tourism with escape and holiday-making is so fixed that we are reluctant to consider it in the same light as a pilgrimage.

25

Pilgrims can be met on almost any train, bus, or mountain trail in India, yet we might not recognize them as pilgrims.

mountain trail : 산길 récognize [rékəgnaiz] v. 인식하다, 알아보다 statístics [stətístiks] n. 통계, 통계학

(A) Statistics on the number of pilgrims in India.

(B) Something about traveling by train or bus in India.

(C) Why the pilgrims might not be recognizable as such.

(D) Other places where pilgrims might be met.

yet we might not recognize them as pilgrims 에 대한 이유나 근거가 제시되는 것이 당연하다.

Focus 7

|지칭어(referents) 찾기|

좋은 글은 문장이 간결하다.

같은 말이 자주 되풀이되지 않는다.

반복을 피하기 위해 흔히 관련 대명사나 대동사를 쓴다.

이 대명사들이 가리키는 말(지칭어)을 빨리 찾는 것이 독해에서 매우 중요하다.

Question Type 1

각 문항의 글에서 밑줄 친 주격대명사 it, she, he, they가 지칭하는 말을 찾아 쓰시오.

1

The administration has decided to give more financial support to the average student. This week <u>it</u> indicated its intention to increase the number of scholarships based on need by 35 precent in the next year.

administrátion [ædminəstréiʃən] *n.* 행정부 fináncial suppórt : 재정지원 the áverage student : 평균학생, 일반학생
inténtion [inténʃən] *n.* 의도 incréase [inkríːs] *v.* 상승시키다, 향상시키다(*opp.* decréase [diːkríːs] *v.* 줄이다, 감소하다)
schólarship [skálərʃip] *n.* 장학금, 장학생 based on ~ : ~을 근거로 need [niːd] *n.* 요구

뒷 문장에서처럼, 비인칭 주어 it로 표현되어 주어 역할을 수행할 수 있는 명사를 앞 문장에서 찾는다.

2

Although Professor Elkins has recently been challenged by Associate Professor Daniel and Professor Taylor, <u>she</u> received the Golden Apple Award for outstanding teaching for the fifth year in a row.

chállenge [tʃǽlindʒ] *v.* 도전하다 outstanding [autstǽndiŋ] *adj.* 뛰어난, 훌륭한 in a row : 한 줄로, 한결같이 〈교수직명〉 proféssor 교수 assóciate proféssor 부교수 assístant proféssor 조교수 hónorary proféssor 명예교수 lécturer 강사

뒷 문장의 주어 역할로 적당한 사람의 이름을 앞 문장에서 찾는다.

3

<u>She</u> has often been compared to her mother, Judy Garland, but Liza Minelli has proven herself to be a star in her own right.

be compáred to ~ : ~에 비유되다, 비교되다 prove [pruːv] *v.* 입증하다, 드러나다 (prove–proved–proven/proved) in one's own right : 자신의 힘으로, 스스로

She가 가리키는 사람은 Judy와 Liza 둘 중임을 쉽게 알 수 있다.

4

Although a woman in the lifeboat shouted to her to jump, the woman standing at the rail of the ship appeared to realize <u>she</u> would not have any chance of being rescued.

lífeboat [láifbout] *n.* 구명정 shout [ʃaut] *v.* 고함치다, 소리치다 rail [reil] *n.* 방책, 난간, 레일 appéar to *do* : ~한 것 같다, ~로 보인다 réscue [réskjuː] *v.* 구조하다, 구출하다 *n.* 구조

she가 a woman in the lifeboat인지 the woman standing at the rail of the ship인지를 확인한다.

5

One thing that Duran did prove about Leonard in their first fight was that <u>he</u> was capable of taking a great deal of punishment.

prove [pruːv] *v.* 증명하다 be cápable of -ing : ~할 수 있다, ~하기 쉽다 púnishment [pʌ́niʃmənt] *n.* 벌, 처벌 take púnishment : 벌점을 받다

Duran과 Leonard 둘 중에 take a great deal of punishment를 하는 사람이 누군지를 알면 된다.

6

A spokesman for the film company discussed the failure of the firm's latest western epic with reporters. <u>He</u> stated that the company would probably lose more than the 15 million dollars it had cost to make the film.

spókesman [spóuksmən] *n.* 대변인 the film company : 영화사 discúss [diskʌ́s] *v.* 의논하다, 협의하다 firm [fəːrm] *n.* 회사 épic [épik] *n.* 서사시(*cf.* lýric [lírik] *n.* 서정시) wéstern épic : 서부서사시, 여기서는 미국의 서부개척사를 다룬 영화를 말한다. repórter [ripɔ́ːrtər] *n.* 기자 state [steit] *v.* 말하다, 언급하다

인칭대명사 He로 받는 명사는 앞 문장에서 A spokesman 하나뿐이다.

7

Michael Cimino, director of Heaven's Gate, which stars Kris Kristofferson, recently reported that <u>he</u> will begin work on another film before the end of the year.

diréctor [diréktər] *n.* 감독 Heaven's Gate : 천국의 문 star [staːr] *v.* ~를 주연시키다

Michael과 Kris 둘 중에서 누가 begin work on anther film 할 것인가를 확인하면 된다.

8

Even though <u>they</u> have been in a more difficult position in recent years, small bankers continue to be able to influence the direction of development in their communities.

even though : 비록 ~일지라도 be in a position : 어떤 지경(위치)에 처하다 bánker [bǽŋkər] *n.* 은행가, 은행 ínfluence [ínfluəns] *v.* 영향을 주다 diréction [dirékʃən] *n.* 방향

they라는 인칭대명사로 받을 수 있는 명사는 하나다.

9

The committee has made the suggestion to all foreign investors that <u>they</u> should study all applicable laws before buying property.

commíttee [kəmíti] *n.* 위원회 make a suggéstion : 제안하다 invéstor [invéstər] *n.* 투자자 fóreign invéstors : 외국인 투자자들 ápplicable [ǽplikəbəl] *adj.* 적용 가능한 próperty [prápərti] *n.* 재산, 소유권

they는 복수형 인칭대명사이므로 다수의 사람을 찾는다.

10

The basketball team never lacked loud supporters, but <u>they</u> rarely responded to this show of enthusiasm.

lack [læk] *v.* ~이 결핍하다, ~이 없다 loud [laud] *adj.* 요란한, 시끄러운 (= noisy) suppórter [səpɔ́ːrtər] *n.* 지지자 rárely [réərli] *adv.* 드물게, 좀체 ~않는 (= seldom) respónd [rispánd] *v.* 반응하다 enthúsiasm [enθúːziæzəm] *n.* 열정, 열광

they가 The basketball team인지 loud supporters인지를 파악하면 알 수 있다.

다음 각 문항의 글에서 밑줄친 him, her, them 등 목적격 대명사가 가리키는 말을 찾아 쓰시오.

11

Scott Fitzgerald, who first introduced <u>him</u> to a publisher, was one of the few contemporary writers that Hemingway did not turn against.

Francis Scott Fitzgerald (1896~1940) 미국의 소설가, 대표작 *The Great Gatsby* (1925) públisher [pʌ́bliʃər] *n.* 출판인, 출판사 contemporary [kəntémpəreri] *adj.* 동시대의, 당대의 Ernest Hemingway (1899~1961) 미국의 소설가, 대표작 *The Sun Also Rises* (1926), *A Farewell to Arms* (1929), *For Whom the Bell Tolls* (1940), *The Old Man and the Sea* (1952), 1954년에 '노벨문학상' 받음. turn against : ~에 반대하다, ~와 대립하다, ~를 배반하다

Scott Fitzgerald : one of the few contemporary writers / Hemingway : him

12

Catching sight of <u>him</u> in a supermarket one day, Archer followed the man with the limp to an apartment in a rundown neighborhood.

catch sight of ~ : ~를 발견하다(보다), ~이 눈에 띄다 limp [limp] *n.* 절뚝거리기 *v.* 다리를 절다 *adj.* 지친, 약한 rundown : 지친, 황폐한

Archer : 주어 (= He who caught sight of him) / the man with the limp : him

13

The award was presented to the playwright by the Chairman of the Committee, who said of <u>him</u> that he brought plesure to literally millions of theatergoers and television viewers.

awárd [əwɔ́ːrd] *n.* 상(賞) presént [prizént] *v.* 주다, 수여하다 pláywright [pleirait] *n.* 극작가 líterally [lítərəli] *adv.* 말 그대로, 글자 그대로 millions of : 수백만의 théatergoer [θíətərgouər] *n.* 관객 víewer[vjúːər] *n.* 시청자

the playwright : him, he / the Chairman of the Committee : 주어 (= the person who said of him that …)

14

While Jane was persuading Mary to ask her for the keys to the car, Mrs. Jones happened to be listening at the door and quickly went downstairs and out of the house.

persuáde [pəːrswéid] v. 설득하다 persuáde A to *do* : ~하도록 A를 설득하다 ask A for ~ : A에게 ~를 요청하다
happen to *do* : 우연히 ~하다 listen at : (문에 귀를 대고) 엿듣다 dównstairs [dáunstɛərz] n. 아래층 *adv.* 아래층으로
(*opp.* úpstáirs [ʌ́pstɛ́ərz] n. 위층 *adv.* 위층으로)

앞 문장의 구조를 보면서 Jane, Mary, her 세 사람의 관계를 잘 파악한 다음에, Mrs. Jones와의 관계를 확인하면 쉽다.

15

Looking at her closely for the first time in months, Elizabeth realized sadly that the woman was indeed beginning to grow old.

for the first time : 처음으로 in months : 여러 달이 지난 후에 grow old : 늙다

Looking at her의 주어는 뒷 문장의 주어인 Elizabeth와 같다.

16

Mrs. Lyon decided that she'd bring Kelly here in the evening and help her pick some clothes out because she liked doing so.

help *someone* do : (누가) ~하는 것을 도와주다 pick *something* out : ~을 고르다

Mrs. Lyon : she / Kelly : her

17

Knowing <u>them</u> well, the Hammonds realized that the Shepherds were unlikely to be on time to meet their guests.

the Hammonds, the Shepherds : 해먼드씨 가족, 셰퍼드씨 가족 (the+성+s) be unlikely to *do* : ~할 것 같지 않다 be on time : 정각에, 시간에 맞춰

the Hammonds : Knowing의 주어, guests / the Shepherds : them

18

Doctors treating patients with diet pills usually warn <u>them</u> of the dangers of addiction.

treat [tri:t] *v.* 치료하다 diet [dáiət] *n.* 다이어트 pill [pil] *n.* 알약 warn A of ~ : A에게 ~을 경고하다 addíction [ədíkʃən] *n.* 중독

Doctors는 them의 주어이다.

19

Though it is not usually difficult to understand <u>them</u>, stutterers often cause parents a lot of worries.

stútter [stʌ́tər] *v.* 말을 더듬다 stutterer *n.* 말더듬이 cause [kɔːz] *v.* 일으키다, ~을 끼치다 wórry [wɔ́ːri] *n.* 근심, 걱정

them이 가리키는 말이 stutterers인지 parents인지는 쉽게 알 수 있다.

20

Intrigued by insects of all kinds, the youngsters spent hours trapping and studying <u>them</u>.

intrígue [intríːg] *v.* 흥미를 유발하다, 호기심을 끌다 ínsect [ínsekt] *n.* 곤충 yóungster [jʌ́ŋstər] *n.* 어린이, 젊은이

them이 가리키는 말이 insects of all kinds인지 they youngsters인지는 쉽게 알 수 있다.

다음 각 문항의 글에서 밑줄친 대명사 소유격 its, her, his, their 등이 가리키는 말을 찾아 쓰시오.

21

    In 1977, the former home of John D. Spreckels acquired the status of Historical Landmark. <u>Its</u> history goes back to 1908, when it was built by Mr. Spreckels.

> fórmer [fɔ́:rmər] *adj.* 이전의, 과거의, 앞의 (= príor)(*cf.* the former : 전자 the latter : 후자) acquíre [əkwáiər] *v.* 얻다, 획득하다 státus [stáitəs] *n.* 지위, 신분 (*cf.* státue [stǽtʃu:] *n.* 상(像)) státure [stǽtʃər] *n.* 신장, 키 státute [stǽtʃu:t] *n.* 법규, 규칙, 정관 lándmark [lǽndmɑːrk] *n.* (여행자를 위한) 표지물, 경계표지, 획기적인 사건, 역사적 의의가 있는 건물 (= histórical lándmark) go back to ~ : ~(언제)까지 거슬러 올라가다

> Its는 사람이 아닌 사물을 받는 소유대명사이다.

22

    Many people visit San Diego every year because of the mild year-round climate, the beaches, and Sea World. But <u>its</u> most famous attraction is probably the exceptionally fine San Diego Zoo.

> mild [maild] *adj.* 온화한(*opp.* strong, bitter : 강한) year-round : 연중, 일년 내내 climate [kláimit] *n.* 기후(*cf.* weather [weðər] *n.* 날씨) beach [bi:tʃ] *n.* 해변 Sea World : 샌디에고에 있는 유명한 해양박물관 attráction [ətrǽkʃən] *n.* 매력, 사람을 끄는 특별한 장소나 행사 excéptionally [iksépʃənəli] *adv.* 예외적으로

> the mild year-round climate, the beach, Sea World 등은 일반적인 샌디에고의 attractions이다

23

    <u>Its</u> usefulness was a thing of the past, but his first bicycle continued to stand in the corner in his bedroom.

> úsefulness [jú:sfəlnis] *n.* 유용성, 쓸모 있음 continue to *do* : ~를 계속하다

> Its로 받는 사물은 his first bicycle 뿐이다.

24

The music teacher reported that <u>her</u> newest pupil, Donna Winter, had the greatest potential of any student she had ever had.

púpil [pjúpil] *n.* 제자, 학생 poténtial [poutén∫əl] *n.* 가능성, 잠재성

The music teacher : her, she / newest pupil = Donna Winter (동격)

25

In an account based on <u>her</u> years sharing an apartment with economist Barbara Ward, Elizabeth Monroe described her as an early-morning writer of extraordinary facility.

accóunt [əkáunt] *n.* 이유, 근거 based on ~ : ~를 바탕으로 한 share [∫ɛər] *v.* 공유하다, 나누다 descríbe [diskráib] *v.* 묘사하다 an early-morning writer : 아침 일찍 일어나 글을 쓴 작가 extraórdinary [ikstrɔ́ːrdəneri] *adj.* 비범한 facílity [fəsíləti] *n.* 재능, 시설

Barbara Ward를 제외하고 인칭명사는 Elizabeth Monroe 뿐이다.

26

<u>His</u> business began to grow when Sterne joined forces with a young lawyer from his hometown.

force [fɔːrs] *n.* 집단, 병력, 힘

Sterne과 a young lawyer 두 사람 중에 주어 역할을 할 수 있는 것을 찾는다.

27

With <u>his</u> sixty acres of land covered with five hundred varieties of lilacs, it is easy to understand why Ken Berdeen of Kennebunk, Maine is known as "The Lilac Man".

ácre [éikər] *n.* 에이커 (1acre = 4,046.71평방미터) cóvered with ~ : ~로 덮여 있는 varíety [vəráiəti] *n.* 다양성, 변화, 갖가지, 종류 be known as ~ : ~로 알려져 있다

his로 받을 사람 이름은 하나뿐이다.

28

    <u>Their</u> neighbors, the Bantu, have begun to have some effect on the way the Bushmen live.

---

the Bantu : 반투족 the Bushmen : 부시맨족 have an efféct on ~ : ~에 영향을 끼치다 the way (which) the Bushmen live

their neighbors = the Bantu (동격)

29

    As it is the ideas and above all the ways these are expressed, rather than <u>their</u> plots, that interest us about Shakespeare's plays, it is a pleasure to see them over and over again.

As = Because above all : 무엇보다도 expréss [iksprés] v. 표현하다 rather than ~ : ~보다는 오히려 ínterest [íntərist] v. 흥미를 끌다 over and over again : 또 다시

가능한 명사들 the ideas, the ways these are expressed, Shakespeare's plays 중에서 plot (플롯)을 가지는 것은 plays (연극)이다.

30

    The defendants insisted on addressing the members of the jury, thus disregarding the advice of <u>their</u> lawyers.

---

deféndant [diféndənt] n. 피고인 insist on -ing : ~을 주장하다 addréss [ədrés] v. 연설하다, 해임하다 júry [dʒúəri] n. 배심원단(보통 12명) (cf. júror [dʒúərər] n. 배심원 judge [dʒʌdʒ] n. 판사, 재판장 láwyer [lɔ́ːjər] n. 변호사 prósecutor [prásəkjuːtər] n. 검사) disregard [disrigáːrd] v. 무시하다

The defendants와 the members of the jury 둘 중에서 lawyers(변호사)를 고용한('their lawyers') 것은 The defendants 들이다.

다음 각 문항의 글에서 밑줄친 소유대명사 hers, his, theirs가 가리키는 말을 찾아 쓰시오.

31

Jean, along with her sisters Doris and May, baked cakes for the annual contest at the county fair. Jean was sorry <u>hers</u> lost, but happy that Doris won a ribbon for her entry.

along with ~ : ~와 함께 bake [beik] *v.* 빵을 굽다(*cf.* báker [béikər] *n.* 빵장수 bakery [béikəri] *n.* 빵집) ánnual [ǽnjuəl] *adj.* 1년의, 해마다의 (*cf.* biénnial [baiéniəl] *adj.* 격년의, 2년마다의 행사, 비엔날레(biennale)) perénnial [pəréniəl] *adj.* 일년 내내 지속되는, 연중의, 다년생의 cóunty [káunti] *n.* 우리의 시(市)나 군(郡)쯤 되는 미국의 지방행정단위 fair [fɛər] *n.* (정기적인) 장날, 바자회, 박람회 *adj.* 아름다운, 공정한

Jean : hers lost / Doris : her entry

32

In her article about teaching dance, Carolyn describes the methods of Marion Rice and points out that <u>hers</u>, more than those of any other local dance teacher, have influenced the aspiring dancers in the neighborhood.

ártical [á:rtikl] *n.* 논문, 기사 descríbe [diskráib] *v.* 묘사하다, 설명하다 point out : 지적하다 ínfluence [ínfluəns] *v.* 영향을 미치다 aspíring [əspáiəriŋ] *adj.* 야심찬, 상승하는

her article : Carolyn's article the / methods of Marion Rice : hers

33

The critic hardly referred to <u>hers</u> at all, but when Sally heard what he had to say about Mary's paintings, she felt relieved rather than disappointed.

crític [krítik] *n.* 비평가 refér to ~ : ~에 대하여 말하다, 언급하다 hardly ~ at all : 결코 ~ 아니하다 (= not ~ at all) relíeve [rilí:v] *v.* 안심시키다, 구제하다 disappóint [disəpóint] *v.* 실망시키다

34

Van Cliburn has given advice and encouragement to many young pianists just beginning their concert careers. <u>His</u> took off in 1958 when he took top honors at Moscow's first Tchaikovsky Competition.

encóuragement [enkɔ́ːridʒmənt] *n.* 격려 caréer [kəríər] *n.* 경력, 활동, 성공 take óff : 이륙하다, 시작하다 *n.* 이륙, 시작 top hónors : 최고의 영예 competítion [kɑmpətíʃən] *n.* 경연, 경쟁(*cf.* compéte [kəmpíːt] *v.* 경쟁하다 compétitive [kəmpétətiv] *adj.* 경쟁적인)

뒷 문장의 주어가 될 만한 핵심어를 앞 문장에서 찾는다.

35

Pierre Cardin has expanded his interests and become a restaurant owner. <u>His</u> is the famous Maxim's of Paris, founded in 1893.

expánd [ikspǽnd] *v.* 확대하다 ínterest [íntərist] *n.* 관심

뒷 문장의 주어 역할을 할 만한 핵심어를 앞 문장에서 찾으면 바로 나온다.

36

After Bill had read Tom Burn's article, he was sure it would win the prize as <u>his</u> dealt with the same subject in a much more superficial manner.

read [riːd]-read [red]-read [red] be sure (that) ~ : ~를 확신하다 win the prize : 상을 타다 deal [diːl] *v.* 다루다, 취급하다 (deal-dealt-dealt) superfícial [suːpərfíʃəl] *adj.* 표면적인, 자세한, 외견상의

Bill : he, his

37

Since theirs was the float which evoked most response from the crowd, the members of the boy's club were disappointed when it placed only second.

Since = Because   float [flout] *n.* 부유물, (낚시의) 찌, (퍼레이드 용) 차   evóke [ivóuk] *v.* 불러일으키다, 환기시키다
respónse [rispáns] *n.* 반응   disappóint [disəpóint] *v.* 실망시키다

문장의 핵심어는 the float와 the members of the boy's club이다.   it = the float

38

David and Roxanna thought that Rose and Charlie's apartment was very luxuriously decorated, but that theirs had a better view.

luxúriously [lʌgʒúəriəs] *adv.* 호화롭게   décorate [dékəreit] *v.* 장식하다, 꾸미다   have a better view : 더 좋은 전망을 가지고 있다, 전망이 더 좋다

역접의 뜻인 but로 앞뒤 문장이 나뉘므로, theirs는 Rose and Charlie's apartment와 대비되는 뜻이다.

39

The English surprisingly beat the French at the battle of Agincourt in 1415 because theirs were the more disciplined archers.

the English : 영국인들   the French : 프랑스인들   surprísingly [sərpráiziŋli] *adv.* 놀랍게도   beat [bi:t] *v.* 물리치다, 쳐부수다 (beat-beat-beat/beaten) 여기서는 과거형이다   báttle [bǽtl] *n.* 전투   díscipline [dísəplin] *v.* 단련하다, 훈련하다 *n.* 징계, 규율, 풍기   árcher [á:rtʃər] *n.* 궁수, 사수

because로 보아 앞 문장의 이유를 설명하는 것이므로 일단 theirs의 인칭은 the English임을 알 수 있다. 그리고 실제 이 전투를 수행한 군인들은 바로 archers들이다.

40

John had entered recipes in so many local contests without success that he was astonished that <u>his</u> was the winning entry in a national competition.

récipe [résəpi] *n.* 조리, 요리, 처방 astónish [əstániʃ] *v.* 놀라게 하다 the winning éntry : 우승 참가품목 entry [éntri] *n.* 참가, 입장, 참가자, 출품물 enter [éntər] *v.* 들어가다

핵심어는 John과 recipes이다.

Question Type 5

다음 각 문항의 글에서 밑줄친 대명사 this, that, these, those가 가리키는 어휘를 찾아 쓰시오

41

The Smith and Philips Research Institute was designated as the recipient of a grant of two million dollars by the Taylor Foundation. <u>This</u> is to be used for the continuation of a study of the cause of warts.

* wart [wɔːrt] *n.* 사마귀, 돌기

reséarch [risɔ́ːrtʃ] *n.* 연구 ínstitute [ínstətjuːt] *n.* 학회, 연구소 désignate [dézigneit] *v.* 지정하다, 임명하다 recípient [risípiənt] *n.* 수령자, 수취인, 수상자 grant [grænt] *n.* 수여품, 하사금, 지원금 foundátion [faundéiʃən] *n.* 재단 be to *do* : ~하기로 되어 있는 continuátion [kəntinjuéiʃən] *n.* 계속, 진행(*cf.* contínue [kəntínjuː] *v.* 계속하다)

'… is to be used for '라는 표현에 적당한 사물이 해당된다.

42

A group of horticulturists in New Jersey has been working on a new project. <u>This</u> involves the development of a completely different type of rose.

* horticúlturist [hɔ̀ːrtəkʌ́ltʃ∂rist] *n.* 원예학자

hórticulture [hɔ́ːrtəkʌ̀ltʃ∂r] *n.* 원예(학) invólve [inválv] *v.* 포함하다

앞 문장에서 지칭어를 this로 받을 수 있는 사물을 찾는다.

43

A daily exercise program results in the need for less sleep for most people. <u>This</u> is partly attributable to the fact that exercisers sleep more soundly than do people who do not exercise regularly.

daily éxercise : 매일 하는 운동 resúlt in ~ : ~의 결과를 낳다, 결과적으로 ~이 되다 attríbutable [ətríbjutəbəl] *adj.* 기인하는, ~에 원인을 돌릴 수 있는(… to) éxerciser [éksərsaizər] *n.* 운동하는 사람 sóundly [sáundli] *adv.* 깊이, 건전하게 sleep soundly : 잠을 깊이 자다, 숙면을 취하다 régularly [régjələrli] *adv.* 정기적으로

This는 앞 문장의 핵심적인 현상, 결과적인 현상을 가리키고 있다.

44

He blamed his failure in business on drink. <u>That</u> was also why he ended up in the hospital with cirrhosis of the liver.

* cirrhósis [siróusis] *n.* 간경화, 간경변

blame [bleim] *v.* ~의 탓으로 돌리다 end up : 결국 마지막에는 ~이 되다, 마지막에는 ~에 살게 되다 cirrhósis [siróusis] *n.* 간경화, 간경변 (간이 딱딱하게 굳어지는 현상) líver [lívər] *n.* 간

drink는 두 가지 좋지 않은 결과를 낳았는데, 하나는 his failure in business이고, 다른 하나는 also why he ended up in the hospital with cirrhosis of liver이다.

45

Many people connect alcohol intake with drunkenness, but <u>that</u> is by no means the only consequence of drinking too much.

connéct A with B : A를 B와 연결짓다 íntake [ínteik] *n.* 흡입구, 섭취량 álcohol íntake : 음주 drúnkenness [drʌ́ŋkənis] *n.* 취기, 알코올 중독 by no means : 결코 ~이 아니다 cónsequence [kánsikwens] *n.* 결과

뒷 문장의 내용으로 보아 앞 문장에서 that으로 지칭될 수 있는 표현은 alcohol intake와 drunkenness이다. 이중에서 the consequence of drinking과 관련되는 말이 정답이다.

46

He insisted on going to the Bahamas for their honeymoon. Fortunately, <u>that</u> was exactly where she wanted to go.

insist on -ing : ~을 주장하다 the Bahamas : 바하마 군도 (여러 개의 섬으로 구성된 군도, 제도 등은 the -s로 표기한다)

지칭어 that가 가리키는 것은 바로 장소(where she wanted to go)이다.

47

Many overweight people blame their condition on physical disorders, but doctors claim that <u>these</u> are seldom the cause of fatness.

óverweight [óuvərweit] *adj.* 무거운, 살찐, 뚱뚱한 (= fat) blame …on ~ : …을 ~ 탓으로 돌리다 phýsical disórder : 신체적 이상 claim [kleim] *v.* 주장하다 séldom [séldəm] *adv.* 결코 ~ 아닌, 좀체 ~ 하지 않는

지칭어 these가 복수형인 점을 생각하면 쉽다.

48

After winning the lottery in Pennsylvania, she bought a Mercedes and a condominium. <u>These</u> were the first two large purchases she had ever been able to pay for in cash.

lóttery [látəri] *n.* 복권 win the lottery : 복권이 당첨되다 a Mercedes : 독일의 자동차회사 벤츠(Benz)사에서 제작한 자동차 이름 condomínium [kɑndəmíniəm] *n.* 콘도 púrchase [pə́ːrtʃəs] *n.* 구매, 구매물품 *v.* 구매하다 in cash : 현찰로(*cf.* in card : 신용카드로)

지칭어 These가 복수형이다.

49

Drinking fine wines and eating Italian food were his favorite pastimes as a young man. Later in his life, <u>these</u> led to his investing all his money in a small Italian restaurant.

pástime [pǽstaim] *n.* 오락, 기분전환, 레크리에이션 lead-led-led invest [invést] *v.* 투자하다

Drinking fine wines and eating Italian food = his favorite pastimes

50

Faulty equipment is sometimes responsible for rollerskating accidents, but problems with balance are <u>those</u> which cause the most falls.

fáulty [fɔ́ːlti] *adj.* 결함 있는(*cf.* fault [fɔːlt] *n.* 결함, 과실, 책임) equípment [ikwípmənt] *n.* 장비 be respónsible for ~ : ~에 책임이 있는 problems with balance : 균형의 문제 (롤러스케이트를 탈 때 필요한 신체균형) fall [fɔːl] *n.* 추락

those = problems with balance (동격)

51

    The first things the new settlers tried to decide on were a flag and a national anthem, <u>those</u> being the most striking symbols of national identity.

séttler [sétlər] *n.* 이주자, 정착민 nátional ánthem : 국가(國歌) stríking [stráikiŋ] *adj.* 인상적인, 두드러진 idéntity [aidéntəti] *n.* 주체성, 정체성

a flag and a national anthem = those (동격)
The first thing (that) the new settlers tried to decide on were

52

    Orange and purple were fashionable that year, but <u>those</u> are by no means the most flattering colors for everyone.

púrple [pə́ːrpəl] *n.* 보라색 fláttering [flǽtəriŋ] *adj.* 아첨하는, 돋보이게 하는

those란 colors를 가리키는 말이다.

53

    Lyndon Johnson was president from 1963 to 1968; <u>those</u> were the years in which the Vietnam War first came to the attention of the American public.

atténtion [əténʃən] *n.* 관심 come to the atténtion : 관심이 되다

1963 to 1968 = those = years in which … (동격)

54

    Signs of aging are unavoidable, but <u>those</u> that can be disguised are of particular interest to cosmetic companies.

sígns of áging : 나이를 먹는 표시, 노화의 증세 unavóidable [ʌnəvóidəbəl] *adj.* 피할 수 없는 disgúise [disgáiz] *v.* 변장(위장)시키다, 감추다 cosmétic [kɑzmétik] *n.* 화장품

다음 각 문항의 글 가운데 밑줄친 말이 지칭하는 어휘를 같은 문장에서 찾아 쓰시오.

55

In 1954, Roger Bannister became the first man to run the mile in four minutes. This time seems incredibly slow by modern-day standards.

mile [mail] *n.* 마일 (1mile = 1,609.3m) incrédibly [inkrédəbli] *adv.* 믿을 수 없을 정도로

앞 문장에서 시간(time)을 찾기는 쉽다.

56

Eventually the two scientists opted to follow their original line. This choice proved to be the right one, and ten years later they were awarded the Nobel Prize for Chemistry.

evéntually [ivéntʃuəli] *adv.* 궁극적으로, 결국 opt [ɑpt] *v.* (~쪽을) 채택하다, 선택하다 oríginal [ərídʒənəl] *adj.* 독자적인, 독창적인 oríginal line : 독자노선 prove to ~ : ~로 판명되다 awárd [əwɔ́:rd] *v.* 상을 주다 chémistry [kémistri] *n.* 화학

opted (to follow their original line)와 choice는 말은 서로 같은 뜻의 표현이다.

57

The conductor was presented with a gold watch at the banquet in his honor. This gift was to commemorate his fifty years of service with the railroad.

condúctor [kəndʌ́ktər] *n.* (기차의) 여객차장 bánquet [bǽŋkwit] *n.* 연회, 잔치 commémorate [kəméməreit] *v.* 기념하다, 축하하다

앞 문장의 'was presented with a gold watch'가 바로 gift를 가리키는 말이다.

58

Many educators now believe that students remember information that they learn on their own better than that presented formally by a teacher. This fact has led to methodological changes in many classrooms.

éducator [édʒukeitər] *n.* 교육자 on their own : 그들 스스로 presént [prizént] *v.* 부여하다, 설명하다, 수여하다 fórmally [fɔ́ːrməli] *adv.* 공식적으로 methodológical [meθədəládʒikəl] *adj.* 방법론적인

methodological changes in many classrooms 라는 현상을 일으킬 정도의 사실은 앞 문장 전체이다.

59

The doctor decided to take out the boy's appendix. This operation was made much more difficult by the circumstances on the island.

take out : 꺼내다, 출발하다 appéndix [əpéndiks] *n.* 부록, 맹장 operátion [apəréiʃən] *n.* 수술, 작전 (*cf.* Caesar's Operation/Section : 제왕절개수술 (Julius Caesar가 이 수술로 태어났다는 전설에서 만들어진 말이다.)) círcumstance [sə́ːrkəmstæns] *n.* 상황

60

The Thunderbird was the most popular American sports car in the fifties. That particular make has changed so greatly, however, that it is no longer considered a sports car by most people.

in the fifties : 1950년대에 make *n.* 구조, 형, 품목, 제조원 no longer ~ : 더 이상 ~이 아닌

61

Somewhat reluctantly, Isabel and Ferdinand agreed to fund Columbus' voyage in search of the Indies. That decision led to perhaps the most important discovery of the last thousand years.

sómewhat [sʌ́mʰwàt] *adv.* 다소 relúctantly [rilʌ́ktəntli] *adv.* 마지못해, 억지로 fund [fʌnd] *v.* 자금을 제공하다 vóyage [vɔ́iidʒ] *n.* 항해 in search of ~ : ~을 찾아서 decísion [disiʒən] *n.* 결정

decision과 agree to do는 같은 의미이다.

62

Albert Einstein was slow to read and write as a child. <u>That surprising fact</u> has lent credence to the idea that not all children should be expected to learn the same things at the same age.

surprísing [sərpráiziŋ] *adj.* 놀라운 lend [lend] *v.* 빌려주다(lend–lent–lent) crédence [krí:dəns] *n.* 신뢰, 신용 expéct [ikspékt] *v.* 기대하다

surprising fact란 앞 문장에서 말하는 사실을 말한다.

63

Wellington defeated Napoleon at Waterloo in 1815. <u>That battle</u> marked the end of one era and the beginning of another.

deféat [difí:t] *v.* 물리치다, 쳐부수다 éra [íərə] *n.* 시대

64

John F. Kennedy was fatally shot on November 22, 1963. <u>That tragedy</u> ended what has been described by some as the Camelot era.

fátally [féitəli] *adv.* 치명적으로, 숙명적으로 shoot-shot-shot descríbe [diskráib] *v.* 묘사하다 Camelot era : 미국의 화려하고 매력 있던 시대, 케네디 정권시대를 가리킨다.

앞 문장의 내용이 바로 비극 (tragedy)이다.

65

He covered his eyes and moaned softly at the sight of insects. Even though he knew <u>these reactions</u> were not rational, he could not control them.

moan [moun] *v.* 신음소리를 내다, 한탄하다 at the sight of ~ : ~을 보고 reáction [ri:ǽkʃən] *n.* 반응 rátional [rǽʃənəl] *adj.* 합리적인, 이성적인, 분별 있는(*opp.* irrátional [irǽʃənəl] *adj.* 분별 없는)

앞 문장에서 행동(reactions)을 나타내는 표현을 찾는다.

66

Our local library receives as many as ten best-sellers each month. These books can be found on a special rack near the entrance.

rack [ræk] *n.* 선반 éntrance [éntrəns] *n.* 출입구(*cf.* éxit [égzit] *n.* 비상구)

67

The map of the new shopping mall shows five restaurants. Those facilities, which are marked in red, are available for business meetings and private banquets.

mall [mɔːl] *n.* 골목길 facílity [fəsíləti] *n.* 시설, 설비 in red : 붉은 글씨로 쓰여진, 붉은 옷을 입은 aváilable [əvéiləbəl] *adj.* 유용한 bánquet [bǽŋkwit] *n.* 연회, 잔치

지칭어 Those facilities가 복수형이라는 것을 인지하고서 앞 문장의 두 facility, the new shopping mall 과 five restaurants 중에서 고른다.

68

He drank and ate to excess, and those problems eventually prevented his becoming a vice-president of the firm.

to/in (an) excéss : 지나치게, 초과하여 prevent -ing : ~을 막다, 못하게 하다 vice-president : 부사장 firm [fəːrm] *n.* 회사

69

As a child, he had taken lessons in tennis and swimming, spent summers at a sports camp, and played Little League Baseball. As a professional athlete, he pointed to those experiences as being responsible for his disciplined attitude.

take lésson : 레슨을 받다 léague [liːg] *n.* 연맹 Little League Baseball : 어린이 야구연맹 áthlete [ǽθliːt] *n.* 운동선수, 육상 선수 dísciplined áttitude : 예의 바른 태도, 훈련된 태도

경험들(experiences)이란 결국 앞 문장에 나열된 사실들이다.

다음 각 문장 가운데 밑줄친 말이 지칭하는 말을 같은 문장에서 찾아 쓰시오.

70

There were clocks of every description in every corner of the shop, but John eventually chose the <u>one</u> he had noticed first.

description [diskrípʃən] *n.* 묘사, 설명(서), 종류, 등급 clocks of every description : 모든 종류의 시계 choose-chose-chosen notice [nóutis] *v.* 발견하다

이 글의 핵심어는 clocks이다.

71

The visitors saw a number of shows during the days they were in New York, but only <u>one</u> of them was really exciting.

이 글의 핵심어는 shows이다.

72

The proposals were discussed at length by the members of the committee, with only <u>one</u> of them emerging intact.

propósal [prəpóuzəl] *n.* 제안, 제의 at léngth : 충분히, 상세히 emérge [imə́ːrdʒ] *v.* 떠오르다, (문제가) 야기되다 intáct [intǽkt] *adj.* 손상되지 않은, 원래대로의

먼저 one of them이 지칭하는 것이 사람인지 아닌지를 확인한다.

73

Sculptures by Grant, Simkins, and several other wellknown artists were on display at the opening, but the only <u>ones</u> to attract favorable comment from the critics were by a relatively unknown artist.

scúlpture [skʌ́lptʃər] *n.* 조각 be on displáy : 전시중인 attráct [ətrǽkt] *v.* 끌다, 얻다 fávorable cómment : 호의적인 평
crític [krítik] *n.* 비평가 rélatively [rélətivli] *adv.* 비교적
〈미술(fine art)관련 용어〉
painting : 회화 (붓으로 그린 경우) drawing : 그림 (연필이나 펜으로 그린 경우) water painting : 수채화 oil painting : 유화
concrete painting : 구상화 abstract painting : 비구상(추상)화 sculpture : 조각 design : 디자인 printing : 판화 lithog-
raphy : 석판화 intaglio printing : 오목판화 relief printing : 볼록판화 brush : 붓 tube : 물감튜브 palette : 빠레트 easel
: 이젤 pastel : 파스텔 cardboard : 두꺼운 종이로 된 판지 canvas : 천으로 된 유화용 화폭 panel : 패널

ones가 지칭하는 것이 사람인지를 먼저 확인한다.

74

Note that the instructions preceding the questions encourage students to concentrate only on the <u>ones</u> they feel they understand.

note [nout] *v.* 주목하다, 유의하다 instrúction [instrʌ́kʃən] *n.* 지시사항 precéde [prisíːd] *v.* ~에 앞서다 encóurage
[enkə́ːridʒ] *v.* 격려하다 cóncentrate [kánsəntreit] *v.* 집중하다 (~ on)

instructions, questions, students 등이 모두 ones로 받을 수 있다. they = students

75

After eliminating the <u>ones</u> which were obviously of no interest, the members of the board passed around the remaining applications for further consideration.

elíminate [ilímineit] *v.* 제거하다 óbviously [ábviəsli] *adv.* 명백히 of no ínterest : 이익이 없는, 관심이 없는 board
[bɔːrd] *n.* 위원회 applicátion [æplikéiʃən] *n.* 원서, 적용 far-further-furthest (정도)(*cf.* far-farther-farthest (거리))
considerátion [kənsidəréiʃən] *n.* 고려, 심사

ones가 지칭하는 것이 사람(the members of the board)인지 사물(applications)인지를 확인한다.

76

American and European tourists visit Yucatan for its archeological sites and for its seaside resorts, <u>the former</u> being among the most varied and most attractive in the world.

Yucatán [ju:kətá:n] *n.* 멕시코 남동부의 반도 archeológical [ɑ:rkiəládʒikəl] *adj.* 고고학의(*cf.* archeólogy [ɑ:rkiálədʒi] *n.* 고고학) site [sait] *n.* 장소 resórt [rizɔ́:rt] *n.* 행락지, 휴양지 the former : 전자(*cf.* the latter : 후자) varied [véərid] *adj.* 변화하는, 다양한

the former : 전자 / the latter : 후자

77

Both graduate and undergraduate students should be interested in the two alternatives, but if <u>the latter</u> is selected it must be completed within two semesters following the end of the course.

gráduate student : 대학원생 undergráduate student : 학부생 be ínterested in ~ : ~에 관심이 있는 altérnative [ɔ:ltə́:rnətiv] *n.* 양자택일, 선택 seléct [silékt] *v.* 선택하다 seméster [siméstər] *n.* 학기

＊2원화 되어 있는 미국대학의 학기제
1. semester system (2학기제)
　① 1st semester : 9월~12월
　② 2nd semester : 1월~4월
　③ term(방학) : 5월~8월

2. quarter system (4학기제)
　① 1st quarter : 9월 말~12월 중순
　② 2nd quarter : 12월 말~3월 중순
　③ 3rd quarter : 3월 말~6월 중순
　④ term(방학) : 6월 말~9월 중순

78

Los Angeles and Minneapolis offer the visitor both a range of major-league sporting attractions and a variety of cultural attractions, but the climate of <u>the former</u> exerts year-round appeal.

a range of ~ : 일정한 범위의 ~ attráction [ətrǽkʃən] *n.* 매력, 사람들의 관심을 끌 만한 행사나 장소 또는 볼거리 a variety of ~ : 다양한 ~ exért [igzə́:rt] *v.* (영향력을) 행사하다, (힘을) 발휘하다 year-round : 일년 내내의, 연중의 appéal [əpí:l] *n.* 매력

79

The NASA scientists and astronauts were equally excited by Al Shepherd's first suborbital flight and by John Glenn's orbital journey, but it was <u>the latter</u> which most caught the attention of the American public.

NASA : 미국항공우주국(National Aeronautics and Space Administration) ástronaut [ǽstrənɔ:t] *n.* 우주비행사 subórbital[sʌbɔ́:rbit] *adj.* 궤도에 진입하지 못한 órbital [ɔ́:rbitl] *adj.* 궤도의 órbit [ɔ́:rbit] *n.* 궤도

80

Both the government and the private sector fund basic and applied research, but grants for <u>the former</u> tend to be relatively restricted in times of economic difficulties.

séctor [séktər] *n.* 영역, 분야 fund [fʌnd] *v.* 자금을 지원하다 basic reséarch : 기초연구 applíed research : 응용연구 grant [grænt] *n.* 지원금 tend to do : ~하는 경향이다 be restrícted : 제한되다 in times of económic dífficulties : 불경기때는

TOEFL Beginner's Reading Comprehension

Part **3**

독해기초연습 2

사실적 이해를 묻는 문제

글에 서술된 단순한 사실을 정확하게 이해하는 것은 우리가 글을 읽는 가장 중요한 이유이다. 사실적 이해를 묻는 문제에서는 본문에 기술된 단순한 사실에 대하여 여러 가지 방식으로 묻는다. 이런 연습을 통해서 우리는 글에 서술된 정보를 정확하고 빠르게 처리할 수 있는 능력을 키울 수 있다.

문제 유형

사실 확인 문제
글의 주제나 요지를 찾는 문제
글의 제목을 고르는 문제
대명사가 가리키는 말(지칭어)을 찾는 문제
본문의 사실과 일치/불일치하는 문장을 찾는 문제

문제 풀이 전략

본문에 기술된 단순한 사실을 묻는 문제이므로 비교적 쉽고 빠르게 답을 찾을 수 있는 문제이다. 이 문제들의 답을 찾고 나면 본문의 내용도 이해하게 되므로, 글의 주제를 비롯한 다른 문제들도 쉽게 풀 수 있는 실마리를 제공하는 셈이 된다.
이런 문제를 푸는 요령은 각 문제의 핵심어(key words)를 찾아 본문에서 같은 말 또는 비슷한 뜻의 영어표현이 있는 곳을 찾으면 쉽게 답을 찾을 수 있다.
위의 문제유형 중 글의 주제나 요지를 찾는 문제, 글의 제목을 고르는 문제는 단순한 사실 확인 문제는 아니지만 사실 확인 문제에 포함시켰다. 영문의 주제문은 글의 첫 문장이 주제문인 경우가 대부분이며, 제목은 흔히 주제문에서 추출된다.

1

Clothing fires are a real kitchen hazard. Long, flowing sleeves have no place in a kitchen—they are too easily caught on pan handles, are easily ignited by range burners, and are generally in the way. Highly flammable synthetic fabrics can be most unsafe. If your range is near a window, you should avoid long curtains that might blow over the range and catch fire.

real [ríːəl] *adj.* 진정한, 말 그대로의 házard [hǽzərd] *n.* 위험(= danger) sleeve [sliv] *n.* 소맷자락 igníte [ignáit] *v.* ~에 불을 붙이다, 불이 붙다 range burner : 레인지 버너, 흔히 우리가 '가스 레인지'라고 하는 것 be in the way : 방해가 되다 flámmable [flǽməbəl] *adj.* 가연성의, 인화성의 híghly flámmable synthétic fábrics : 인화성이 강한 합성섬유 catch fire : 불이 붙다

주제문 : 첫 문장(Clothing fires are a real kitchen hazard.) 핵심어 : clothing fire, kitchen hazard

1. What hazard is this paragraph chiefly concerned with?

(A) Hazardous kitchens

(B) Impractical clothing

(C) Fires

(D) Curtains, long sleeves, and so forth getting in the way

2. What is dangerous about synthetic fabrics?

(A) Long sleeves

(B) They get in the way

(C) The wind might blow them over the burners

(D) Some are highly flammable

1. 문제의 핵심어 : hazard
   본문의 정답찾기(scanning) : 1행(Clothing fires are a real kitchen hazard.)
2. 문제의 핵심어 : synthetic fabrics, dangerous
   본문의 정답찾기 : 3~4행(Highly flammable synthetic fabrics can be most unsafe.)

2

The rattles with which a rattlesnake warns of its presence are formed by loosely connecting hollow rings of hard skin, which make a buzzing sound when its tail is shaken. As a baby, the snake begins to form its rattles from the button at the very tip of its tail. Thereafter, each time it sheds its skin, a new ring is formed. Popular belief holds that a snake's age can be told by counting the rings, but this idea is fallacious. In fact, a snake may lose its old skin as often as four times a year. Also, rattles tend to wear or break off with time.

rattle [rǽtl] *n.* 방울뱀 꼬리의 음향기관 ráttlesnake [rǽtlsneik] *n.* 방울뱀 warn of ~ : ~을 경고하다, 알리다 its présence : 자기의 존재(출현) hóllow [hálou] *adj.* 속이 빈 a buzzing sound : 붕붕거리는 소리 shed [ʃed] *v.* 허물 벗다 fallácious [fəléiʃəs] *adj.* 허위의, 잘못된 break off : 끊다, 파기하다 with time : 시간이 지남에 따라

주제문 : 첫 문장 핵심어 : rattle, rattlesnake, formed by … hard skin, make a buzzing sound

1. A rattlesnake's rattles are made of
   (A) skin.
   (B) bone.
   (C) wood.
   (D) muscle.

2. How often does a rattlesnake shed its skin?
   (A) Once every four years
   (B) Once every four months
   (C) Up to four times every year
   (D) Four times more often than other snakes

1. 문제의 핵심어 : rattles, made of
   본문의 정답찾기 : 첫 문장(The rattles … are formed by … rings of hard skin). 보기의 bone, word, muscle 등은 본문에 없는 말이다.
2. 문제의 핵심어 : How often, shed its skin
   본문의 정답찾기 : 7~8행(a snake may lose its old skin as often as four times a year)
   ※ 보기의 표현들 중에서 본문에 있는 표현과 같은 것을 찾는 것이 도움이 된다.

3

Williamsburg is a historic city in Virginia situated on a peninsula between two rivers, the York and the James. It was settled by English colonists in 1633, twenty-six years after the first permanent English colony in America was settled at Jamestown. In the beginning the colony at Williamsburg was named Middle Plantation because of its location in the middle of the peninsula. The site for Williamsburg had been selected by the colonists because the soil drainage was better there than at the Jamestown location, and there were fewer mosquitoes.

sítuated on ~ : ~에 자리잡은 península [pinínsələr] *n.* 반도 the York : 요크강 the James : 제임스강(*cf.* 강 이름에 the를 붙인다) colonist [kálənist] *n.* 식민지 주민 cólony [káləni] *n.* 식민지 séttle [sétl] *v.* 정착하다 plantátion [plæntéiʃən] *n.* 농장, 플랜테이션 soil [sɔil] *n.* 흙 dráinage [dréinidʒ] *n.* 배수(장치), 하수, 배수로 mosquíto [məskí:tou] *n.* 모기

주제문 : 첫 문장 핵심어 : Williamsburg, situated on, site, Middle Plantation

1. According to the passage, Williamsburg is located

   (A) on an island.
   (B) in the middle of a river.
   (C) where the York and the James meet.
   (D) on a piece of land with rivers on two sides.

2. The passage states that the name Middle Plantation

   (A) is a more recent name than Williamsburg.
   (B) derived from the location of the colony on the peninsula.
   (C) refers to the middle part of England that was home to the colonists.
   (D) was given to the new colony because it was located in the middle of several plantations.

1. 문제의 핵심어 : Williamsburg is located
   본문의 정답찾기 : 1~2행(Williamsburg is ··· situated on a peninsula between two rivers, the York and the James.)
2. 문제의 핵심어 : Middle Plantation, name
   본문의 정답찾기 : 5행(···was named Middle Plantation because of its location in the middle of the peninsula.)

4

Marianne Moore was born in St. Louis in 1887, and graduated from Bryn Mawr College in 1909. She taught stenography for a few years, and then worked as a librarian in New York. She was a member of the editorial staff of the famous literary magazine, *The Dial*, from 1925 to 1929. Although a book of her poems, titled *Observations*, was published in America in 1924, Miss Moore has only recently received the full acclaim she deserves.

stenógraphy [stənágrəfi] *n.* 속기(술)(= shorthand) librárian [laibrɛ́əriən] *n.* 도서관 사서 editórial staff : 편집직원 líterary [lítəreri] *adj.* 문학의 líterary mágazine : 문학잡지 accláim [əkléim] *n.* 갈채, 환호 (= acclamátion) desérve [dizə́ːrv] *v.* ~을 받을 가치가 있다, 받을 만하다

Marianne Moore가 살아온 과정과 직업이 연대순으로 나열되어 있다.

1. When did Miss Moore graduate from college?
   (A) 1887
   (B) 1909
   (C) 1925
   (D) 1924

2. The one profession not mentioned as being pursued by Miss Moore is that of
   (A) poet.
   (B) teacher.
   (C) scientist.
   (D) librarian.

1. 문제의 핵심어 : Moore, graduate from college, When
   본문의 정답찾기 : 1~2행(Marianne Moore was … and graduated from Bryn Mawr College in 1909.)
2. 문제의 핵심어 : profession
   본문의 정답찾기 : Marianne Moore가 가졌던 직업은, 2행(taught stenography), 3행(worked as a librarian), 3~4행(a member of the editorial staff of … The Dial.), 5행(a book of her poems.)에 차례로 나타나 있다.

5

Ice ages, those periods when ice covered extensive areas of the earth, are known to have occurred at least six times. Past ice ages can be recognized from rock strata that show evidence of foreign materials deposited by moving walls of ice or melting glaciers. Ice ages can also be recognized from land formations that have been produced from moving walls of ice, such as Ushaped valleys, sculptured landscapes, and polished rock faces.

ice ages : 빙하시대 exténsive [iksténsiv] *adj.* 넓은, 광범위한 stráta [stréitə] *n.* 층, 지층, 계층(strátum의 복수형)
depósit [dipázit] *v.* 저장하다 glácier [gléiʃər] *n.* 빙하 mélting gláciers : 녹는 빙하 land formation : 육지의 형태
U-shaped válleys : U자형 계곡 scúlptured lándscapes : 조각된 풍경 pólished rock faces : 매끄러운 바위표면

주제문 : 첫 문장 핵심어 : Ice ages

1. According to the passage, what happens during an ice age?

    (A) Rock strata are recognized by geologists.

    (B) Evidence of foreign materials is found.

    (C) Ice covers a large portion of the earth's surface.

    (D) Ice melts six times.

2. The passage covers how many different methods of recognizing past ice ages?

    (A) One

    (B) Two

    (C) There

    (D) Four

3. According to the passage, what in the rock strata is a clue to geologists of a past ice age?

    (A) Ice

    (B) Melting glaciers

    (C) U-shaped valleys

    (D) Substances from other areas

1. 문제의 핵심어 : Ice age, what happen
   본문의 정답찾기 : 1행(Ice ages, those periods … areas of the earth)에서 빙하시대의 개념을 설명
   하고 있다. / ice ages = those periods (동격)
2. 문제의 핵심어 : methods of recognizing past Ice ages
   본문의 정답찾기 : 2~3행(Past ice ages can be recognized from rock strata that …) / 4~5행
   (Ice ages can also be recognized from land formations that …)

3. 문제의 핵심어 : past ice age, clue, rock strata, what?
  본문의 정답찾기 : 2~4행(Past ice ages can be recognized from rock strata that show evidence of foreign materials deposited by …) / foreign materials = substances from other areas

6

In the philosophy of John Dewey a sharp distinction is made between "intelligence" and "reasoning." According to Dewey, intelligence is the only absolute way to achieve a balance between realism and idealism, between practicality and wisdom of life. Intelligence involves "interacting with other things and knowing them," while reasoning is merely the act of an observer, "… a mind that beholds or grasps objects outside the world of things …" With reasoning, a level of mental certainty can be achieved, but it is through intelligence that control is taken of events that shape one's life.

distínction [distíŋkʃən] *n.* 차이, 구별, 특징 ábsolute [æbsəluːt] *adj.* 절대적인 achíeve [ətʃíːv] *v.* 성취하다 practicálity [præktikǽləti] *n.* 실용성 interáct [intərǽkt] *v.* 상호작용하다 behóld [bihóuld] *v.* 바라보다 grasp [græsp] *v.* 움켜쥐다 méntal [méntl] *adj.* 마음의, 정신의 shape [ʃeip] *v.* 형성하다, 모양짓다

주제문 : 첫 문장 핵심어 : philosophy, John Dewey, distinction, intelligence, reasoning

1. What is the topic of this passage?

  (A) The intelligence of John Dewey

  (B) Distinctions made by John Dewey

  (C) Dewey's ideas on the ability to reason

  (D) How intelligence differs from reasoning in Dewey's philosophy.

Nitrogen fixation is a process by which additional nitrogen is continuously fed into biological circulation. In this process, certain bacteria turn nitrogen into ammonia(NH_3). This newly created ammonia is then for the most part absorbed by plants.

The opposite process of denitrification returns nitrogen to the air. During the process of denitrification, bacteria cause some of the nitrates from the soil to change into gaseous nitrogen or nitrous oxide(N_2O). In this gaseous form the nitrogen returns to the atmosphere.

＊ nitrógen fixátion : 질소고정 denitrificátion·[di:naitrəfikáiʃən] *n*. 탈질소작용 nítrate [náitreit] *n*. 질산염
nítrous óxide : 질소산화물

nítrogen fixátion : 질소고정, 공중의 유기질소를 생물이 섭취하여 암모니아로 환원시키는 과정(*cf.* fix [fiks] *v.* 고정시키다 fixátion [fikséiʃən] *n.* 고정) prócess [práʃes] *n.* 과정, 공정 feed [fi:d] *v.* 먹이다, 공급하다 (feed-fed-fed) biólogy [baiálədʒi] *n.* 생물학(*cf.* biológical) circulátion [sə:rkjəléiʃən] *n.* 순환, 유통, 신문·잡지·도서의 발행 부수, 배포 absórb [æbsɔ́:rb] *v.* 흡수하다 denitrificátion [dinaitrəfikéiʃən] *n.* (박테리아에 의한) 탈질소작용 soil [sɔil] *n.* 흙 gáseous [gǽsiəs] *adj.* 가스의, 기체의 nítrous [náitrəs] *adj.* 질소를 함유한 óxide [áksaid] *n.* 산화물 átmosphere [ǽtməsfiər] *n.* 대기, 공기

주제문 : 단락이 둘이므로 주제(topic)가 둘이다. 각 단락의 첫 문장.
핵심어 : nitrogen fixation, biological circulation, denitrification
단락을 알 수 있는 연결어 : In this process …, The opposite process …

1. Which of the following would be the best title for this passage?

(A) The Process of Nitrogen Fixation

(B) Two Nitrogen Processes

(C) The Return of Nitrogen to the Air

(D) The Effects of Nitrogen on Plant Life

Fort Knox, Kentucky, is the site of a U.S. army post, but it is even more renowned for the Fort Knox Bullion Depository, the massive vault that contains the bulk of the U.S. government's gold deposits. Completed in 1936, the vault is housed in a two-story building constructed of granite, steel, and concrete; the vault itself is made of steel and concrete and has a door that weighs more than twenty tons. Naturally, the most up-to-date security devices available are in place at Fort Knox, and the army post nearby provides further protection.

* Fort Knox Bullion Depository : 포트녹스 금괴보관처

---

site [sáit] *n.* 장소(= place) army post : (육)군부대 주둔지 be renówned for ~ : ~로 명성을 얻다 búllion [búljən] *n.* 금괴 depósitory [dipázitɔːri] *n.* 저장소, 창고 depósit [dipázit] *n.* 보관물, 퇴적물, 보증금 vault [vɔːlt] *n.* 저장실 bulk [bʌlk] *n.* 대부분, 용적, 화물 house [hauz] *v.* 수용하다 a two-story building : 2층 건물 gránite [grǽnit] *n.* 화강암 weigh [wei] *v.* 무게가 나가다(*cf.* weight [weit] *n.* 무게) up-to-date : 최신의 secúrity devíce : 보안장치 be in place : 적절한 자리에 놓여 있는 protéction [prətékʃən] *n.* 보호

주제문 : 첫 문장 핵심어 : the Fort Knox Bullion Depository, the U.S. governmen's gold deposits

1. Which of the following best describes the topic of the passage?

(A) The city of Fort Knox, Kentucky

(B) The federal gold depository

(C) The U.S. army post at Fort Knox

(D) Gold bullion

2. Which of the following would be the best title for this passage?

(A) The Massive Concrete Vault

(B) Fort Knox Security

(C) Where the U.S. Keeps Its Gold

(D) A Visit to Kentucky

---

1. 윗글의 핵심어인 Bullion Depository, U.S. government's gold deposits 등이 들어 있는 표현을 고른다.
2. 1번 문제와 같은 핵심어가 있는 표현을 찾는다.

One identifying characteristic of minerals is their relative hardness, which can be determined by scratching one mineral with another. In this type of test, a harder mineral can scratch a softer one, but a softer mineral is unable to scratch the harder one. The Mohs' hardness scale is used to rank minerals according to hardness. Ten minerals are listed in this scale, ranging from talc with a hardness of 1 to diamond with a hardness of 10. On this scale, quartz (number 7) is harder than feldspar (number 6) and is therefore able to scratch it; however, feldspar is unable to make a mark on quartz.

* the Mohs' hárdness scale : 모스경도 talc [tælk] *n.* 활석, 운모 féldspar [féldspaːr] *n.* 장석

idéntify [aidéntəfai] *v.* 확인하다, 식별하다 detérmine [ditə́ːrmin] *v.* 결정하다 scratch [skrætʃ] *v.* 긁다 the Mohs' hardness scale : 모스경도, 광물의 경도기준, 독일의 광물학자 Friedrich Mohs (1773~1839)의 성을 따서 나눈 10단계의 경도기준 rank [ræŋk] *v.* 등급을 정하다 accórding to ~ : ~에 따라서 range [reindʒ] *v.* (범위가) 오르내리다, 걸치다 talc [tælk] *n.* 활석, 운모 quartz [kwɔːrts] *n.* 석영, 수정 féldspar [féldspaːr] *n.* 장석

주제문 : 첫 문장 핵심어 : one identifying characteristic of minerals, hardness, scratching one mineral with another, Mohs' hardness scale, rank minerals according to hardness

1. Which of the following best describes the subject of this passage?
   (A) The hardness of diamonds
   (B) Identifying minerals by means of a scratch test
   (C) Feldspar on the Mohs' scale
   (D) Recognizing minerals in their natural state

2. The main idea of this passage is that
   (A) the hardness of a mineral can be determined by its ability to make a mark on other minerals.
   (B) diamonds, with a hardness of 10 on the Mohs' scale, can scratch all other minerals.
   (C) a softer mineral cannot be scratched by a harder mineral.
   (D) talc is the first mineral listed on the Mohs' scale.

2. 지나치게 지엽적인 것을 표현하거나, 반대로 너무 일반적인 표현은 요지로서 적절하지 않다.

10

Hurricanes generally occur in the North Atlantic from May through November, with the peak of the hurricane season in September; only rarely will they occur December through April in that part of the ocean. The main reason for the occurrence of hurricanes during this period is that the temperature on the water's surface is at its warmest and the humidity of the air is at its highest.

Of the tropical storms that occur each year in the North Atlantic, only about five, on the average, are powerful enough to be called hurricanes. To be classified as a hurricane, a tropical storm must have winds reaching speeds of at least 117 kilometers per hour, but the winds are often much stronger than that; the winds of intense hurricanes can easily surpass 240 kilometers per hour.

---

húrricane [hə́:rekein] *n.* 태풍, 허리케인 peak [pi:k] *n.* 꼭대기, 절정 occúrrence [əkə́:rəns] *n.* 발생(*v.* occur) humídity [hju:mídətii] *n.* 습기, 습도 trópical storm : 열대성 폭풍 inténse [inténs] *adj.* 강한, 맹렬한 surpáss [sərpǽs] *v.* 능가하다, 초월하다

주제문 : 단락이 둘이므로 화제(topic)도 둘이다. 각 단락의 첫 문장.
핵심어 : hurricane, the tropical storms

1. This passage mainly discusses

  (A) how many hurricanes occur each year.

  (B) the strength of hurricanes.

  (C) the weather in the North Atlantic.

  (D) hurricanes in one part of the world.

2. The best title for this passage would be

  (A) The North Atlantic Ocean.

  (B) Storms of the Northern Atlantic.

  (C) Hurricanes: the Damage and Destruction.

  (D) What Happens May through November.

---

1. 두 단락 모두 허리케인에 대한 글이다.
2. tropical storms 중에서 강한 것이 Hurricanes이다.

11

The human heart is divided into four chambers, each of which serves its own function in the cycle of pumping blood. The atria are the thin-walled upper chambers that gather blood as it flows from the veins between heartbeats. The ventricles are the thick-walled lower chambers that receive blood from the atria and push it into the arteries with each contraction of the heart. The left atrium and ventricle work separately from those on the right. The role of the chambers on the right side of the heart is to receive oxygen-depleted blood from the body tissues and send it on the lungs; the chambers on the left side of the heart then receive the oxygen-enriched blood from the lungs and send it back out to the body tissues.

* átrium [éitriəm] *n.* (좌우)심방(*pl.* atria) véntricles [véntrikəls] *n.* (좌우)심실 ártery [á:rtəri] *n.* 동맥

fúnction [fʌ́ŋkʃən] *n.* 기능 pump [pʌmp] *v.* 펌프질하다, 퍼내다 átrium [éitriəm] *n.* (심장) 좌우심방(*pl.* atria) vein [vein] *n.* 혈관 héartbeat [hartbi:t] *n.* 심장박동 véntricles [véntikəl] *n.* (심장) 좌우심실 ártery[á:rtəri] *n.* 동맥 contráction [kəntrǽkʃən] *n.* 수축(*cf.* cóntract [kántrækt] *v.* 수축하다, 계약하다) depléte [diplí:t] *v.* 고갈시키다, 써 버리다 óxygen-depléted : 산소가 고갈된 bódy tíssue : 신체조직 lung [lʌŋ] *n.* 폐, 허파 óxygen-enríched : 산소가 풍부한(*opp.* óxygen-depléted)

주제문 : 첫 문장 핵심어 : human heart, four chambers, atria, ventricles

1. All of the following are true about ventricles EXCEPT that

(A) they have relatively thick walls.

(B) they send blood to the atria.

(C) they are lower than the atria.

(D) there are two ventricles, a right one and a left one.

2. When is blood pushed into the arteries from the ventricles?

(A) As the heart beats

(B) Between heartbeats

(C) Before each contraction of the heart

(D) Before it is received by the atria

3. According to the passage, which part of the heart gets blood from the body tissues and passes it on to the lungs?

(A) The atria

(B) The ventricles

(C) The right atrium and ventricle

(D) The left atrium and ventricle

12

The Golden Age of railroads refers to the period from the end of the Civil War to the beginning of World War I when railroads flourished and in fact maintained a near monopoly in mass transportation in the United States. One of the significant developments during the period was the notable increase in uniformity, particularly through the standardization of track gauge and time.

At the end of the Civil War, only about half of the nation's railroad track was laid at what is now the standard gauge of 1.4 meters; much of the rest, particularly in southern states, had a 1.5-meter gauge. During the post-war years tracks were converted to the 1.4-meter gauge, and by June 1, 1886, the standardization of tracks was completed, resulting in increased efficiency and economy in the rail system.

A further benefit to railroad efficiency was the beginning of Standard Time in 1883. With the adoption of Standard Time, four time zones were established across the country, thus simplifying railroad scheduling and improving the efficiency of railroad service.

flóurish [flə́:riʃ] v. 번성하다 monópoly [mənápəli] n. 독점 transportátion [trænspərtéiʃən] n. 교통, 운송 signíficant [signífikənt] adj. 중요한 nótable [nóutəbəl] adj. 현저한 unifórmity [ju:nəfɔ́:rməti] n. 단일화, 획일성 gauge [geidʒ] n. 계측기, 기준, (철도의) 선로 폭, 궤간 post-: 접두어로 쓰일 경우, 후기, 다음이라는 뜻 convért [kənvə́:rt] v. 변화하다(= change, turn) resúlt in ~ : ~의 결과를 낳다 bénefit [bénəfit] n. 혜택, 이익 adóption [ədápʃən] n. 채택, 채용 estáblish [istǽbliʃ] v. 설립하다, 확립하다 símplify [símpləfai] v. 단순화시키다 impróve [imprú:v] v. 향상시키다

주제문 : 첫 단락의 첫 문장
핵심어 : 첫 단락 — the Golden Age of railroads, the standardization of track gauge and time
       둘째 단락 — the standardization of tracks, efficiency and economy in the rail system
       셋째 단락 — the beginning of standard time

1. Which of the following is NOT true about the Golden Age of railroads according to the passage?

   (A) It occurred prior to the first World War.
   (B) Most of U.S. mass transportation was controlled by the railroads.
   (C) Track gauge was standardized before the Golden Age of railroads.
   (D) Standard Time was implemented during the Golden Age of railroads.

2. According to the passage, the establishment of uniformity of track gauge resulted in which of the following?

   (A) The Civil War
   (B) Improved economy in the transportation system
   (C) Standardization of time zones
   (D) Railroad schedules

3. According to the passage, when was Standard Time implemented in the United States?

   (A) Before the Civil War
   (B) On June 1, 1886
   (C) After World War I
   (D) Before standardized track gauge was established throughout the U.S.

---

1. the Golden Age of railroads가 핵심어인 첫 문단의 내용과 다른 표현이 정답이다.
2. 문제의 핵심어 : uniformity of track gauge, result in
   본문의 정답찾기 : 12~13행 (resulting in …)
3. 문제의 핵심어 : beginning of Standard Time
   본문의 정답찾기 : 15행 (… in 1883.)
   철도 선로의 단일화가 완성된 것이 1886년이다.

13

Lincoln's now famous Gettysburg Address was not, on the occasion of its delivery, recognized as the masterpiece it is today. Lincoln was not even the primary speaker at the ceremonies, held at the height of the Civil War in 1863, to dedicate the battlefield at Gettysburg. The main speaker was orator Edward Everett, whose two-hour speech was followed by Lincoln's shorter remarks. Lincoln began his small portion of the program with words that today are immediately recognized by most Americans: "Four score and seven years ago our fathers brought forth on this continent a new nation, conceived in liberty and dedicated to the proposition that all men are created equal." At the time of the speech, little notice was given to what Lincoln had said, and Lincoln considered his appearance at the ceremonies rather unsuccessful. It was after his speech appeared in print that it began receiving the growing recognition that today places it among the greatest speeches of all time.

on the occásion of ~ : ~하던 때에는, ~할 경우에는 delívery [dilívəri] *n.* 전달, 발표 másterpiece [mǽstərpiːs] *n.* 걸작, 명작 height [hait] *n.* 높이, 고지, 절정(*cf.* high) dédicate [dédikeit] *v.* 헌정하다, 바치다 báttlefield [bǽtlfiːld] *n.* 전쟁터 órator [ɔ́(ː)rətər] *n.* 연설자, 변사, 웅변가(*cf.* óral [ɔ́ːrəl] *adj.* 구두의, 구술의 oratório [ɔrətɔ́ːriou] *n.* 오라토리오, 종교적 주제의 대규모 서사음악) remárk [rimáːrk] *n.* 소견, 촌평 pórtion [pɔ́ːrʃən] *n.* 부분, 몫 four score and seven : 87 bring forth : 낳다 cóntinent [kántənənt] *n.* 대륙 concéive [kənsíːv] *v.* 마음에 품다, 상상하다 líberty [líbərti] *n.* 자유(*cf.* líberal [líbərəl] *adj.* 자유로운) proposition [prɑpəzíʃən] *n.* 의제, 명제 recognítion [rekəgníʃən] *n.* 인식, 알아봄

주제문 : 첫 문장   결론문 : 마지막 문장   핵심어 : Gettysburg Address

1. The main idea of this passage is that
   (A) the Gettysburg Address has always been regarded as a masterpiece.
   (B) at the time of its delivery the Gettysburg Address was truly appreciated as a masterpiece.
   (C) it was not until sometime after 1863 that Lincoln's speech at Gettysburg took its place in history.
   (D) Lincoln is better recognized today than he was at the time of his presidency.

2. According to the passage, when Lincoln spoke at the Gettysburg ceremonies,
   (A) his words were immediately recognized by most Americans.
   (B) he spoke for only a short period of time.
   (C) he was enthusiastically cheered.
   (D) he was extremely proud of his performance.

3. When did Lincoln's Gettysburg Address begin to receive public acclaim?

(A) After it had been published

(B) Immediately after the speech

(C) Not until the present day

(D) After Lincoln received growing recognition

1. 글의 요지는 흔히 주제문(첫 문장)과 결론(마지막 문장)에 있다.
2. 문제의 핵심어 : Lincoln, Gettysburg, speak
   본문의 정답찾기 : 사실확인 문제이다. 설명문인 두 번째 문장부터 읽어 내려가며 사실을 확인한다.
3. 문제의 핵심어 : Gettysburg Address, public acclaim, when
   본문의 정답찾기 : 12~15행(It was after his speech appeared in print that it began receiving the growing recognition that …)

14

Hay fever is a seasonal allergy to pollens; the term hay fever, however, is a less than adequate description since an attack of this allergy does not cause fever and since such an attack can be brought on by sources other than hay-producing grasses. Hay fever is generally caused by air-borne pollens, particularly ragweed pollen. The amount of pollen in the air is largely dependent on geographical location, weather, and season. In the eastern section of the United States, for example, there are generally three periods when pollen from various sources can cause intense hay fever suffering: in the springtime months of March and April when pollen from trees is prevalent, in the summer months of June and July when grass pollen fills the air, and at the end of August when ragweed pollen is at its most concentrated levels.

* hay fever: 꽃가루 알레르기 póllen [pálən] n. 꽃가루 rágweed [rǽgwiːd] n. 돼지풀

háy féver : 꽃가루 알레르기(= pollenósis) hay [hei] n. 건초, 풀 állergy [ǽlərdʒi] n. 알레르기 póllen [pálən] n. 꽃가루, 화분 áir-borne póllens : 공기로 운반되는 꽃가루 rágweed póllen : 돼지풀 꽃가루 be depéndent on ~ : ~에 의지하는, ~따라 결정되는 prévalent [prévələnt] adj. 널리 퍼진, 유행한 at most cóncentrated lévels : 고농도의

주제문 : 첫 문장 핵심어 : hay fever

1. Which of the following would be the best title for the passage?

    (A) The Relationship Between Season and Allergies

    (B) Misconceptions and Facts about Hay Fever

    (C) Hay Fever in the Eastern U.S.

    (D) How Ragweed Causes Hay Fever

2. According to the passage, which of the following helps to explain why the term hay fever is somewhat of a misnomer?

    (A) A strong fever occurs after an attack.

    (B) The amount of pollen in the air depends on geographical location.

    (C) Hay fever is often caused by ragweed.

    (D) Grass pollen is prevalent in June and July.

3. Which of the following is NOT discussed in the passage as a determining factor of the amount of pollen in the air?

    (A) Place

    (B) Climate

    (C) Time of year

    (D) Altitude

1. 문제의 핵심어 : 제목(title)은 주로 주제문에 포함되어 있다.
   본문의 정답찾기 : 첫 문장. 윗글의 핵심어가 hay fever 임을 명심.
2. 문제의 핵심어 : the term hay fever
   본문의 정답찾기 : 주제(1~4행)에 대한 이유는 4~5행이다.
3. 문제의 핵심어 : the amount of pollen in the air, determining
   본문의 정답찾기 : 5~7행

15

According to the theory of continental drift, the continents are not fixed in position but instead move slowly across the surface of the earth, constantly changing in position relative to one another. This theory was first proposed in the eighteenth century when mapmakers noticed how closely the continents of the earth fit together when matched up. It was suggested then that the present-day continents had once been one large continent that had broken up into pieces which drifted apart.

Today the modern theory of plate tectonics has developed from the theory of continental drift. The theory of plate tectonics suggests that the crust of the earth is divided into six large and many small plates. These plates drift on the lava that composes the inner core of the earth. These plates consist of ocean floor and continents that quite probably began breaking up and moving relative to one another more than 200 million years ago.

* cóntinent drift : 대류이동설 plate tectónics : 지각표층 구조학

continéntal drift : 대류이동(설) rélative to ~ : ~와 관련하여,~에 비례하여 one another : 서로서로 fit togéther : 들어맞다, 함께 어울리다 match up : 짝을 맞추다 break up into ~ : ~로 부서지다 drift apárt : 분리되어 표류하다 plate [pleit] *n.* 지각 표층부의 암반 tectonics [tektániks] *n.* 구조(지질)학(*cf.* tectónic *a.* 지질구조의, 지각변동하는) plate tectonics : 지각표층 구조학 crust [krʌst] *n.* 지각, 지구표면 láva [láːvə] *n.* 용암 compóse [kəmpóuz] *v.* 구성하다 (= consíst of) core [kɔːr] *n.* 핵, 핵심

주제문 : 첫 단락의 첫 문장 핵심어 : 첫 단락－continental drift / 둘째 단락－plate tectonics

1. The topic of this passage is

   (A) continental drift.

   (B) the theory of plate tectonics.

   (C) the development of ideas about the movement of the earth's surface.

   (D) eighteenth-century mapmakers.

2. The passage states that the theory of continental drift developed as a resurt of

   (A) the fixed positions of the continents.

   (B) the work of mapmakers.

   (C) the rapid movement of continents.

   (D) the fit of the earth's plates.

3. Which of the following is NOT true about the theory of plate tectonics?

   (A) It is not as old as the theory of continental drift.

   (B) It evolved from the theory of continental drift.

   (C) It postulates that the earth's surface is separated into plates.

   (D) It was proposed by mapmakers.

4. According to the passage, what constitutes a tectonic plate?

   (A) The inner core of the earth

   (B) Only the continents

   (C) Lava

   (D) The surface of the land and the floor of the oceans

2. 문제의 핵심어 : theory of continental drift, first proposed
   본문의 정답찾기 : 3~6행
3. 문제의 핵심어 : theory of plate tectonics
   본문의 정답찾기 : 9행 이하
4. 문제의 핵심어 : a tectonic plate, constitute
   본문의 정답찾기 : 13~14행

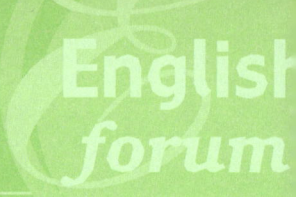

Group 2

추론적 이해를 묻는 문제

추론적 이해를 묻는 문제는 글에 서술된 사실을 바탕으로 글에 서술되지 않은 내용들을 유추하는 문제이다. 글을 읽으면서 다음에 이어질 내용을 미리 예측해 보는 것은 효과적인 영문독해를 위해서 꼭 필요하다. 추론적 이해를 묻는 문제를 통해서 다음에 전개될 글의 내용을 유추하고 종합하는 능력을 키울 수 있다.

문제 유형

원인/결과를 추론하는 문제
본문 앞에 서술된 글의 내용을 유추하는 문제
본문 다음에 이어질 글의 내용을 유추하는 문제
글 전체의 결론을 파악하는 문제

문제 풀이 전략

주로 본문의 내용을 이해한 뒤 그것을 바탕으로 유추(implication/inference)할 수 있는 사항을 묻는 간접적인 문제들이다. 따라서 문제의 내용이 그대로 본문에 기술되어 있지는 않다. 추론 문제는 문제에서 무엇을 묻고 있는가를 정확히 파악한 후에 즉, 문제의 핵심어를 파악한 후에 본문의 관련된 부분을 찾아 정확하게 읽는 것이 요령이다. 다른 유형의 문제보다 난이도가 높은 편이기 때문에 많은 연습을 필요로 한다.

1 _____

The most conservative sect of the Mennonite Church is the Old Order Amish, with 33,000 members living mainly today in the states of Pennsylvania, Ohio, and Indiana. Their lifestyle reflects their belief in the doctrines of separation from the world and simplicity of life. The Amish have steadfastly rejected the societal changes that have occurred in the previous three hundred years, preferring instead to remain securely rooted in a seventeenth-century lifestyle. They live without radios, televisions, telephones, electric lights, and cars; they dress in plainly styled and colored old-fashioned clothes; and they farm their lands with horses and tools rather than modern farm equipment. They have a highly communal form of living, with barn raisings and quilting bees as commonplace activities.

* the Mennonite Church : 메논 교파 the Óld Órder Ámish : (메논파 소속의) 암만 종파 barn raising : 헛간 상량식 quilting bee : (미) 누비이불을 만드는 여성들의 모임

---

consérvative [kənsə́:rvətiv] *adj.* 보수적인 sect [sekt] *n.* 교파 the Ménnonite Church : 메논 교회 the Óld Órder Ámish : (메논파 소속의) 암만 종파 refléct [riflékt] *v.* 반영하다 stéadfast[stédfæst] *adj.* 확고부동한 socíetal [səsáiətl] *adj.* 사회의 prefér (instead) to (remain) : ~하기를 택하다 secúrely [sikjúər] *adv.* 안전하게 equípment [ikwípmənt] *n.* 장비 a highly commúnal form of life : 매우 공동체적인 삶의 한 형태 barn raising : 헛간의 상량식 quilting bee : (미) 누비이불을 만드는 여성들의 모임, 잡담을 즐기는 친목회 cómmonplace actívities : 평범한 활동

주제문 : 첫 문장 핵심어 : the most conservative sect

1. The paragraph preceding this passage most probably discusses

(A) other more liberal sects of Mennonites.

(B) where Mennonites live.

(C) the communal Amish lifestyle.

(D) the most conservative Mennonites.

2. Which of the following would probably NOT be found on an Amish farm?

(A) A hammer

(B) A cart

(C) A long dress

(D) A refrigerator

---

1. 앞 단락의 주제를 유추하는 문제. 첫 문장의 The most conservative sect of the Mennonite를 단서로 하여 유추한다. liberal(자유주의인) ↔ conservative(보수주의적인)
2. 문제의 핵심어 : Amish farm(암만종파의 농가)
   본문의 정답찾기 : 7~10행

The extinction of many species of birds has undoubtedly been hastened by modern man; since 1600 it has been estimated that approximately 100 bird species have become extinct over the world. In North America, the first species known to be annihilated was the great auk, a flightless bird that served as an easy source of food and bait for Atlantic fishermen through the beginning of the nineteenth century.

Shortly after the great auk's extinction, two other North American species, the Carolina parakeet and the passenger pigeon, began dwindling noticeably in numbers. The last Carolina parakeet and the last passenger pigeon in captivity both died in September 1914. In addition to these extinct species, several others such as the bald eagle, the peregrine falcon, and the California condor are today recognized as endangered; steps are being taken to prevent their extinction.

* great auk : (북태평양 연안의) 바다쇠오리 Carolína párakeet : 캐롤라인 앵무새 pássenger pígeon : 여행비둘기 bald eagle : 북미산 흰머리 수리 péregrine fálcon : 송골매 Califórnia cóndor : 캘리포니아 콘도르

extínction [ikstíŋkʃən] *n.* 소멸, 멸종 extínct [ikstíŋkt] *adj.* 멸종된 spécies [spíːʃiz] *n.* 종, 종족(*pl.* species) hásten [héisn] *v.* 서둘러~하다 éstimate [éstəmeit] *v.* 평가하다 anníhilate [ənáiəleit] *v.* 전멸시키다 flíghtless [fláitlis] *adj.* 날지못하는 bait[beit] *n.* 미끼, 먹이 párakeet [pǽrəkiːt] *n.* 작은 앵무새 Carolína párakeet : 캐롤라 인 앵무새 pássenger pígeon : 여행비둘기, 북미에서 하늘이 어두워질 정도로 큰 무리를 지어 이동했으나 남획으로 1914년 멸종 dwindle [dwindl] *v.* 점점 작아지다, 줄어들다 in numbers : 수적으로 in captívity : 감금(보호)상태에서, 갇혀 지내다가 endánger [endéindʒər] *v.* 위태롭게 하다 take steps : 조치를 취하다

주제문 : 첫 문장 핵심어 : The extinction of many species of birds, hastened by modern man

1. The passage implies that the great auk disappeared

   (A) before 1600.

   (B) in the 1600s.

   (C) in the 1800s.

   (D) in the last fifty years.

2. It can be inferred from the passage that the great auk was killed because

   (A) it was eating the fishermen's catch.

   (B) fishermen wanted to eat it.

   (C) it flew over fishing areas.

   (D) it baited fishermen.

3. The paragraph following this passage most probably discusses

(A) what is being done to save endangered birds.

(B) what the bald eagle symbolizes to Americans.

(C) how several bird species became endangered.

(D) other extinct species.

3

The Mason-Dixon Line, often considered by American to be the demarcation between the North and the South, is in reality the boundary that separates the state of Pennsylvania from Maryland and parts of West Virginia. Prior to the Civil War, this southern boundary of Pennsylvania separated the non-slave states to the north from the slave states to the south.

The Mason-Dixon Line was established well before the Civil War, as a result of a boundary dispute between Pennsylvania and Maryland. Two English astronomers, Charles Mason and Jeremiah Dixon, were called in to survey the area and officially mark the boundary between the two states. The survey was completed in 1767, and the boundary was marked with stones.

demarcátion [dima:rkéiʃən] *n.* 경계를 설정하다, 구획을 정하다 in reálity : 실제로는 bóundary [báundəri] *n.* 국경, 경계 séparate A from B : B로부터 A를 분리하다 prior to = before slave [sleiv] *n.* 노예 a bóundary dispúte : 국경 분쟁 survéy [sə:rvéi] *v.* 조사하다 offícially [əfíʃəli] *adv.* 공식적으로

주제문 : 첫 문장 핵심어 : The Mason-Dixon Line

1. The best title for this passage would be

    (A) Dividing the North and the South.

    (B) The Meaning of the Mason-Dixon Line.

    (C) Two English Astronomers.

    (D) The History of the Mason-Dixon Line.

2. It can be inferred from the passage that before the Civil War

    (A) Pennsylvania was south of the Mason-Dixon Line.

    (B) Pennsylvania was a non-slave state.

    (C) the states south of the Mason-Dixon Line had the same opinion about slavery as Pennsylvania.

    (D) the slave states were not divided from the non-slave states.

3. According to the passage, the Mason-Dixon Line was established because of a disagreement

    (A) about borders.

    (B) about slaves.

    (C) between two astronomers.

    (D) over surveying techniques.

4. The passage indicates that the Mason-Dixon Line was identified with

    (A) pieces of rock.

    (B) a fence.

    (C) a stone wall.

    (D) a border crossing.

1. 제목이나 핵심어는 주제문에 있다. the Mason-Dixon Line의 연대기적 역사를 기술하고 있다.
2. 문제의 핵심어 : before the Civil War
   본문의 정답찾기 : 4행 이하(Prior to the Civil War, …)
3. 문제의 핵심어 : Mason-Dixon Line, established because of~
   본문의 정답찾기 : 7~8행(Mason-Dixon Line, established as a result of a boundary dispute)
4. 문제의 핵심어 : identified with
   본문의 정답찾기 : 마지막문장 …marked with stones.

4

Manic depression is another psychiatric illness that mainly affects the mood. A patient suffering from this disease will alterate between periods of manic excitement and extreme depression, with or without relatively normal periods in between. The changes in mood suffered by a manic-depressive patient go far beyond the day-to-day mood changes experienced by the general population. In the period of manic excitement; the mood elevation can become so intense that it can result in extended insomnia, extreme irritability, and heightened aggressiveness. In the period of depression, which may last for several weeks or months, a patient experiences feeling of general fatigue, uselessness, and hopelessness, and in serious cases may contemplate suicide.

* mánic depréssion : 조울증 insómnia [insámniə] *n*. 불면증

---

psychiátric [saikiǽtrik] *adj*. 정신의학적인 súffer from ~ : ~로 고생을 하다, ~을 앓다 álternate [ɔ́:ltərnit] *v*. 번갈아 오 다 mánic excítement : 조기흥분증세 day-to-day : daily irritabílity [irətəbíləti] *n*. 과민성, 성급함 héighten [háitn] *v*. 높이다, 고양하다 aggréssiveness [əgrésivnis] *n*. 공격성 fatígue [fətí:g] *n*. 피로 cóntemplate [kántəmpleit] *v*. 응시하다, 심사숙고하다

주제문 : 첫 문장 핵심어 : Manic depression

1. The paragraph preceding this passage most probably discusses

(A) when manic depression develops.

(B) a different type of mental disease.

(C) how moods are determined.

(D) how manic depression can result in suicide.

2. According to the passage, a manic-depressive patient in a manic phase would be feeling

(A) highly emotional.

(B) unhappy.

(C) listless.

(D) relatively normal.

3. The passage indicates that most people

(A) never undergo mood changes.

(B) experience occasional shifts in mood.

(C) switch wildly from highs to lows.

(D) become highly depressed.

4. The passage implies that

(A) changes from excitement to depression occur frequently and often.

(B) only manic-depressive patients experience aggression.

(C) the depressive phase of this disease can be more harmful than the manic phase.

(D) suicide is inevitable in cases of manic depression.

1. 문제의 핵심어 : 앞 단락의 내용 유추
   본문의 정답찾기 : 첫 문장에 암시되어 있다. ··· another psychiatric illness ···
2. 문제의 핵심어 : a manic-depressive patient, a manic phase
   본문의 정답찾기 : 6~9행
3. 문제의 핵심어 : most people
   본문의 정답찾기 : 4~6행

5

Another program instrumental in the popularization of science was *Cosmos*. This series, broadcast on public television, dealt with topics and issues from varied fields of science. The principal writer and narrator of the program was Carl Sagan, a noted astronomer and Pulitzer Prize winning author.

séries [síəri:z] *n.* 시리즈, (신문, 방송의) 연재물 (= sérial) broadcast [brɔ́:dkæst] *v.* 방송하다 (broadcast–broadcast–broadcast) deal with ~ : ~을 다루다 príncipal [prínsəpəl] *adj.* 주요한, 주된 (= chief, leading, main) astrónomer [əstránəmər] *n.* 천문학자 Púlitzer Príze : 퓰리처상, 헝가리 태생의 미국 신문경영자였던 Joseph Pulitzer (1847~1911)가 만든 상으로, 매년 언론, 문학, 음악 분야에서 공이 큰 미국인에게 수여된다. 1917년부터 첫 수상이 시작됨.

주제문 : 첫 문장 핵심어 : program instrumental in the popularization of science, Cosmos, series, varied field of science, Carl Sagan 연결어 : Another program

1. The paragraph preceding this passage most probably discusses

(A) a different scientific television series.

(B) Carl Sagan's scientific achievements.

(C) the Pulitzer Prize won by Carl Sagan.

(D) public television.

1. 앞의 글을 유추하는 문제, 첫 문장의 연결어 Another program 을 단서로 유추한다.
   another program = another scientific television program

6

The 1960 presidential campaign featured the politically innovative and highly influential series of televised debates in the contest between the Republicans and the Democrats. Senator John Kennedy established an early lead among the Democratic hopefuls and was nominated on the first vote at the Los Angeles convention to be the representative of the Democratic party in the presidential election. Richard Nixon, then serving as Vice-President of the United States under Eisen-hower, received the nomination of the Republican party. Both Nixon and Kennedy campaigned vigorously throughout the country and then took the unprecedented step of appearing in face-to-face debates on television. Political experts contend that the debates were a decisive force in the elections. In front of a viewership of more than 100 million citizens, Kennedy masterfully overcame Nixon's advantage as the better-known and more experienced candidate and reversed the public perception of him as too inexperienced and immature for the presidency.

presidéntial campáign : 대통령선거운동 féature [fíːtʃər] v. 특징으로 하다 ínnovative [ínouveitiv] adj. 혁신적인 influéntial [influénʃəl] adj. 영향을 미치는 téleviside debátes : 텔레비전으로 방영된 토론 the Repúblicans : 미국 공화당 (= the Repúblican party) the Démocrats : 미국 민주당 (= the Democrátic party) sénator [sénətər] n. 상원의원 the Democrátic hópefuls : 민주당 예비주자들 nóminate [náməneit] v. 지명하다(cf. nominátion [namənéiʃən] n. 지명) convéntion [kənvénʃən] n. 전당대회, 집회 represéntative [reprizéntativ] n. 대표자 presidéntial eléction : 대통령선거 vígorously [vígərəsli] adj. 활발하게 unprécedented step : 전례 없는 진보 face-to-face debáte : 직접(대면)토론 conténd [kənténd] v. 논쟁하다, 경쟁하다 decísive force : 결정적인 힘 víewership [vjúːərʃip] n. 시청률, 시청자 másterfully [mǽstərfəli] adv. 훌륭하게 overcóme [ouvərkʌ́m] v. 극복하다 cándidate [kǽndədeit] n. 후보자 revérse [rivə́ːrs] v. 뒤집다, 역전시키다 públic percéption : 대중적 인지도 immatúre [imətjúər] adj. 성숙하지 못한(opp. mátune [mɔ́tjuər] adj. 성숙한) présidency [prézidənsi] n. 대통령직무(수행)

주제문 : 첫 문장 핵심어 : presidential campaign, televised debates, contest between the Republicans and the Democrats

1. Which of the following best expresses the main idea of the passage?

(A) Kennedy defeated Nixon in the 1960 presidential election.

(B) Television debates were instrumental in determining the outcome of the 1960 presidential election.

(C) Television debates have long been a part of campaigning.

(D) Kennedy was the leading Democratic candidate in the 1960 presidential election.

2. The passage implies that Kennedy

   (A) was a long shot to receive the Democratic presidential nomination.

   (B) won the Democratic presidential nomination fairly easily.

   (C) was not a front runner in the race for the Democratic presidential nomination.

   (D) came from behind to win the Democratic presidential nomination.

3. The passage states that the television debates between presidential candidates in 1960

   (A) did not establish a precedent.

   (B) were the final televised presidential debates.

   (C) were fairly usual in the history of presidential campaigns.

   (D) were the first presidential campaign debates to be televised.

4. The passage states that in the debates with Nixon, Kennedy demonstrated to the American people that he was

   (A) old enough to be president.

   (B) more experienced than Nixon.

   (C) better known than Nixon.

   (D) too inexperienced to serve as president.

---

1. 문제의 핵심어 : main idea
   본문의 정답찾기 : 주제나 요지는 흔히 첫 문장에 실린다.
2. 문제의 핵심어 : Kennedy
   본문의 정답찾기 : Kennedy에 관한 내용이므로, 윗글에서 'Kennedy'가 주어인 문장들을 차례로 훑어본다.
3. 문제의 핵심어 : television debates
   본문의 정답찾기 : 첫 문장을 포함해서 'television debates'가 들어있는 문장을 차례로 읽는다.
4. 문제의 핵심어 : debates, demonstrate
   본문의 정답찾기 : '… reserved the public perception of him as …'

7

Another noteworthy trend in twentieth-century music in the U.S. has been the use of folk and popular music as a base for more serious compositions. The motivation for these borrowings from traditional sources might be a desire on the part of a composer to return to simpler forms, to enhance patriotic feelings, or to establish an immediate rapport with an audience. For whatever reason, composers such as Charles Ives and Aaron Copland offered compositions featuring new musical forms flavored with refrains from traditional Americana. Ives employed patriotic songs, hymns, jazz, and popular songs in his compositions, while Copland drew upon folk music, particularly as sources for his ballets *Billy the Kid*, *Rodeo*, and *Appalachian Spring*.

* rappórt [ræpɔ́:r] *n.* 친밀한 관계, 공감대 refráin [rifréin] *n.* 반복구, 후렴

---

nóteworthy [nóutwəːrði] *adj.* 주목할 만한, 눈에 띄는 trend[trend] *n.* 경향, 추세 composítion [kampəzíʃən] *n.* 작곡(*cf.* compóser [kəmpóuzər] *n.* 작곡가) motivátion [moutəvéiʃən] *n.* 동기 bórrowings : 차용물, 빌린 것 tradítional sóurces : 전통적인 소재 enhánce[enhǽns] *v.* 높이다, 고양하다 patriótic féelings : 애국적인 감정 Charles Ives (1874~1954) 미국의 작곡가 Aaron Copland (1900~) 미국의 작곡가 flávor [fléivər] *v.* 맛(멋)을 내다, 풍미하다 hymn [him] *n.* 찬송가, 성가 draw upon ~ : ~을 이용하다, ~을 의지하다 bállet [bǽlei] *n.* 발레

주제문 : 첫 문장 핵심어 : another trend, twenty-century music in the U.S., use of folk and popular music

1. The paragraph preceding this passage most probably discusses

(A) nineteenth-century music.

(B) one development in music of this century.

(C) the works of Aaron Copland.

(D) the history of folk and popular music.

2. Which of the following best describes the main idea of the passage?

(A) Traditional music has flavored some American musical compositions in this century.

(B) Ives and Copland have used folk and popular music in their compositions.

(C) A variety of explanations exist as to why a composer might use traditional sources of music.

(D) Traditional music is composed of various types of folk and popular music.

3. It can be inferred from this passage that the author is not sure

(A) when Ives wrote his compositions.

(B) that Ives and Copland actually borrowed from traditional music.

(C) why certain composers borrowed from folk and popular music.

(D) if Copland really featured new musical forms.

4. Which of the following is not listed in the passage as a source for Ives' compositions?

(A) National music

(B) Religious music

(C) Jazz

(D) American ballets

5. The passage would most probably be assigned reading in which of the following courses?

(A) American History

(B) The History of Jazz

(C) Modern American Music

(D) Composition

1. 문제의 핵심어 : preceding this passage
   본문의 정답찾기 : 앞의 글을 유추하는 문제는 첫 문장을 읽으면 유추가 가능하다. one~, another~
2. 문제의 핵심어 : main idea
   본문의 정답찾기 : 주제는 주로 첫 문장에 실려 있다.
3. 문제의 핵심어 : infer
   본문의 정답찾기 : 6~8행(For whatever reason, ··· Americana.)
4. 문제의 핵심어 : sources for Ives' compositions
   본문의 정답찾기 : 9~10행(Ives employed patriotic songs, hymns, jazz, and popular songs in his compositions)
5. 제목은 대개 주제문에서 찾을 수 있다.

Group 3

종합적 판단을 묻는 문제

종합적 판단을 묻는 문제에서는 글의 정서, 저자의 의도나 목적, 글의 성격 등을 파악하고 있는지를 묻는다. 글에 서술된 단순한 사실은 글쓴이의 의도에 의해서 여러 가지로 해석될 수 있다. 따라서 글쓴이의 의도나 목적을 잘 이해하는 것은 사실적 정보를 정확하게 이해하는 데에 필수적이다.

문제 유형

글의 성격을 묻는 문제
글의 분위기를 묻는 문제
글을 쓴 목적을 묻는 문제

문제 풀이 전략

추론적 이해를 요구하는 문제와 같이 글의 내용을 충분히 이해한 뒤에 판단이 가능한 종합적인 문제들이다. 글의 성격/분위기(tone)를 묻는 문제는 글이 설명문인 경우는 주제를 보충 설명하는 서술문을 종합해서 판단해야 하며, 비설명문은 글에 감정을 나타내는 단어들 즉, humorous(해학적), sarcastic(풍자적), outraged(격분한), sentimental(감상적), melancholy (우울한) 등에 주의를 기울여야 한다. 글의 목적을 묻는 문제는 주제문이나 주제문을 보충 설명하는 서술을 읽고 판단하면 쉽다.

Military awards have long been considered symbolic of royalty, and thus when the United States was a young nation just finished with revolution and eager to distance itself from anything tasting of monarchy, there was strong sentiment against military decoration. For a century, from the end of the Revolutionary War until the Civil War, the United States awarded no military honors. The institution of the Medal of Honor in 1861 was a source of great discussion and concern. From the Civil War until World War I, the Medal of Honor was the only military award given by the United States government, and today it is awarded only in the most extreme cases of heroism. Although the United States is still somewhat wary of granting military awards, several awards have been instituted since World War I.

míltary awárd : 군사 포상 symbólic [simbálik] *n.* 상징이 되는(*cf.* sýmbol [símbəl] *n.* 상징) éager to do : ~을 하고 싶어하다 dístance [dístəns] *v.* 거리를 두다, 떼어놓다 distance A from B : A를 B로부터 떼어놓다 taste [teist] *v.* 맛이 나다, 맛보다 mónarchy [mánərki] *n.* 군주제 séntiment [séntəmənt] *n.* 정서, 감정 míltary decorátion : 군용 장식 míltary hónors : 군대 훈장 héroism [hérouizəm] *n.* 영웅주의 wáry [wɛ́əri] *adj.* 경계하는 grant [grænt] *v.* 주다, 수여하다 ínstitute [ínstətjuːt] *v.* 제정하다, 실시하다

주제문 : 첫 문장 핵심어 : military awards

1. The tone of the passage is

(A) angered.

(B) humorous.

(C) outraged.

(D) informational.

2. The author's purpose in this passage is to

(A) describe the history of military awards from the Revolutionary War to the Civil War.

(B) demonstrate an effect of America's attitude toward royalty.

(C) give an opinion of military awards.

(D) outline various historical symbols of royalty.

3. This passage would probably be assigned reading in a course on

(A) military science.

(B) sociology.

(C) american history.

(D) interior decoration.

2

    In Cold Blood (1966) is a well-known example of the "non-fiction novel," a recently popular type of writing based upon factual events in which the author attempts to describe the underlying forces, thoughts, and emotions that lead to actual events. In Truman Capote's book, the author describes the sadistic murder of a family on a Kansas farm, often showing the point of view of the killers. To research the book, Capote interviewed the murderers, and he maintains that his book presents a faithful reconstruction of the incident.

nonfíction nóvel : 논픽션 소설 fáctual evénts : 사실에 입각한 사건 underlíe [ʌndərlái] *v.* ~의 밑에 눕다, 기초가 되다 sadístic [sədístik] *adj.* 가학성의(*cf.* sadism [sǽdizəm] *n.* 가학성 *opp.* másochism [mǽsəkizəm] *n.* 피학성, 자기학대) presént [prizént] *v.* 주다, 상연하다, 싣다 reconstrúction [riːkənstrʌ́kʃən] *n.* 재건

주제문 : 첫 문장 핵심어 : nonfiction novel

1. The purpose of this passage is to

(A) discuss an example of a new literary genre.

(B) tell the story of *In Cold Blood*.

(C) explain Truman Capote's reasons for writing *In Cold Blood*.

(D) describe how Truman Capote researched his nonfiction novel.

2. Which of the following best describes the tone of the passage?

(A) Cold

(B) Sadistic

(C) Emotional

(D) Descriptive

Up to now confessions that have been obtained from defendants in a hypnotic state have not been admitted into evidence by courts in the United States. Experts in the field of hypnosis have found that such confessions are not completely reliable. Subjects in a hypnotic state may confess to crimes they did not commit for one of two reasons. Either they fantasize that they had committed the crimes or they believe that others want them to confess.

A landmark case concerning a confession obtained under hypnosis went all the way to the U.S. Supreme Court. In the case of *Leyra* vs. *Denno*, a suspect was hypnotized by a psychiatrist for the district attorney; in a post-hypnotic state the suspect signed three separate confessions to a murder. The Supreme Court ruled that the confessions were invalid because of the mental intimidation used to obtain them. The suspect was then released because the confessions had been the only evidence against him.

* hypnósis [hipnóusis] *n.* 최면상태

up to now : 지금까지 conféssion [kənféʃən] *n.* 자백, 고백 obtáin [əbtéin] *v.* 얻다(= get) deféndant [diféndənt] *n.* 피고 hypnótic [hipnátik] *adj.* 최면상태의 hýpnotize [hípnətaiz] *v.* 최면을 걸다, 무력하게 하다 a post-hypnótic state : 최면후의 상태 éxpert [ékspəːrt] *n.* 전문가 súbject [sʌ́bdʒikt] *n.* 환자, 조사대상자 commít [kəmít] *v.* 저지르다 fántasize [fǽntəsaiz] *v.* 공상에 잠기다, 상상 속에 그리다 lándmark [lǽndmaːrk] *n.* 표지물 landmark case : 획기적인 사건 all the way : 줄곧, 모처럼 suspéct [səspékt] *n.* 용의자, 피의자 psychíatrist [saikáiətrist] *n.* 정신과의사 attórney [ətɔ́ːrni] *n.* 검사 dístrict attórney : 지방검사 inválid [inǽlid] *adj.* 부당한 (*opp.* valid [vǽlid] *adj.* 타당한) intimidátion [intimədéiʃən] *n.* 위협, 협박(*cf.* tímid [tímid] *adj.* 겁 많은, 소심한) reléase [rilíːs] *v.* 석방하다 agáinst [əgénst] *prep.* ~에 반대하는, ~에 불리한

주제문 : 첫 문장 핵심어 : confession, hypnosis

1. Which of the following best describes the author's purpose in this passage?

(A) To describe the history of hypnosis

(B) To demonstrate why confessions made under hypnosis are not reliable

(C) To clarify the role of the Supreme Court in invalidating confessions from hypnotized subjects

(D) To explain the legal status of hypnotically induced confessions

2. The tone of this passage could best be described as

(A) outraged.

(B) judicious.

(C) hypnotic.

(D) informative.

4

The rate at which the deforestation of the world is proceeding is alarming. In 1950 approximately 25 percent of the earth's land surface had been covered with forests, and less than 25 years later the amount of forest land was reduced to 20 percent. This decrease from 25 percent to 20 percent from 1950 to 1973 represents an astounding loss of 20 million square kilometers of forests. Predictions are that an additional 20 million square kilometers of forest land will be lost by 2020.

The majority of deforestation is occurring in tropical forests in developing countries, fueled by the developing countries' need for increased agricultural land and the desire on the part of developed countries to import wood and wood products. More than 90 percent of the plywood used in the United States, for example, is imported from developing countries with tropical forests. By the mid-1980's, solutions to this expanding problem were being sought, in the form of attempts to establish an international regulatory organization to oversee the use of tropical forests.

* deforestation [di:fɔːristéiʃən] *n.* 산림벌채 plýwood [pláiwud] *n.* 합판

alárming [əlá:rmiŋ] *adj.* 놀라운 astóunding [əstáundiŋ] *adj.* 놀라운 predíction [pridíkʃən] *n.* 예보 trópical fórests : 열대림 fúel[fjú:əl] *v.* 연료를 공급하다 solútion [səlú:ʃən] *n.* 해답 seek[si:k] *v.* 찾다, 추구하다(seek-sought-sought) internátional regulátory organizátion : 국제적인 규제조직 oversée [ouvərsí:] *v.* 감독하다, 감시하다

1. The author's main purpose in this passage is to

    (A) cite statistics about an improvement on the earth's land surface.

    (B) explain where deforestation is occurring.

    (C) make the reader aware of a worsening world problem.

    (D) blame developing countries for deforestation.

2. Which of the following best describes the tone of the passage?

    (A) Concerned

    (B) Disinterested

    (C) Placid

    (D) Exaggerated

3. This passage would probably be assigned reading in which of the following courses?

    (A) Geology

    (B) Geography

    (C) Geometry

    (D) Marine Biology

---

1. 문제의 핵심어 : author's purpose
   본문의 정답찾기 : 윗글의 두 문단에서 각각 첫 문장을 읽고 유추할 수 있다. 대개 첫 문장들이 글의 주제나 목적을 내포하고 있다.
2. 문제의 핵심어 : tone
   산림채벌로 인하여 지구의 산림면적이 줄어드는 것을 염려하는 논조이다.

5

The rattlesnake has a reputation as a dangerous and deadly snake with a fierce hatred for mankind. Although the rattlesnake is indeed a venomous snake capable of killing a human, its nature has perhaps been somewhat exaggerated in myth and folklore.

The rattlesnake is not inherently aggressive and generally strikes only when it has been put on the defensive. In its defensive posture the rattlesnake raises the front part of its body off the ground and assumes an S-shaped form in preparation for a thrust forward. At the end of a forward thrust, the rattlesnake pushes its fangs into the victim, thereby injecting its venom.

There are more than thirty species of rattlesnakes, varying in length from 20 inches to six feet and also varying in toxicity of venom. In the United States there are only a few deaths annually from rattlesnakes, with a mortality rate of less than 2 percent of those attacked.

* vénom [vénəm] *n.* 독(= póisonous flúid, tóxin) fang [fæŋ] *n.* 독니, 독이 든 방울뱀의 송곳니 toxícity [tɑksísəti] *n.* (유)독성

ráttlesnake [rǽtlsneik] *n.* 방울뱀, 북미산 독사 déadly [dédli] *adj.* 치명적인 fíerce [fíərs] *adj.* 맹렬한, 지독한 hátred [héitrid] *n.* 증오 vénomous [vénəməs] *adj.* 독이 있는 cápable of -ing : ~할 수 있는 (= can) exággerate [igzǽdʒəreit] *v.* 과장하다 fólklore [fóuklɔːr] *n.* 민속, 민속학 inhérently [inhíərentli] *adv.* 본래, 타고난 대로 strike [straik] *v.* 치다, 두드리다 the defénsive : 방어자 pósture [pástʃər] *n.* 자세 assúme [əsjúːm] *v.* ~인 체 하다, (모습을) 취하다, 띄다 in preparátion for : ~을 준비하여 thrust [θrʌst] *n.* 찌르기, 돌진 fang [fæŋ] *n.* 독니, 독이 든 방울뱀의 송곳니 injéct [indʒékt] *v.* 주사하다 váry [véəri] *v.* 변하다(= change) a mortálity rate : 사망률, 치사율 mortálity [mɔːrtǽləti] *n.* 죽음(= death) (*cf.* immortálity [imɔːrtǽləti] *n.* 불멸)

주제문 : 첫 문단의 첫 문장 핵심어 : rattlesnake

1. Which of the following would be the best title for this passage?

   (A) The Exaggerated Reputation of the Rattlesnake

   (B) The Dangerous and Deadly Rattlesnake

   (C) The Venomous Killer of Humans

   (D) Myth and Folklore about Killers

2. According to the passage, which of the following is true about rattlesnakes?

   (A) They are always ready to attack.

   (B) They are always dangerous and deadly.

   (C) Their fierce nature has been underplayed in myth and folklore.

   (D) Their poison can kill people.

3. When a rattlesnake is ready to defend itself, it

   (A) lies in an S-shape on the ground.

   (B) lunges with the back part of its body.

   (C) is partially off the ground.

   (D) assumes it is prepared by thrusting its fangs into the ground.

4. The author's purpose in this passage is to

    (A) warn readers about the extreme danger from rattlesnakes.

    (B) explain a misconception about rattlesnakes.

    (C) describe a rattlesnake attack.

    (D) clarify how a rattlesnake kills humans.

---

1. 문제의 핵심어 : title
   본문의 정답찾기 : 각 문단의 첫 문장을 읽되, 특히 첫 문단의 첫 문장을 참고한다.
2. 문제의 핵심어 : about rattlesnake, true
   본문의 정답찾기 : 3행
3. 문제의 핵심어 : defend
   본문의 정답찾기 : 6~8행('In its defensive posture …')
4. 문제의 핵심어 : author's purpose
   본문의 정답찾기 : 주제가 실린 첫 문단을 읽고 유추한다.

6

    A massive banking crisis occurred in the United States in 1933. In the two preceding years, a large number of banks had failed, and fear of lost savings prompted many depositors to remove their funds from banks. Problems became so serous in the state of Michigan that Governor William A. Comstock was forced to declare a moratorium on all banking activities in the state on February 14, 1933. The panic in Michigan quickly spread to other states, and by March 6, President Franklin D. Roosevelt had declared a banking moratorium throughout the United States that left the entire country without banking services.

    Congress immediately met in a special session to solve the banking crisis and on March 9 passed the Emergency Banking Act of 1933 to assist financially healthy banks to reopen. By March 15, banks controlling 90 percent of the country's financial reserves were again open for business.

a mássive bánking crísis : 대단위 금융위기 prompt [prɑmpt] *v.* 자극하다, 촉발하다 depósitor [dipázitər] *n.* 예금주 moratórium [mɔːrətɔ́ːriəm] *n.* 지불중지 a bánking moratórium : 예금지불중지 pánic [pǽnik] *n.* 공황, 금융공황 séssion [séʃən] *n.* 회기 the Emérgency Bánking Áct : 비상금융조례 resérve [rizə́ːrv] *n.* 비축, 준비

주제문 : 첫 문장 핵심어 : A massive banking crisis

1. The author's purpose in this passage is to

   (A) discuss a problem and its resolution.

   (B) warn depositors about potential banking problems.

   (C) assess blame for a problem that had occurred.

   (D) praise Congress for its actions.

2. The passage states that all the following occurred prior to 1933 EXCEPT
   that

   (A) many banks went under.

   (B) many bank patrons were afraid of losing their deposits.

   (C) a lot of money was withdrawn from accounts.

   (D) Governor Comstock cancelled all banking activities in Michigan.

3. Which of the following is implied in the passage?

   (A) Congress did not give any special priority to the banking situation.

   (B) The Emergency Banking Act helped all banks to reopen.

   (C) Ninety percent of the banks reopened by the middle of March.

   (D) Ten percent of the country's money was in financially unhealthy
       banks.

4. Which of the following best describes the tone of the passage?

   (A) Romantic

   (B) Critical

   (C) Historical

   (D) Angry

TOEFL Beginner's Reading Comprehension

Part 4

독해종합연습

|독해종합연습|

1

A grade report is mailed to the student at the end of each semester. This cumulative record, known as a "student copy," is not valid for transfer or certification purposes. Additional student copies may be obtained at a cost of $3.00 each.

1. How does the student receive his grades?

   (A) In an envelope
   (B) Over the telephone
   (C) Directly from the professor
   (D) From a notice posted on the bulletin board

2. According to the passage, the "student's copy" is NOT

   (A) reproduceable.
   (B) permanent.
   (C) a complete record.
   (D) an official transcript.

3. How often are the grades reported?

   (A) Every month
   (B) At the end of the term
   (C) Once a year
   (D) Whenever the student wants them

4. Where would this paragraph most probably be found?

    (A) In a test booklet

    (B) In a letter from a student

    (C) In a college catalog

    (D) In a class schedule

2

    If robots ever come to enjoy a prominent place in the future, they may owe at least a small debt of gratitude to a "micromouse" named Moonlight Special. The micromouse is a robot rodent that can "feel" its way through a maze and memorize the correct path after two passes. On the third run through the maze, Moonlight Special can crawl from start to finish without bumping into a wall or making a wrong turn.

1. What is Moonlight Special?

    (A) A bionic mouse

    (B) A species of rodent

    (C) A small robot

    (D) An electronic game

2. What can the micromouse do?

    (A) Memorize a maze.

    (B) Construct maze variations.

    (C) Distinguish between two lights.

    (D) Remember one path out of two.

3. What will the micromouse do after two runs through a maze?

    (A) Run rather than crawl.

    (B) Alter its course.

    (C) Avoid turns and bumps.

    (D) Perform without errors.

3

When used for studies of learning and memory, the octopus is a more interesting subject than the squid. Unlike the free-swimming squid, which relies exclusively on its eyes to guide it to a tasty fish or crab, the octopus often feeds off the bottom of the sea. It uses not only its eyes but its tentacles to identify a likely meal. The brain of the octopus has two separate memory-storage areas—one for visual memories and one for tactile memories.

1. How does the squid find its food?

   (A) By sight only

   (B) By touch only

   (C) Both by sight and by touch

   (D) In none of the ways described above

2. The passage is mainly about

   (A) a new way of feeding fish.

   (B) biological differences between two animals.

   (C) how to go deep-sea fishing.

   (D) a warning to deep-sea divers.

3. According to the passage, which of the following can describe the octopus?

   (A) Its brain is simpler than that of the squid.

   (B) It cannot look and touch at the same time.

   (C) Its brain does not function very well.

   (D) The memory of what it has seen and touched is contained in separate areas.

4

Economic expansion continued in May. Government reports showed gains in industrial production, personal income, and housing starts. Housing construction, however, remained sluggish, mainly because the cost of new homes has risen much faster than average incomes, but housing starts did show a small increase over those of April.

1. The author's claims concerning economic expansion seem to be based on
   (A) government data in three areas.
   (B) government budgetary reports.
   (C) the author's own research.
   (D) the author's personal insight.

2. According to the passage, which of the following is true of housing starts?
   (A) They were the same as in previous months.
   (B) They were lower in May than in April.
   (C) They were slightly higher in May than in April.
   (D) They were much higher in May than in April.

3. According to the passage, housing construction is recovering slowly because
   (A) the cost of a new home is higher than the government's price guidelines.
   (B) new homes are being built at a faster rate than needed.
   (C) prices or new homes have been going up faster than increases in people's incomes.
   (D) new homes are selling faster than anticipated.

5

It is common knowledge that ability to do a particular job and performance on the job do not always go hand in hand. Persons with great potential ability sometimes fall down on the job because of laziness or lack of interest in the job, while persons with ordinary talents have often achieved excellent results through their industry and their loyalty to the interests of their employers. It is clear, therefore, that the final test of any employee is his performance on the job.

1. The most accurate of the following statements, on the basis of the above paragraph is that

   (A) employees who lack ability are usually not industrious.

   (B) an employee's attitudes are more important than his abilities.

   (C) mediocre employees who are interested in their work are preferable to employees who possess great ability.

   (D) superior capacity for performance should be supplemented with proper attitudes.

2. On the basis of the above paragraph, the employee of most value to his employer is not necessarily the one who

   (A) achieves excellent results.

   (B) best understands the significance of his duties.

   (C) possesses the greatest talent.

   (D) produces the greatest amount of work.

3. According to the above paragraph, an employee's efficiency is best determined by an

   (A) appraisal of his interest in his work.

   (B) evaluation of the work performed by him.

   (C) appraisal of his loyalty to his employer.

   (D) evaluation of his potential ability to perform his work.

6

Most students are unwilling to believe that their teachers are human beings with human weaknesses. However, when a student gets to know a teacher well, he invariably finds that this authority figure possesses all sorts of flaws and bad habits-anything from drinking too much to being late for appointments. His office may be untidy, his children may be ill-mannered, he may even lie on his income tax returns. In short, the evidence suggests that teachers are just as human as their students.

1. According to the passage, most students think that

    (A) their teachers are dishonest.

    (B) their teachers are authority figures.

    (C) their teachers have no human flaw.

    (D) it is impossible to know teachers well.

2. The passage states that teachers are

    (A) ill-mannered.

    (B) perfect.

    (C) well-educated.

    (D) human.

7

The influenza virus is a single molecule composed of millions of individual atoms. While bacteria can be considered as a type of plant, secreting poisonous substances into the body of the organism they attack, viruses, like the influenza virus, are living arganisms themselves. We may consider them as regular chemical molecules since they have strictly defined atomic structure; but on the other hand, we must also consider them as being alive since they are able to multiply in unlimited quantities.

1. According to this passage, bacteria are

    (A) poisons.

    (B) very small.

    (C) larger than viruses.

    (D) plants.

2. The writer says that viruses are alive because they

    (A) have a complex atomic structure.

    (B) move.

    (C) multiply.

    (D) need warmth and light.

3. The atomic structure of viruses

    (A) is variable.

    (B) is strictly defined.

    (C) cannot be analyzed chemically.

    (D) is more complex than that of bacteria.

8

Character is a respect for human beings and the right to interpret experience differently. Character admits self-interest as a natural trait, but puts its faith on man's hesitant but heartening instinct to cooperate. Character is allergic to tyranny, irritable with ignorance, and always open to improvement. Character implies the ability to laugh whole-heartedly and weep unashamedly. Character is, above all, a tremendous humility before the facts—an automatic alliance with truth even when that truth is bitter medicine.

1. The title below that best expresses the ideas of the paragraph is

    (A) The Bitter Medicine of Truth.

    (B) Respect for Character.

    (C) Character and Experience.

    (D) A Definition of Character.

2. A quality of character not mentioned by the author is

    (A) sympathy.

    (B) humbleness.

    (C) humor.

    (D) patientce.

3. The author indicates that the man of character

    (A) expects people to be entirely unselfish.

    (B) recognizes selfishness as the dominating trait of all mankind.

    (C) realizes that people are naturally interested in themselves.

    (D) admits that tyranny and ignorance are worse than selfishness.

9

Although most universities in the United States are on a semester system which offers classes in the fall and spring, some schools observe a quarter system comprised of fall, winter, spring, and summer quarters. The academic year, September to June, is divided into three quarters of eleven weeks each beginning in September, January, and March; the summer quarter, June to August, is composed of shorter sessions of varying length. Students may take advantage of the opportunity to study year around by enrolling in all four quarters. Most students begin their programs in the fall quarter, but they may enter at the beginning of any of the other quarters.

1. The academic year is

    (A) September to August.

    (B) June to August.

    (C) August to June.

    (D) September to June.

2. A semester system

    (A) has eleven-week sessions.

    (B) is not very popular in the United States.

    (C) gives students the opportunity to study year around.

    (D) has two major sessions a year.

3. Which of the following would be the best title for this passage?

   (A) Universities in the United States

   (B) The Academic Year

   (C) The Quarter System

   (D) The Semester System

10

Plutarch loved those who could use life for grand purposes and depart from it as grandly, but he would not pass over weaknesses and vices which marred the grandeur. His hero of heroes is Alexander the Great; he loves him above all other men, while his abomination of abominations is bad faith, dishonorable action. Nevertheless he tells, with no attempt to extenuate, how Alexander promised a safe conduct to a brave Persian army if they surrendered, and then, "even as they were marching away he fell upon them and put them all to the sword," "a breach of his word," Plutarch says sadly, "which is a lasting blemish to his achievements." He adds piteously, "but the only one," He hated to tell that story.

1. How did Plutarch feel about Alexander the Great?

   (A) He loved him without reservation.

   (B) He loved him except for one action.

   (C) He thought he had treated the Persian army bravely.

   (D) He hated his achievements.

2. What human failure did Plutarch hate?

   (A) Treachery

   (B) Abomination

   (C) Murder

   (D) Defeat in battle

3. The author indicates that Plutarch, in his account of Alexander's treatment of the Persians, was speaking

   (A) impulsively.

   (B) forgivingly.

   (C) reluctantly.

   (D) spitefully.

11

Precipitation, commonly referred to as rainfall, is a measure of the quantity of water in the form of either rain, hail, or snow which reaches the ground. The average annual precipitation over the whole of the United States is thirty-six inches. It should be understood however, that a foot of snow is not equal to a foot of precipitation. A general formula for computing the precipitation of snowfall is that thirty-eight inches of snow is equal to one inch of precipitation. In New York State, for example, seventy-six inches of snow in one year would be recorded as only two inches of precipitation. Forty inches of rain would be recorded as forty inches of precipitation. The total annual precipitation would be recorded as forty-two inches.

1. The term precipitation includes
   (A) only rainfall.
   (B) rain, hail, and snow.
   (C) rain, snow, and humidity.
   (D) rain, hail, and humidity.

2. What is the average annual rainfall in inches in the United States?
   (A) Thirty-six inches
   (B) Thirty-eight inches
   (C) Forty inches
   (D) Forty-two inches

3. If a state has 152 inches of snow in a year, by how much does this increase the annual precipitation?
   (A) By two feet
   (B) By four inches
   (C) By four feet
   (D) By 152 inches

4. Another word which is often used in place of precipitation is
   (A) humidity.
   (B) wetness.
   (C) rainfall.
   (D) rain-snow.

12

The Oneida were an Iroquoian-speaking North American Indian tribe who were one of the original five nations of the Iroquois league. Like other Iroquois tribes the Oneida practiced corn agriculture. They were divided into three clans, each having three representatives in the confederation. Each community also had a local council that guided the chief or chiefs. The Oneida supported the colonist cause in the American Revolution and consequently experienced the robbery of the pro-British Iroquois under Chief Joseph Brant. They retired within American lines, where they served as scouts. They returned to their homes after the war and were compensated by the United States for their losses.

* clan [klæn] *n.* 씨족

1. According to the passage, the way of life of the Oneida Indians can be characterized as

   (A) primitive.
   (B) agricultural.
   (C) industry-oriented.
   (D) commercial.

2. In the next-to-last sentence of the passage, the statement "They retired" is used to indicate that the Oneida

   (A) protected their elderly members.
   (B) ceased to do any work.
   (C) withdrew as a group.
   (D) released their captives.

3. According to the passage, what happened to the Oneida after the American Revolution?

   (A) They received reparation from the United States.
   (B) They became citizens of the United States.
   (C) Their families were forced to relocate in new regions.
   (D) Their numbers continued to dwindle at a rapid rate.

13

Both the Sun and the Moon appear larger when they are rising or setting, although there is no real difference in the distance they are from the Earth. This perceptual phenomenon, known as the "Moon illusion," has been studied over the years. Various explanations, including the muscle strain for the person looking up and the comparison of the Moon with other things on the horizon that make it appear larger, have been disputed by scientists, but thus far there is no widely accepted explanation of the phenomenon.

1. Which of the following would be the most appropriate title for the passage?

(A) Perceived Sizes of the Sun and Moon

(B) Comparisons of Objects on the Horizon

(C) Perceptions of Distance

(D) The Rising and Setting of the Sun and Moon

2. The "Moon illusion" of the Sun can be seen at

(A) evening.

(B) dawn and dusk.

(C) mid-morning and mid-afternoon.

(D) midday.

3. According to the passage, the true cause of the "Moon illusion" is

(A) well known.

(B) different at different times.

(C) rarely disputed.

(D) still under study.

14

Sometimes certain eras or events from our past receive little or no attention. This might be because there is little information available on these subjects, or because the subjects are controversial or shameful, and we are reluctant to face them. But when we ignore or deny a part of our past, we fail to learn the lessons that history can teach us, and we neglect people who are part of that history. These people—and their history—can become "invisible," and in time we can forget that they ought to be part of what we think of as history.

1. What is the author's main point?

(A) History tends to repeat itself.

(B) Historians should not write about disputed matters.

(C) More people should study history.

(D) No part of history should be ignored.

2. It can be inferred from the passage that the best motivation for studying history is to

(A) learn from its past lessons.

(B) appreciate the perspectives of writers of historical texts.

(C) become more well-rounded students.

(D) compare the life-styles of major historical characters.

3. The author implies that the work of historians would be more valuable if they

(A) asked current world leaders to write down their views of history.

(B) includes accounts of unpleasant events in their texts.

(C) wrote psychological discussions about incidents in history.

(D) emphasized a biographical viewpoint in history books.

15

As the result of several discoveries and the development of new techniques and equipment, the importance of the shellfish industry has increased since 1950. One shellfish, the oyster, has been cultivated in great numbers by means of the new technology. Marine biologists discovered that by using chemicals and raising the water temperature, they could induce oysters to lay eggs not only in the summer, but also in the fall, winter, and spring. They also succeeded in breeding new strains of oysters that were resistant to diseases and grew faster and larger. In addition, the cultivated oysters taste better!

1. The main topic of this passage is
   (A) an explanation of marine biology.
   (B) new locations for oyster beds.
   (C) improvements in the oyster industry.
   (D) the shellfish industry before 1950.

2. It can be inferred from the passage that before the use of the new technology, oysters laid their eggs each year during
   (A) one season.
   (B) two seasons.
   (C) three seasons.
   (D) four seasons.

3. According to the passage, all of the following are characteristics of the new strains of oysters EXCEPT
   (A) resistant to illness.
   (B) more rapid growth.
   (C) a larger size.
   (D) flawless pearls.

16

What carried the new men of Europe and Asia to the ends of the earth was their ability to invent new kinds of tools and use them in new ways to increase their efficiency as hunters, fishermen, collectors, and travelers. The first of these inventions included tools designed for making other implements. Flint chisels could be used for fine work with horn, ivory, bone, and wood. Fabrics could be woven from rushes and bark. Baskets could be made for storing grain, and gourds could be collected for storing water. Harpoons and spears and other missiles extended the range of the animals man could kill. Perhaps the most significant inventions were those man used to carry him over the water. They not only increased his power and his means of subsistence; they also spread his populations over rivers and oceans.

1. The passage is mainly about
   (A) the uses of flint.
   (B) the invention of weapons.
   (C) the expansion of modern colonial powers.
   (D) early man's technological development.

2. The device used for fashioning other materials was the
   (A) harpoon.
   (B) flint chisel.
   (C) gourd.
   (D) basket.

3. The word 'missile' in this passage probably means
   (A) a variety of wood.
   (B) an animal that was hunted.
   (C) a weapon for throwing.
   (D) a vessel for holding water.

17

There are many ways of communicating without using speech. Signals, signs, symbols, and gestures may be found in every known culture. The basic function of a signal is to impinge upon the environment in such a way that it attracts attention, as, for example, the dots and dashes of a telegraph circuit. Coded to refer to speech, the potential for communication is very great. While less adaptable to the codification of words, signs contain greater meaning in and of themselves. A stop sign or a barber pole conveys meaning quickly and conveniently. Symbols are more difficult to describe than either signals or signs because of their intricate relationship with the receiver's cultural perceptions. In some cultures, applauding in a theater provides performers with an auditory symbol of approval. Gestures such as waving and handshaking also communicate certain cultural messages.

1. According to this passage, a signal is

   (A) more difficult to describe than other forms of communication.

   (B) an interruption in the environment.

   (C) less able to be adapted to refer to speech.

   (D) a gesture.

2. Applauding was cited as an example of

   (A) a signal.

   (B) a sign.

   (C) a symbol.

   (D) a gesture.

3. It may be concluded from this passage that

   (A) signals, signs, symbols, and gestures are forms of communication.

   (B) symbols are very easy to define and interpret.

   (C) only some cultures have signals, signs, and symbols.

   (D) waving and handshaking are not related to culture.

18

When there is no distance between people, the only way that anyone can keep his distance is by a code of etiquette that has acceptance in a community. Manners are the antidote to adjustment to the group. They make social intercourse possible without any forfeit of one's personal dignity. They are armor against invasion of privacy; they are the advance patrols that report whether one should withdraw or advance into intimacy. They are the friendly but noncommittal gestures of civilized people. The manners of crowded countries are, I believe, always more formal than those of open countries, (as they are, for example, in Europe and Japan), and it may be that we are seeing a rising concern about American manners precisely because we encounter more people in closer distance than we ever have before. We feel the need to find ways in which to be part of the group without selling out our privacy or our individuality for a mess of adjustment.

1. The author suggests that in Europe good manners are
   (A) informal.
   (B) excessive.
   (C) essential.
   (D) not practiced.

2. According to the author, manners serve to
   (A) facilitate relationships among people.
   (B) preserve certain ceremonies.
   (C) help people to make friends quickly.
   (D) reveal character traits.

3. The passage indicates that people cherish their
   (A) superior manners.
   (B) advanced civilization.
   (C) personal identity.
   (D) ability to make friends.

19

The general principles of dynamics are rules which dem-onstrate a relationship between the motions of bodies and the forces which produce those motions. Based in large part on the work of his predecessors, Sir Isaac Newton deduced three laws of dynamics which he published in 1687 in his famous *Principia.*

Prior to Newton, Aristotle had established that the natural state of a body was a state of rest, and that unless a force acted upon it to maintain motion, a moving body would come to rest. Galileo had succeeded in correctly describing the behavior of falling objects and in recording that no force was required to maintain a body in motion. He noted that the effect of force was to change motion. Huygens recognized that a change in the direction of motion involved acceleration, just as did a change in speed, and further, that the action of a force was required. Kepler deduced the laws describing the motion of planets around the sun. It was primarily from Galileo and Kepler that Newton borrowed.

1. Which of the following scientists established that the natural state of a body was a state of rest?

(A) Galileo
(B) Kepler
(C) Aristotle
(D) Newton

2. The first scientist to correctly describe the behavior of falling object was

(A) Aristotle.
(B) Newton.
(C) Kepler.
(D) Galileo.

3. According to this passage, Newton based his laws primarily upon the work of

(A) Galileo and Copernicus.
(B) Ptolemy and Copernicus.
(C) Huygens and Kepler.
(D) Galileo and Kepler.

4. What was the main purpose of this passage?

(A) To demonstrate the development of Newton's law

(B) To establish Newton as the authority in the field of physics

(C) To discredit Newton's laws of motion

(D) To describe the motion of planets around the sun

20

William Faulkner of Oxford was not a native of Oxford; nor was he born with the name Faulkner. He was born in New Albany, Mississippi, on September 25, 1897, and the family spelled the name Falkner. He published his first book when he was twenty-seven. He was awarded the Nobel Prize for Literature when he was fifty-three. He was generally acknowledged as the major American writer of his time when he died on July 6, 1962. Faulkner or Falkner, he spent almost the whole of his life in the Mississippi town which millions who read his works know not as Oxford but as Jefferson. Even to the people of Oxford, Faulkner was a kind of legend in his own lifetime. There was, for example, the mystery of who put the "u" in William's last name. For many years the commonly accepted story was that it was a careless printer, in setting type for *The Marble Faun* (1924). Faulkner biographer Carvel Collins demonstrates that the writer himself added it, and, at least occasionally, as early as 1918.

1. At the time of his death, Faulkner was

(A) twenty-seven.

(B) fifty-three.

(C) sixty-two.

(D) sixty-four.

2. Faulkner lived most of his life in

    (A) Jefferson.

    (B) Oxford.

    (C) New Albany.

    (D) his birthplace.

3. The "u" in Faulkner's name was added by

    (A) a careless printer.

    (B) Faulkner's biographer Carvel Collins.

    (C) Faulkner himself.

    (D) Faulkner's great-grandfather.

Step 2

| 독해종합연습 |

1

The term "satellite city" is used to describe the relationship between a large city and neighboring smaller cities and towns that are economically dependent upon it. Satellite cities may be collection and distribution points in the commercial linkages of a trading metropolis, or they may be manufacturing or mining centers existing with one-industry economies as the creatures of some nearby center. This latter form is what is generally meant when one uses the term "satellite city." Taken in this sense, nineteenth-century Chicopee and Lowell, Massachusetts, were satellites of Boston. Both were mill towns created by Boston investors to serve the economy of that New England metropolis. Located on cheap land along water-power sites in the midst of a farming region that could supply ample labor, they were satellites in the fullest sense of the term. Pullman, Illinois, and Gary, Indiana, were likewise one-in-dustry towns created in conjunction with the much broader economy of nearby Chicago. Such places, as Vera Schlakman and Stanley Buder have pointed out in their excellent urban biographies, had a one-dimensional quality and little social vigor. These cities could not stand alone; they were in a sense colonies of a multifunctional mother city.

1. Which of the following is characteristic of a satellite city?

(A) It is a self-sufficient community.

(B) It offers cheap land to people.

(C) It tends to concentrate on a single product.

(D) It lies within a space station orbiting Earth.

2. According to the passage, Chicopee and Lowell were ideal locations for the development of towns because they had

(A) fully developed electric power plants.

(B) an adequate number of workers.

(C) Farmland that would not be flooded.

(D) extremely rich investors.

3. The author describes each of the following as being economically dependent on another city EXCEPT

(A) Chicopee, Massachusetts.

(B) Lowell, Massachusetts.

(C) Pullman, Illinois.

(D) Chicago, Illinois.

2

Belize, capital of British Honduras, has always been the colony's administrative, cultural, and geographic center. It is a unique waterfront community characterized by large frame houses with screened verandas. Located on the periphery of the hurricane zone, and at an average elevation of two feet above sea level, the town is vulnerable to any tidal wave. Hence most buildings are on stilts, and many others have Spartan furnishings at the street level. The cooling effect of sea breezes in a community surrounded on three sides by salt water relieves the otherwise oppressive climate. Located on the Caribbean coast of Central America slightly more than eight hundred miles south of New Orleans and about the same distance west of Jamaica, Belize had a population of nearly six thousand in 1859, ten thousand in 1900, and reached thirty thousand in the 1960's.

* stilt [stilt] *n.* (건조물을 버티는) 지주, 버팀목

1. Jamaica is located

(A) about eight hundred miles south of New Orleans.

(B) about eight hundred miles east of Belize.

(C) about eight hundred miles west of Belize.

(D) about eight hundred miles north of New Orleans.

2. Because of the dangers from storms and waves, the houses of Belize

   (A) are on the waterfront.

   (B) have large, screened verandas.

   (C) enjoy cooling sea breezes.

   (D) are built on stilts.

3. Between 1900 and 1960 the population of Belize

   (A) almost doubled.

   (B) increased by an unspecified amount.

   (C) tripled.

   (D) stayed about the same.

3

One of the most important weapons used during the Second World War was not a weapon used against people, but rather a drug used against disease. The wartime use of penicillin saved thousands of lives. In the First World War, for example, pneumonia was responsible for eighteen percent of all the deaths in the United States army. In the Second World War, the rate went down to less than one percent. In addition, penicillin was instrumental in keeping wounds from getting infected and in helping to speed the healing process of those wounds that did become infected.

1. Which of the following would be the best title for the passage?

   (A) A Dangerous Weapon

   (B) Guns in the Second World War

   (C) An Epidemic of Pneumonia

   (D) An Important Drug

2. According to the passage, one of the leading causes of death during the First World War was

   (A) gas.

   (B) accident.

   (C) disease.

   (D) drugs.

3. Compared with the death rate from pneumonia in the First World War, the rate in the Second World War was

(A) much higher.

(B) the same.

(C) slightly lower.

(D) significantly lowe.

4. According to the passage, penicillin was useful in the Second World War for all of the following purposes EXCEPT

(A) treating pneumonia.

(B) preventing infection.

(C) healing wounds.

(D) hurting the enemy.

4

Over the years, jazz has changed and developed, but it has retained its basic quality. One of the forms of music that contributed to the development of jazz was the blues. About a third of jazz music is in the blues form. So are over half of the popular rock 'n' roll pieces. Even some of the country and western music of the United States is in the blues form.

A major step in the development of jazz was taken by musicians in New Orleans. New Orleans jazz, sometimes called Dixieland, had the deep emotion of the blues and the Black spiritual as well as elements of ragtime and European folk music.

1. What is the main purpose of the passage?

(A) To trace the musical origins of jazz

(B) To distinguish between classical and popular music

(C) To change the composition of jazz music

(D) To cite examples of regional music

2. Which of the following statements about rock 'n' roll in the United States is supported by the passage?

(A) It is the second most popular music.

(B) It is only half as lively as jazz.

(C) It is the least developed of all musical forms.

(D) It is often written in blues form.

3. Which of the following types of music is NOT mentioned in the passage as having a blues form?

(A) Rock 'n' roll

(B) Jazz

(C) European folk music

(D) Country and western

4. According to the passage, what is one characteristic of Dixieland music?

(A) Its use of drums

(B) Its slow beat

(C) Its religious symbolism

(D) Its depth of feeling

* 미국음악

① Jazz Music : 19세기 말부터 20세기 초에 걸쳐 미국의 흑인 음악에 클래식이나 행진곡 등의 요소가 가미되어 발달한 대중음악의 한 장르. 약동적인 독특한 리듬과 감각이 있으며, 즉흥적 연주를 중시한다.뉴 올리언즈 재즈에서 시작되어 스윙, 모던재즈, 프리재즈 등으로 발전하였다.

② The Blues (블루스) : 2/4 또는 4/4박자의 애조띤 가곡이나 또는 그에 맞춰 느리게 추는 춤. 미국 흑인 사이에서 불리어진 애가(哀歌)로 출발하여 후에 재즈에 도입되어 재즈의 음악적 기반을 이루기도 하였다.

③ Rock 'N' Roll (로큰롤) : 강렬한 리듬의 컨트리, 포크, 블루스의 요소가 섞인 것으로, 1950년대에 미국에서 세계로 유행한 대중 음악

④ Country and Western : 미국 동남부 산악지대의 백인 개척민들 사이에서 생긴 대중 음악. mountain music, country song, cowboy song등이 있다.

⑤ Black Spiritual (흑인영가) : 흑인이 부르는 종교적인 민요를 가리킨다. 구약성서에서 소재를 얻었는데, 괴로운 현실에서 벗어나려는 소원과 신의 은혜에 감사하는 기도를 담고있는 것이 특징이다.

⑥ Ragtime [rǽgtaim] : 미국 미주리주 시더리아 지방의 흑인 피아노 연주자들 사이에 생긴 재즈 연주 형식과 그 곡(= Ragtime Music)

5

A new atomic clock being developed for navigation satellites will perform better than previous devices. The clock, which incorporates a hydrogen maser, will use a new microwave cavity design to provide a compact and lightweight package, and new electronic techniques to maintain long-term stability. The clock can provide precise navigation information because it is stable to one second in three million years. The differences in the time when signals from four satellites arrive at one location can be used to calculate that position to within a few yards.

1. From the passage it can be inferred that which of the following characteristics of the clock mentioned will be most impressive?
   (A) Its compact size
   (B) Its weight
   (C) Its accuracy
   (D) Its ability to measure distance

2. It can be inferred from the passage that the new clock will be
   (A) long-lasting
   (B) harmful to humans
   (C) produced in great numbers
   (D) very attractive looking

3. According to the passage, signals from how many satellites will be used to calculate a position?
   (A) 1
   (B) 2
   (C) 3
   (D) 4

4. What is the primary purpose of the passage?
   (A) To teach a lesson
   (B) To sell a product
   (C) To support a theory
   (D) To provide information

6

When, during the first quarter of the twentieth century, echo sounding was developed to allow ships while under way to record the depth of the bottom, probably no one suspected that it would also provide a means of learning something about deep-sea life. But operators of the new instruments soon discovered that the sound waves, directed downward from the ship like a beam of light, were reflected back from any solid object they met. Answering echoes were returned from intermediate depths, presumably from schools of fish, whales, or submarines; then a second echo was received from the bottom.

1. The author writes about something that happened during which of the following periods of time?
   (A) 1800-1850
   (B) 1850-1900
   (C) 1900-1925
   (D) 1925-195

2. What did the operators send down into the water?
   (A) Beams of light
   (B) Small, solid objects
   (C) New instruments
   (D) Sound waves

3. Which of the following enterprises would most likely be interested in using the instruments mentioned?
   (A) Sports equipment stores
   (B) Commercial fishing businesses
   (C) Sound-recording studios
   (D) Shipbuilding yards

4. For what purpose was the instrument originally designed?
   (A) Recording ocean depths
   (B) Communicating with divers
   (C) Locating deep-sea life
   (D) Detecting submarines

7

Archaeologists have excavated ancient pyramids in Egypt and more recent ones in Central and South America. Similarities have been noted in the design and construction of these structures found thousands of miles apart. Some researchers have wondered if contact could have existed between these pyramid builders. Thor Heyerdahl, the Norwegian explorer, put together a ship based on ancient Egyptian drawings and set sail for Barbados to lend support to the theory of cultural contact. Heyerdahl ran into various problems in his first attempt to reach Barbados and had to abandon his efforts. On a second try he did reach Barbados, as the ancient Egyptians might have done.

1. According to this passage, the first pyramid builders were probably

    (A) Central Americans.
    (B) Barbadians.
    (C) South Americans.
    (D) Egyptians.

2. Thor Heyerdahl was testing the theory that

    (A) Contact between pyramid builders was possible.
    (B) Egyptian drawings were borrowed from another culture.
    (C) Excavation of pyramids is possible without damaging them.
    (D) South Americans sailed to Egypt.

3. Thor Heyerdahl finally reached

    (A) Egypt.
    (B) Mexico.
    (C) Barbados.
    (D) South America.

4. According to the passage, Thor Heyerdahl's ship was built

    (A) in an Egyptian shipyard.
    (B) with an ancient sail.
    (C) from Norwegian pine.
    (D) by ancient Egyptian drawings.

8

At the battle of Gettysburg, General George G. Meade, who succeeded General Hooker as commander of the Army of the Potomac, threw back Lee's attacks and hurt the Confederate army badly. Meade had fought a skillful defensive battle, but he was satisfied with his victory as it was. He was content to see Lee leave his front, and his principal concern was to "herd" Lee back over the Potomac. Like other Federal generals, he lacked the killer instinct, which all the great battle captains have had, to finish off the enemy. After the engagement he issued a congratulatory order to his troops in which he praised them for having driven the enemy from "out soil." After all, this was a civil war! When Lincoln read the order, he exclaimed in anguish, "My God! Is that all?"

1. The battle of Gettysburg

   (A) was won by the Confederate army.

   (B) was won by Hooker.

   (C) was won by Lee.

   (D) was won by the Federal army.

2. George G. Meade did not

   (A) hurt the Confederate army.

   (B) fight a good defensive battle.

   (C) force Lee to retreat.

   (D) completely destroy the enemy.

3. When Lincoln heard of Meade's order, he

   (A) was delighted.

   (B) congratulated the troops.

   (C) was dismayed.

   (D) prayed.

4. The implication of the paragraph is that

   (A) Meade was totally incompetent.

   (B) Meade was ruthless.

   (C) Meade should have finished off the enemy.

   (D) Meade was well-loved by his men.

Embodying the bad as well as the good of America, Theodore Roosevelt was admired by his countrymen almost as much for his failings as for his "finer qualities." His defects were those of a majority of the people. Harry Thurston Peck noted that "the self-consciousness, the touch of the swagger, the love of applause and of publicity, the occasional lapse of official dignity, even the reckless speech, the unnecessary frankness, and the disregard of form" which characterized Roosevelt were in reality "traits that were national." One of Roosevelt's bitterest critics wrote, "Roosevelt is popular—as popular as any President in our history. America has a hysterical element. Official hysterics appeal to them. With some of our people physical size means greatness. In them Roosevelt touches a responsive chord. Many of our people are boastful and self-assertive. Roosevelt is their ideal. Swaggering and clamorousness appeal to some of us. Roosevelt satisfies us."

1. Roosevelt's defects

(A) were peculiarly his own.

(B) were similar to those of other Americans.

(C) far outweighed his good qualities.

(D) were well-hidden.

2. Roosevelt's personality was clearly

(A) shy and retiring.

(B) cautious and prudent.

(C) bold and informal.

(D) dignified and tactful.

3. Physically, Roosevelt was probably

(A) short and fat.

(B) thin and sickly.

(C) a big man.

(D) a small man.

4. The unidentified critic quoted in this passage
   (A) admired Roosevelt as a man, but he questioned his ability as a president.
   (B) thought that Roosevelt was popular mainly because he was different from the average American.
   (C) believed that Roosevelt was seen clearly and judged accurately by the American people.
   (D) disliked and disapproved of Roosevelt.

10

There are five kinds of apes in the world today. Two of them—gibbons and siamangs—are true swingers. They move by swinging like pendulums from branch to branch. Their arms are exceedingly long, their hands and fingers elongated and specialized. Their bodies are short and light, their legs shrunken. With that design—a minimum of weight at the bottom of the pendulum—they can move remarkably rapidly through the trees, swinging from branch to branch with a sureness and smoothness that must be seen to be appreciated, often negotiating gaps of ten feet or more. When they come to the ground, which is almost never, gibbons stand erect, waddling along on their short, weak legs, holding out their long arms to either side for balance. A strolling gibbon reminds one of a tightrope walker.

* tightrope walker : 줄타기 곡예사

1. According to the passage, brachiation is a way of
   (A) 2.   (B) 3.
   (C) 4.   (D) 5.

2. The apes discussed in the passage can most easily travel from place to place by
   (A) leaping from tree to tree.
   (B) waddling on the ground.
   (C) swinging between branches.
   (D) walking on a tightrope.

3. Based on information in the passage, a gibbon's movement in the trees could best be described as

(A) clumsy and awkward.

(B) graceful and rhythmic.

(C) nervous and tentative.

(D) slow and careful.

4. As described in the passage, a strolling gibbon brings to mind a

(A) disco dancer.

(B) circus performer.

(C) jogger.

(D) negotiator.

11

All living languages are characterized by sound changes that have occurred and will continue to occur in the course of their history. Some linguists choose to consider the sound change process as something that operates with the regularity of physical laws. "Sound law" is a term devised by linguist August Leskien to describe the absolute regularity of this kind of structural change in language. The term "sound law" means that, in a given area and at a given period, if a sound changes, the change will be universal and will have no exceptions. This rule loses some of its inflexibility by amendments to the effect that, if apparent exceptions are found, they are due to some extraneous factor, such as learned influence, foreign or dialectal borrowing, or analogy.

1. What is the main topic of the passage?

(A) Sound changes that have occurred in language

(B) A theory of sound change

(C) Some exceptions to the rule of sound change

(D) Some reasons for sound change

2. Leskien developed the term "sound law" because he believed that

(A) sounds change in a certain pattern without exception.

(B) amendments were needed to existing sound change theories.

(C) physical laws should not be applied to linguistic theory.

(D) a general law and several qualifiers could explain sound change.

3. The author of the passage implies that regular sound change is caused by

(A) knowledge of linguistic and physical law.

(B) new pronunciations being proposed by linguists.

(C) influence from foreign languages.

(D) structural forces within language.

12

The different textures in tree bark result from changes in the cork cambium and the stretching of the bark as the tree increase in circumference. In the beech tree the cambium remains close to the surface, expanding when necessary and producing a smooth gray cork that appears tightly stretched over the trunk. In most species, however, successive cork cambiums are formed beneath the original one: the new layer of cork that forms cuts off and kills the outer cambium under pressure from the expanding trunk. Some trees have secondary cork cambiums that occur in patches. With time, these patches result in layers of scales easily seen in a fragment of pine bark. Like pines, ash trees have patches of secondary cork cambium. As the trunk expands, the fibers pull apart, creating a net of diamond-shaped furrows, but the bark does not flake off in scales.

* bark [bɑːrk] *n.* 나무껍질 cámbium [kǽmbiəm] *n.* (식물의) 형성층 circúmference [sərkʌ́mfərəns] *n.* 원주, 원둘레
 beech tree : 너도밤나무 ash tree : 물푸레나무

1. What is the main topic of the passage?

(A) The art of identifying species of trees by their bark.

(B) How changes in the cambium layer affect a tree's bark.

(C) The killing of the bark by the expanding tree.

(D) How phloem tissue is produced in trees.

2. According to the passage, what happens to the original cork cambium in most species as a tree grows?

(A) It is hidden beneath new cambium layers.

(B) It becomes part of the phloem tissue.

(C) It grows with the tree.

(D) It dies.

3. How are the barks of ash and pine trees similar?

(A) They are both smooth.

(B) Their surfaces are lose and fragmented.

(C) They lack successive cork cambium layers.

(D) Their secondary cork cambium appears in patches.

13

At the center of our solar system is a star called the Sun. It is a ball of very hot gases. Its diameter is more than 100 times as big as that of the Earth. It gives off powerful rays of light in the form of radiant energy. This energy travels to the Earth at a speed of approximately 300,000 kilometers per second. This means that sunlight takes 8.33 minutes to get to Earth.

The temperature on the surface of the Sun is about 5,520 Celsius, and it is much hotter inside. Scientists now believe that the heat of the Sun comes from natural atomic energy. In this process, hydrogen is believed to be changed to helium with an enormous amount of energy given off. The mass (matter) is changed to energy. This energy is in the form of heat, light, and other forms of radiation.

1. The author makes all of the following statements about the Sun EXCEPT that it

(A) is a star.

(B) emits light rays.

(C) lies at the edge of the solar system.

(D) is 100 times bigger than Earth.

2. It can be inferred from the passage that the temperature of the outer rim of the Sun is

(A) hotter than the Earth's interior.

(B) cooler than the Sun's interior.

(C) as hot as the Earth's interior.

(D) as hot as the Sun's interior.

3. According to the passage, which of the following best describes the manner in which the Sun is thought to produce energy?

(A) Helium heats hydrogen, which gives off light.

(B) heat and light melt hydrogen, which releases helium.

(C) Light produces hydrogen and helium, which release heat.

(D) Hydrogen changes to helium, which gives off light and heat.

14

By the end of the first quarter of the nineteenth century a number of our Eastern institutions–Harvard, Yale, Columbia, and Pennsylvania– had some of the necessary ingredients of a university, but hardly yet the point of view. They were little groups of schools and institutes. Indeed, just after the Revolution, the schools of Pennsylvania and Harvard had assumed the somewhat pretentious title of university, and, shortly after, the University of Virginia was founded under the guidance of Thomas Jefferson. In the South, Georgia and later North Carolina began to rise. The substance in all these was mainly lacking, though the title was honored. There were rather feeble law, medical, and divinity schools, somewhat loosely attached to these colleges. It has been commonly recognized, however, that the first decade after the close of the War Between the States, that is, from about 1866 to 1876, was the great early flowering of the university idea in America.

1. In 1825

(A) no American educational institution called itself a university.

(B) all American higher educational institutions called themselves universities.

(C) those institutions which called themselves universities were not justified in doing so.

(D) no American institution of higher education had any of the necessary ingredients of a university.

2. Thomas Jefferson founded

    (A) The University of Pennsylvania.

    (B) Harvard University.

    (C) The University of Virginia.

    (D) The University of Georgia.

3. The War Between the States ended

    (A) about 1866.

    (B) about 1876.

    (C) about 1856.

    (D) during the decade from 1866-1876.

4. The University idea really began to develop

    (A) in the first quarter of the nineteenth century.

    (B) just after the Revolution.

    (C) during the last quarter of the nineteenth century.

    (D) just after the War Between the States.

15

In the nineteenth century many people accepted as scientifically valid not only facereading, or physiognomy, but also head-reading, or phrenology. The bumps on a person's cranium, they thought, revealed his or her personality; so did the shape of the mouth or the tilt of the nose. Today's thinking has it that what goes on in the brain does not depend on the face, and yet, just as astrology continues to flourish in a scientific world, so too does "phys/phren," as the combination has come to be called, remain with us in the 1980's.

1. What is the main topic of the passage?

    (A) Physiognomy

    (B) Phrenology

    (C) Astrology

    (D) Phys/phren

2. The ideas mentioned in the passage gained acceptance in

    (A) In the 1800's.   (B) In 1900.   (C) In 1919.   (D) In 1950.

3. Physiognomy can best be described as a

   (A) branch of astrology.

   (B) measurement of the potential of an individual's brain.

   (C) highly accurate psychological science.

   (D) personality analysis of facial features.

4. Phrenology can best be described as a method of

   (A) healing bumps on the head.

   (B) preventing severe and recurring nosebleeds.

   (C) curing diseases that enter the body through the mouth.

   (D) analyzing character by the bumps on the skull.

5. The tone of the passage can best be described as

   (A) negative.

   (B) objective.

   (C) prophetic .

   (D) frightening.

16

Prejudice means literally prejudgement, the rejection of a contention out of hand before examining the evidence. Prejudice is the result of powerful emotions, not of sound reasoning. If we wish to find out the truth of a matter, we must approach the question with as nearly open a mind as we can and with a deep awareness of our own limitations and predispositions. On the other hand, if after carefully and openly examining the evidence we reject the proposition, that is not prejudice. It might be called "post-judice." It is certainly a prerequisite for knowledge.

1. With what subject is the passage mainly concerned?

   (A) Knowledge   (B) Evidence

   (C) Judgements   (D) Limitations

2. According to the passage, prejudice is caused by

   (A) feelings.   (B) past experiences.

   (C) sound reasoning.   (D) wisdom.

3. The author implies that everyone's judgment is sometimes affected by

    (A) partiality.   (B) competition.

    (C) ill health.   (D) legal considerations.

4. "On the other hand," as it is used in the fourth sentence, could best be replaced by which of the following words?

    (A) Supposedly   (B) Therefore

    (C) Additionally   (D) But

5. Which of the following maxims best applies to the situation described in the passage?

    (A) Birds of a feather flock together.

    (B) Never judge a book by its cover.

    (C) Still waters run deep.

    (D) Words are the gateway to knowledge.

17

    Several different bison species have lived on the North American continent since the Ice Age; today only two exist. The wood bison is the larger of the two, and is now found mostly in western Canada. Better known in the United States is the Plains bison, or buffalo. At one time, herds of these animals could be sighted almost everywhere from the Appalachian Mountains in the East to the Rocky Mountains in the West.

1. What does the passage mainly discuss?

    (A) The cause of the extinction of bison

    (B) Two existing species of bison

    (C) Animals on the North American Continent

    (D) Effects of the Ice Age

2. The author implies that several types of bison

    (A) live outside the United States and Canada.

    (B) existed before the Ice Age.

    (C) are well adapted to swampy terrain.

    (D) have been killed or have died out.

3. According to the passage, how many species of bison are well-known in the United States?

(A) 1   (B) 2   (C) 3   (D) 4

4. It can be inferred from the passage that the Plains bison usually

(A) stay in groups.

(B) have good eyesight.

(C) are more popular than buffalo.

(D) travel short distances.

5. In the last sentence, the phrase "At one time" most probably means

(A) at a glance.

(B) on a single day.

(C) during one historical period.

(D) at any moment.

18

At the time of the writing of the Constitution, there were no political parties. However, it wasn't long before different ideas about how the United States government should be run caused people to take sides. Two opposing parties—the Federalists headed by Alexander Hamilton and the Anti-Federalists headed by Thomas Jefferson—soon formed. The Federalists wanted a stronger national government to make important decisions for the individual states and for the nation as a whole. The Anti-Federalists wanted the states to make their own decisions without the national government interfering. Even today, the Republican and Democratic parties argue whether the state or national government should have more control.

1. With what topic is the passage mainly concerned?

(A) The writing of the Constitution

(B) The development of political parties

(C) Republican and Democratic leadership

(D) The running of local goverments

2. It can be inferred from the passage that the Anti-Federalists wanted

(A) two opposing political parties.

(B) money from the national government.

(C) immediate removal of state governments.

(D) a weak central government.

3. According to the passage, what happened to arguments concerning how the government should be run?

(A) Solutions to them were quickly found.

(B) Republicans and Democrats opposed them.

(C) They ended when Jefferson and Hamilton died.

(D) They have continued to the present day.

4. It can be inferred from the passage that the Federalist and Anti-Federalist parties

(A) had no effect on future parties.

(B) have become lobbying groups.

(C) currently have control over the President.

(D) are no longer active in politics.

19

Besides feeling the soil and sniffing the air, farmers can now point gun-shaped infrared meters at their crops to find out when the plants need watering. These portable meters give digital readouts that indicate the difference between a plant's temperature and that of the surrounding air. When it is short of water, a plant, which normally uses evaporation as a means of cooling, cannot rid itself of the heat it absorbs from sunlight or the heat that may build up from its own metabolism. Therefore, if the meter indicates that a plant is warmer than the air, it may mean that it is time to irrigate.

＊ ínfrared méters : 적외선 계량기 metábolism [mətǽbəlizəm] n. 신진대사

1. Which of the following would be the most appropriate title for the passage?

(A) A New Aid for Farmers

(B) Plant Temperatures and Evaporation

(C) Checking Crop Yields

(D) The Metabolism of Plants

2. According to the passage, farmers feel the soil in order to

   (A) check its ability to absorb heat.

   (B) check the moisture content of the air.

   (C) determine its mineral content.

   (D) determine the time to water crops.

3. According to the passage, what do the meters measure?

   (A) The quality of crops being grown.

   (B) The temperatures of plants and air.

   (C) The water content of plants.

   (D) The rate of evaporation.

4. Which of the following plays the most important role in a plant's cooling?

   (A) Evaporation   (B) Sunlight

   (C) Absorption of water   (D) Infrared rays

5. According to the passage, a plant can no longer cool itself if

   (A) outside temperatures are high.

   (B) the soil becomes too warm.

   (C) it absorbs infrared rays.

   (D) it needs water.

20

So long as the bulk of the population remains on the land as subsistence farmers, a modern industrial society cannot develop. The farmers do not produce enough extra food to feed the workers needed in nonagricultural pursuits. Nor can workers be released from the farms to the factories while so many hands are needed for traditional methods of cultivation. And farmers who are not producing anything for the market cannot go to the market as purchasers themselves. Local demand for consumer goods does not expand. There is thus no stimulus to local industrial production. Agriculture must, therefore, yield workers and savings to the new industrialized, urbanized sectors if a modern economy is to be achieved.

＊ subsístence fármers : (겨우 생계나 유지하는 영세한) 자족농민

1. What is the author's main point?

   (A) Traditional farming methods can enrich civilization.

   (B) The development of an urban economy depends on the modernization of agriculture.

   (C) People who work on farms tend to eat more than people who live in cities.

   (D) The industrialization of modern society stabilizes the agricultural economy.

2. According to the passage, a characteristic of food production in a subsistence economy is that farmers

   (A) must bring in workers from urban communities.

   (B) cannot produce all their own food.

   (C) must buy some foods to achieve a balanced diet.

   (D) cannot grow enough food to support nonfarmers.

3. According to the passage, what is a disadvantage of traditional farming methods?

   (A) Farmers do not enjoy their jobs.

   (B) Farmers do not get enough to eat.

   (C) Too many farmers are necessary.

   (D) Too many jobs are poorly paid.

4. The paragraph following the passage most probably discusses

   (A) the creation of a demand for more agricultural products.

   (B) the difficult transition from an agricultural to an industrial economy.

   (C) guidelines for hiring greater numbers of farm workers.

   (D) the recent revival of the family farm system.

Step 3 |독해종합연습|

1

A tree frog is less than an inch long, yet its loud, clear call can be heard almost a mile away. This sound is hard to locate even though the creature may be sitting nearby. Probably more persons hear than ever see the tiny animal. Only the full-grown male can sing, and the performance is an amazing sight to watch. The tree frog sits on its hind legs, leans back, and sings. Its white throat swells up until it looks like a shiny bubble about to burst. With its mouth closed, the frog makes four two-toned notes. The sac under its chin is then a bag of loose skin. To call again, it must take another breath. A spell of cool weather may quiet the frogs for a while, but the next warm spring night they will be singing again.

* four two-toned notes : 두 음색으로 된 네 마디 가락

1. Which of the following best preserves the meaning of the first sentence in the passage?

(A) The tree frog's song is not loud, but it can be heard a mile away.

(B) Because it is small, the tree frog's song cannot be heard a mile away.

(C) Although the tree frog is small, its song can be heard a mile away.

(D) When it is an inch long, the tree frog can be heard a mile away.

2. The word "creature" (line 3) refers to the

(A) hiding place of the frog.

(B) person who is listening to the sound.

(C) mate of the frog.

(D) frog that is making the sound.

3. According to the author, the frog sings without

    (A) leaving its hiding place.

    (B) making much noise.

    (C) opening its mouth.

    (D) repeating its songs.

4. It is clear from the passage that the tree frog is

    (A) relatively inconspicuous.

    (B) not friendly to humans.

    (C) a common sight in most woods.

    (D) easily frightened by noise.

2

    Historians generally agree that the English alphabet descended from ancient Egyptian hieroglyphics, or "sacred writings," that were first recorded by priests more than 5,000 years ago. Hieroglyphics are pictures carved in stone or inscribed on papyrus. For centuries after Egypt's decline, explorers who discovered hieroglyphic carvings in Egypt were mystified as to their meaning. But in 1799 an officer in Napoleon's army discovered near the Egyptian village of Rosetta a smooth, thick black stone covered with carvings that were divided into three separate sections. One section was a historical account in Greek, one was in hieroglyphics, and one was in demotics or simplified hieroglyphics. The Greek account said that it was exactly the same as the Egyptian writing and this finding enabled scholars to decipher the mysterious ancient carvings.

* hieroglýphics [haiərəglífiks] *n.* 상형문자 demótics [dimátiks] *n.* (고대 이집트의) 민중문자, 상형문자의 간체

1. Which of the following facts about hieroglyphics is stated in the passage?

    (A) They were used until 1799.

    (B) They were the basis of ancient Greek writing.

    (C) They were sometimes written on papyrus.

    (D) They were first discovered by Napoleon's army.

2. The Rosetta stone was found by

   (A) a history scholar.

   (B) a military officer.

   (C) an explorer.

   (D) an Egyptian priest.

3. The Rosetta stone is important because it

   (A) was written in Latin.

   (B) proved that hieroglyphics were used in Rosetta.

   (C) showed that hieroglyphics were very ancient.

   (D) provided a key for deciphering hieroglyphics.

4. Hieroglyphics were a mystery because

   (A) the priests refused to translate them.

   (B) no one could decipher them.

   (C) they resembled Greek writing.

   (D) no papyrus had been preserved.

3

   The tap dancer, like the flamenco performer, is basically an improviser. Thus looking at tap one wants to savor the personality and inventiveness of the individual. When Bill Robinson danced in the movies, his technical skill and sophisticated rhythms could be heard as well as seen. The Nicholas Brothers ran up walls or the proscenium arch of the theater or jumped off platforms and landed in splits on the floor. Peg Leg Bates, who had lost a leg, made a specialty out of dancing with his wooden leg. Sandman Sims scattered sand on the floor (as Fred Astaire did in one of his films) and tapped ever so softly, slid and turned in dances as soothing as lullabies.

* ímproviser [ímprəvaizər] *n.* 즉흥연주가 proscénium arch : 무대앞 아치

1. What does the passage mainly discuss?

    (A) The styles of various tap dancers

    (B) The structure of the modern dance theater

    (C) The difference between flamenco and tap dancing

    (D) The use of dance in certain movie productions

2. According to the passage, in what way is a flamenco dancer similar to a tap dancer?

    (A) Both perform the same kinds of steps.

    (B) Both rely on individual inventiveness.

    (C) Both are trained in classical techniques.

    (D) Both make very little noise.

3. An acrobatic style of dancing was most closely associated with which of the following performers?

    (A) Peg Leg Bates

    (B) Bill Robinson

    (C) The Nicholas Brothers

    (D) Fred Astaire

4. Which two dancers used sand in their routines?

    (A) Robinson and Slims

    (B) The Nicholas Brothers

    (C) Bates and Robinson

    (D) Sims and Astaire

5. The author implies which of the following about tap dancing?

    (A) It is more complex than flamenco dancing.

    (B) It is meant to be heard as well as seen.

    (C) It became popular primarily because of the movies.

    (D) It should be performed by at least two people.

4

But the success of science, both its intellectual excitement and its practical application, depends upon the self-correcting character of science. There must be a way of testing any valid idea. It must be possible to reproduce any valid experiment. The character or beliefs of scientists are irrelevant; all that matters is whether the evidence supports their contentions. Arguments from authority simply do not count; too many authorities have been mistaken too often. I would like to see these very effective scientific modes of thought communicated by the schools and the media; and it would certainly be an astonishment and delight to see them introduced into politics. Scientists have been known to change their minds completely and publicly when presented with new evidence or new arguments. I cannot recall the last time a politician displayed a similar openness and willingness to change.

1. What does the passage mainly discuss?

   (A) The rewards of intellectual excitement
   (B) Practical applications of an abstract theory
   (C) An important characteristic of science
   (D) Some similarities between politics and science

2. What did the paragraph preceding the passage most probably discuss?

   (A) The achievements of science
   (B) The scientific community
   (C) Self-correction
   (D) Faulty information

3. According to the passage, if a scientist repeats an experiment several times and does not produce similar results each time, the experiment must be

   (A) extremely complex.
   (B) incorrectly recorded.
   (C) invalid.
   (D) scientific.

4. According to the passage, which of the following is most essential to scientists' work?

(A) Character   (B) Beliefs

(C) Authority   (D) Evidence

5. The author implies that, in science, arguments from authority are

(A) irrelevant.   (B) effective.

(C) uncomplicated.   (D) accountable.

5

Magnesium is another mineral we now obtain by collecting huge volumes of ocean water and treating it with chemicals, although originally it was derived only from brines or from the treatment of such magnesium-containing rocks as dolomite, of which whole mountain ranges are composed. In a cubic mile of seawater there are about four million tons of magnesium. Since the direct extraction method was developed about 1941, production has increased enormously. It was magnesium from the sea that made possible the wartime growth of the aviation industry, for every airplane made in the United States (and in most other countries as well) contains about half a ton of magnesium metal. And it has innumerable uses in other industries where a lightweight metal is desired, besides its longstanding utility as an insulating material, and its use in printing inks, medicines, and toothpastes.

＊brine [brain] *n.* 염수, 간수 dólomite [dóuləmait] *n.* 백운석(암) ínsulating matérial : 절연재료

1. What is the main topic of this passage?

(A) Uses of seawater

(B) Treatment of seawater

(C) Chemical properties of magnesium

(D) Derivation and uses of magnesium

2. According to the passage, magnesium was first obtained from

(A) rocks found on land.

(B) great amounts of ocean water.

(C) the sea floor.

(D) major industrial sites.

3. According to the passage, which of the following was a direct consequence of the new method of obtaining magnesium?

(A) The development of insulation materials
(B) Increased airplane production
(C) Improved medical facilities
(D) The development of cheap inks for printing

4. According to the passage, why is magnesium important to industry?

(A) It is strong.
(B) It conducts heat well.
(C) It weighs little.
(D) It is inexpensive to produce.

5. It can be inferred from the passage that during the past fifty years the demand for magnesium has

(A) declined greatly.
(B) remained stable.
(C) increased slightly.
(D) risen dramatically.

6

In ancient times wealth was measured and exchanged tangibly, in things that could be touched: food, tools, and precious metals and stones. Then the barter system was replaced by coins, which still had real value since they were pieces of rare metal. Coins were followed by fiat money, paper notes that have value only because everyone agrees to accept them.

Today electronic monetary systems are gradually being introduced that will transform money into even less tangible forms, reducing it to arrays of "bits and bytes," or units of computerized information, whizzing between machines at the speed of light. Already, electronic fund transfer allows money to be instantly sent and received by different banks, companies, and countries through computers and telecommunications devices.

1. Which of the following would be the most appropriate title for the passage?

(A) International Banking Policies

(B) The History of Monetary Exchange

(C) The Development of Paper Currencies

(D) Current Problems in the Economy

2. According to the passage, which of the following was the earliest kind of exchange of wealth?

(A) Bartered goods

(B) Coin currency

(C) Fiat money

(D) Intangible forms

3. The author mentions food, tools, and precious metals and stones together because they are all

(A) material objects.

(B) useful items.

(C) articles stored in museums.

(D) difficult things to obtain.

4. According to the passage, coins once had real value as currency because they

(A) represented a great improvement over barter.

(B) permitted easy transportation of wealth.

(C) could become collector's items.

(D) were made of precious metals.

5. Which of the following statements about computerized monetary systems is NOT supported by the passage?

(A) They promote international trade.

(B) They allow very rapid money transfers.

(C) They are still limited to small transactions.

(D) They are dependent on good telecommunications systems.

7

Margaret Bourke-White, one of the most prolific photojournalists of the twentieth century, was a witness to world events from the 1920's through the 1950's. During her student days Bourke-White made a photographic record of campus life. Her career blossomed at a time when the American art world had embraced Modernism and found a new beauty in technology. Aesthetic principles were applied to such banal objects as furnaces and washing machines, and Bourke-White became one of the best industrial photographers of the period. During her career she also photographed such important subjects as the serious midwestern drought of the 1930's and the Second World War, and she saw her work published in some of the world's most famous magazines.

1. What is the main subject of the passage?

   (A) Modern and twentieth-century art
   (B) Industrial photography as a career
   (C) The career of Margaret Bourke-White
   (D) The journals of Margaret Bourke-White

2. Margaret Bourke-White was most well known as

   (A) photographer.
   (B) publisher.
   (C) reporter.
   (D) model.

3. Margaret Bourke-White's career lasted for about how many years?

   (A) Ten
   (B) Twenty
   (C) Forty
   (D) Fifty

4. It can be inferred from the passage that Modernism primarily represented a

   (A) glorification of the mundane.
   (B) serious effort to record recent world.
   (C) set of principles for photography.
   (D) fashionable journalistic technique.

5. According to the passage, Margaret Bourke-White used all of the following as subjects for her work EXCEPT

(A) academic life.

(B) natural disasters.

(C) industrial environments

(D) glamorous models.

8

Magnetism is an important force of nature acting between objects called magnets. Magnets are most commonly known for their ability to attract metallic substances. The Earth itself behaves as if a large magnet runs through its center, with the strongest areas being at the north and south poles. Surprisingly, the magnetic field surrounding the Earth is a million times weaker than the field surrounding an atom, yet it is a million times stronger than that surrounding our own galaxy. Magnetism plays an essential role in creating large amounts of electricity, without which complex industrial techniques would be infeasible.

* inféasible [infíːzəbəl] *adj.* 실현 불가능한

1. Which of the following is the best title for the passage?

(A) The Uses of Magnets

(B) Important Forces in the Physical World

(C) The Nature of Magnetism

(D) One Source of Electricity

2. According to the passage, magnets are best known

(A) for their role in industry.

(B) as a minor process in nature.

(C) for the strength of their attraction.

(D) for their capacity to draw metallic objects.

3. The passage states that the Earth

(A) is immune to magnetic forces.

(B) has a large magnet on its surface.

(C) acts as if a large magnet runs through its core.

(D) has a weak magnetic field at its north and south poles.

4. The word "it" in line 6 refers to

  (A) an atom's magnetic field.

  (B) the Earth's surface.

  (C) the Earth's magnetic field.

  (D) the galaxy's magnetic field.

5. It can be inferred from the passage that

  (A) the larger an object, the weaker its magnetic field.

  (B) the larger an object, the stronger its magnetic field.

  (C) the smaller an object, the weaker its magnetic field.

  (D) the strength of a magnetic field is not related to the size of an object.

9

   People who travel frequently on business or for pleasure often suffer some form of health problem, yet over half of these problems can easily be prevented. The most common ailment, a headache, can be avoided by taking along an ample supply of aspirin or other pain reliever. Another common affliction is motion sickness caused by the constant movement of a vehicle. Ginger capsules, sold in most health-food stores, have been found effective as a remedy. Other familiar problems include sunburn, which can be prevented by using an effective sunscreen, and insect bites, which can be controlled with use of a repellent spray or ointment. For everyday cuts and scratches, a first-aid kit containing bandages and antiseptic cream is recommended.

* páin relíever : 진통제 mótion síckness : 멀미 repéllent spráy : 방충제 antiséptic créam : 살균제

1. What is the best title for this passage?

  (A) Frequent Travelers

  (B) Avoiding Travel Ailments

  (C) Common Health Problems

  (D) Traveling for Business or Pleasure

2. According to the passage, travelers are most commonly bothered by

  (A) sunburn.

  (B) motion sickness.

  (C) insect bites.

  (D) headaches.

3. According to the passage, what can be used to remedy motion sickness?

(A) A moving vehicle

(B) Pain-killers

(C) Ginger capsules

(D) A first-aid kit

4. Which of the following is NOT mentioned in the passage as a solution to a health problem?

(A) Sunscreen

(B) Cold cream

(C) Repellent spray

(D) Aspirin

5. It can be inferred from the passage that many travelers

(A) do not take simple health precautions.

(B) reject the use of remedies to health problems.

(C) are not afflicted by health problems.

(D) rarely complain about their ailments to others.

10

The cheetah is a large, catlike animal known for its great speed. The fastest creature over short distances, the cheetah is capable of sprinting up to 70 miles per hour. At one time its range of movement included the Middle East and parts of central Asia and India, but today the effects of hunting and farming have restricted the cheetah mostly to central and eastern Africa.

An adult cheetah usually lives alone within a well-defined territory. Male and female cheetahs meet only briefly for the purpose of mating. The cheetah keeps enemies away with its sharp claws which, unlike those of other cats, cannot be fully retracted. The cheetah is also one of the few big cats that can purr as well as roar.

1. What is the cheetah best known for?

    (A) Its size and strength

    (B) Its similarity to the cat

    (C) Its range of movement

    (D) Its sprinting ability

2. Where is the cheetah primarily found today?

    (A) Asia

    (B) India

    (C) Africa

    (D) Middle East

3. It can be inferred from the passage that the number of cheetahs

    (A) has fluctuated greatly.

    (B) has somewhat increased.

    (C) has remained stable.

    (D) has declined over the years.

4. The author indicates that an adult cheetah

    (A) leads a lone existence.

    (B) does not mate very often.

    (C) maintains family life within a given territory.

    (D) has a wide range of movement.

5. It can be inferred from the passage that most big cats

    (A) can only purr.

    (B) cannot purr or roar.

    (C) can only roar.

    (D) purr as well as roar.

11

Of all the natural wonders of the world, few are as spectacular as Niagara Falls. Located on the Niagara River along the border between the United States and Canada, Niagara Falls actually consists of two falls, the American Falls and the Horseshoe Falls. The former is on the U.S. side of the border, in the state of New York, while the latter is on the Canadian side. About 85% of the water in Niagara River flows over the Horseshoe Falls, which is the more impressive of the two falls.

About 10 million people visit the falls each year, most during the summer tourist season. Sightseers can ride steamers up close to the boiling water of the falls, or view them from parks on both sides of the river. Niagara Falls has long been a popular honeymoon destination for newlyweds.

1. What is the best title for this passage?

(A) Natural Wonders of the World

(B) Popular Tourist Attractions

(C) Two Spectacular Waterfalls

(D) Honeymoon Attractions

2. Which of the following is entirely on the U.S. side of the border with Canada?

(A) Niagara River

(B) American Falls

(C) Niagara Falls

(D) Horseshoe Falls

3. It can be inferred from the passage that Horseshoe Falls

(A) is the larger of the two falls.

(B) is the less impressive fall.

(C) has 15% of the Niagara River flowing over its edge.

(D) is in the state of New York.

4. According to the passage, where can people watch the falls?

(A) From trains

(B) From airplanes

(C) From parks or boats

(D) From cars or buses

5. According to the passage, Niagara Falls

(A) is a favorite spot of newlyweds.

(B) generates very hot water.

(C) can be viewed from only one side of the Niagara River.

(D) is only impressive during the summer tourist season.

12

Up to about 1915, movies were short and programs were made up of several works. Then, D.W. Griffith and others began to make full-length films which provided the same powerful emotional appeal as did melodrama and presented spectacles far beyond what the theatre could offer. Consequently, after World War I increasing numbers of spectators deserted the theatre for the movies. This trend was accelerated in the late 1920's as a result of two new elements; In 1927 sound was added to the previously silent film, and thus one of the theatre's principal claims to superiority vanished. In 1929 a serious economic depression began. Since audiences could go to the movies for a fraction of what it cost to see a play, theatregoing became a luxury which few could afford, especially as the depression deepened.

By the end of World War II, the American theatre had been reduced to about thirty theatres in New York City and a small number of touring companies originating there.

1. One thing that movies could do better than the theatre was

(A) provide longer programs.

(B) provide emotional appeal.

(C) provide more melodrama.

(D) provide greater spectacle.

2. Up to the 1920's one objection to films was that

    (A) they were too short.

    (B) they were silent.

    (C) they were too expensive.

    (D) they did not tell a complete story.

3. One thing that made people choose the movies over the theatre was

    (A) world War I.

    (B) a depression.

    (C) the fact that films were silent.

    (D) the fact that films were shorter.

4. By the end of World War II,

    (A) theatre had become entertainment for the masses.

    (B) the theatre was no longer considered a luxury.

    (C) professional theatrical performances were confined mainly to New York City.

    (D) there were no theatrical performances outside of New York City.

5. When the author of this paragraph says "this trend was accelerated in the late 1920's" (lines 6 and 7), he means that

    (A) many more people went to the theatre than to the movies.

    (B) the shift away from the movies the theatre was slowed down.

    (C) the popularity of the theatre was gradually increasing.

    (D) the shift away from the theatre to the movies was speeded up.

13

Barbara Tuchman was an American Pulitzer-winning historian who knew how to stand out from the crowd. Author of books such as *The First Salute*, her bestselling account of the American Revolution, Tuchman had a special talent for making history appealing to common people. Unlike other published historians, Tuchman did not limit herself to a dry retelling of fact. Her prose skillfully combined scholarly treatment with high drama.

Tuchman also distinguished herself by declining to pursue a

doctorate degree, which won her the disrespect of many of her mainstream colleagues. To them, the lack of advanced training made her books suspect as literary works and teaching tools. A few others, however, maintained that her art of historical investigation might actually have suffered if she had acquired a Ph. D. degree. They point to the boring efforts of historians whose works, for the most part, lie buried on library shelves. Tuchman, on the other hand, succeeded in bringing history to the attention of the masses.

1. Which of the following is the best title for the passage?

    (A) Pulitzer Prize-Winning Historians

    (B) The Works of Barbara Tuchman

    (C) An Account of the American Revolution

    (D) Barbara Tuchman: A Unique Historian

2. According to the passage, Barbara Tuchman had the special ability to

    (A) make historical facts interesting.

    (B) write many bestselling books.

    (C) overcome the effects of advanced training.

    (D) limit her accounts to historical facts.

3. In line 11, the word "others" could best be replaced by which of the following?

    (A) literary works

    (B) colleagues

    (C) teaching tools

    (D) common people

4. It can be inferred from the passage that many mainstream historians

    (A) viewed Tuchman with great respect.

    (B) suffered as a result of Tuchman's literary success.

    (C) dismissed Tuchman's works as popular prose.

    (D) never attained advanced degrees.

14

A professor of anthropology at the University of Tucson has created an entirely new field of science called garbology. William Rathje and his students have been studying the garbage left for collection in front of Tucson homes since 1973. With the help of the local sanitation company, they have inspected and categorized some 120 tons of garbage and have arrived at some interesting conclusions.

One result is that middle-income families waste more food than lower- or upper-income families. Another fact is that poor families pay more for their food and household items than wealthy families because they cannot afford to buy it in bulk. Finally, the overall waste figure is down to 15 percent, about half the figure from the first quarter of this century. This can be attributed to modern methods of refrigeration, transportation, processing, and packaging.

* garbólogy [ɡɑːrbάlədʒi] *n.* 쓰레기 처리학

1. What does the passage mainly discuss?

   (A) The creation of a new science
   (B) The job of an anthropology professor
   (C) Results from work in the field of garbology
   (D) Methods of handling food products

2. According to the passage, who is William Rathje?

   (A) A sanitation engineer
   (B) A university student
   (C) A government scientist
   (D) An anthropology professor

3. What did William Rathje and his students examine?

   (A) A local sanitation company
   (B) The fronts of homes in Tucson, Arizona
   (C) Garbage left on streets for collection
   (D) Modern methods of refrigeration

4. Which of the following is NOT mentioned as a reason for the decrease in waste since the first quarter of this century?

(A) Better eating habits of Americans

(B) Improved methods of refrigerating food

(C) Faster means of transporting perishable foods

(D) Superior methods of packaging products

5. According to the passage, why do the poor pay more for their food than the rich?

(A) They are more careless with their money.

(B) They are unable to purchase large quantities at a time.

(C) They shop at more expensive stores.

(D) They do not earn as much money

15

People commonly complain that they never have enough time to accomplish tasks. The hours and minutes seem to slip away before many planned chores get done. According to time management experts, the main reason for this is that most people fail to set priorities about what to do first. They get tired down by trivial, time-consuming matters and never complete the important ones.

One simple solution often used by those at the top is to keep lists of tasks to be accomplished daily. These lists order jobs from most essential to least essential and are checked regularly through the day to assess progress. Not only is this an effective way to manage time, but also it serves to give individuals a much-deserved sense of satisfaction over their achievements. People who do not keep lists often face the end of the work day with uncertainty over the significance of their accomplishments, which over time can contribute to serious problems in mental and physical health.

1. Which of the following is the best title for the passage?

(A) Common Complaints About Work

(B) Accomplishing Trivial Matters

(C) Achieving Job Satisfaction

(D) Learning to Manage Time

2. According to the passage, why do many people never seem to have enough time to accomplish things?

   (A) They do not prioritize tasks.

   (B) They get tied down by one difficult problem.

   (C) They fail to deal with trivial matters.

   (D) They do not seek the advice of time management experts.

3. In line 7, the word "those" refers to

   (A) daily lists.

   (B) trivial matters.

   (C) priorities.

   (D) people.

4. The passage states that one solution to time management problems is to

   (A) consult a time management expert.

   (B) accomplish time-consuming matters first.

   (C) keep daily lists of priorities and check them regularly.

   (D) spend only a short time on each task.

5. The paragraph following the passage most probably discusses

   (A) mental and physical health problems.

   (B) another solution to time management problems.

   (C) ways to achieve a sense of fulfillment.

   (D) different types of lists.

16

Most educational specialists believe that early schooling should provide children with an awareness of their own abilities and the self-confidence to use these abilities. One approach recognized by many experts as promoting these qualities is the Montessori method, first practiced by Maria Montessori of Italy in the early 1900s. Nancy McCormick Rambusch is credited with popularizing the method in the United States, where today there are over 400 Montessori schools. The method helps children learn for themselves by providing them with instructional materials and tasks that facilitate acts of discovery and manipulation. Through such exploration, children develop their sense of touch and learn how to do everyday tasks without adult assistance. Other benefits include improvement in language skills, and acquaintance with elements of science, music, and art.

1. What is the main purpose of this passage?
   (A) To explain the role of early education in child development
   (B) To describe the development of the Montessori method
   (C) To discuss the life and work of Maria Montessori
   (D) To demonstrate how children learn social and cultural values

2. According to the passage, who was first responsible for spreading the Montessori method in the United States?
   (A) Nancy McCormick Rambusch
   (B) A prominent educational expert
   (C) Maria Montessori
   (D) An administrator in the Department of Education

3. Which of the following is NOT mentioned as a benefit of the Montessori method?
   (A) Development of tactile senses
   (B) Improvement of language ability
   (C) Capacity to perform adult tasks
   (D) Knowledge of arts and sciences

4. The following paragraph most likely discusses
   (A) another educational approach beneficial to children.
   (B) details on the life of Maria Montessori.
   (C) additional practitioners of the Montessori method.
   (D) elements of science, music, and art.

17

Canning is a method of preserving food over extended periods of time. The process involves sealing food in containers and heating it in order to kill bacteria that could eventually cause spoilage. While most canned food is produced by commercial companies, some is done at home.

Homegrown fruits and vegetables such as apples and tomatoes are the most popular foods to can. Even certain kinds of meats are suitable for canning. However, it is not advisable to heat produce such as avocados because of the changes in taste and texture that occur. Other foods, including cucumbers and peppers, can be canned only if they are first pickled and then cooked at very low temperatures.

Properly canned food can be saved for as long as three years. If not properly sealed, the food can be spoiled by the growth of organisms. In severe cases, bacteria can cause a fatal form of poisoning called botulism. For this reason, it is very important to check the seal of the jar or bottle regularly to make sure it has remained undisturbed.

* avocádo [ǽvəkádou] *n.* 아보카도 (농작물 이름) bótulism [bátʃəlizəm] *n.* 보툴리누스 중독, 소시지 중독

1. What is the best title for this passage?
   (A) Several Techniques for Canning Produce
   (B) The Use of Sealed Containers
   (C) Detecting Harmful Organisms
   (D) The Nature of the Canning Method

2. According to the passage, what is needed to kill bacteria that spoil food?
   (A) Sealing
   (B) Heat
   (C) A commercial company
   (D) Homegrown produce

3. According to the passage, which of the following is NOT suitable for canning?
   (A) Apples
   (B) Tomatoes
   (C) Cucumbers
   (D) Avocados

4. It can be inferred from the passage that bacteria

   (A) It is rarely harmful.

   (B) It develops very slowly.

   (C) It is one type of organism.

   (D) It is a result of canning foods.

5. According to the passage, botulism can be avoided by

   (A) disturbing the container from time to time.

   (B) properly sealing a jar or bottle.

   (C) reheating the canned food.

   (D) promoting the growth of beneficial organisms.

TOEFL Beginner's Reading Comprehension

정답과 해설

Translations and Explanatory Answers

Translations and Explanatory Answers

Part 2. 독해기초연습 I

Focus 1. 문단의 주제 찾기

[Question Type 1]

[1] 전세계의 모든 대도시들은 같은 문제를 안고 있다. 그 문제는 바로 대기오염이다. 멕시코 시는 대기가 아주 나쁘다. 그곳의 대기는 더럽고 건강에 아주 나쁘다. 자동차들이 오염된 공기의 한 원인이다. 현재 많은 멕시코인들은 자동차를 소유하고 시내를 달린다. 지역내의 공장들도 대기를 오염시킨다. 이 공장들이 대기 중에 많은 매연을 내놓는다. 대도시에서 공기를 정화시키기는 쉽지 않다. 정부가 새로운 법을 만들어야 하고, 모두가 도와야 한다.

(A) 대기오염 .... 너무 포괄적인 표현
(B) 멕시코시의 대기오염 .... 적절한 표현
(C) 공장들이 어떻게 대기를 오염시키는가 .... 너무 지엽적인 표현

【정답】 B

[2] 미국에서는 두 종류의 텔레비전 방송국이 있다. 하나는 상업용이다. 미국에 있는 텔레비전 방송국의 약 841개가 상업방송국이다. 이 방송국들은 기업체이다. 돈을 벌기 위해 광고를 방영한다. 다른 한 종류의 텔레비전 방송국은 공영방송이다. 이 방송국들은 광고를 일체 방영하지 않는다. 이들은 정부로부터 어느 정도의 돈을 받는다. 그리고 공영방송을 시청하는 사람들에게서도 돈을 받는다.

(A) 미국 텔레비전 방송국의 두 가지 종류 ....
적절한 표현
(B) 공영 방송국들 .... 너무 지엽적인 표현
(C) 미국의 텔레비전 .... 너무 포괄적인 표현

【정답】 A

[3] 넓은 숲은 여러 가지로 우리에게 중요하다. 그것은 우리에게 건축이나 난방용으로 목재를 제공한다. 많은 종류의 동식물에게는 집이다. 많은 도시인들에게 숲은 휴가를 가는 장소이다. 사람들은 거기서 자연에 대해 배울 수 있다. 그들은 신선한 공기를 마시고 조용한 곳에서 잠잘

수 있다. 그런데 숲이 모두에게 중요한 이유가 한 가지 더 있다. 숲 속의 나무들의 잎들은 공기를 맑게 하는 데 도움이 된다. 더러운 공기는 세계 곳곳에서 문제이다. 우리의 숲이 없으면 이 문제는 훨씬 더 악화될 것이다.

(A) 숲의 중요성 .... 적절한 표현
(B) 숲에서 갖는 휴가 .... 너무 지엽적인 표현
(C) 넓은 숲 .... 너무 포괄적인 표현

【정답】 A

[4] 좋은 차를 한 잔 만들기는 쉽다. 다음 단계를 따라하면 된다. 첫째, 물을 조금 끓인다. 다음, 뜨거운 물을 찻주전자에 조금 넣어 따뜻하게 데운다. 주전자의 물을 쏟아내고 찻잎을 조금 넣는다. 찻잎은 필요한 각 찻잔에 찻숟가락으로 한 숟갈 정도씩 필요할 것이다. 그런 다음, 끓는 물을 찻주전자에 붓는다. 주전자 뚜껑을 덮고 몇 분을 기다린다. 그러면 이제 차를 마셔도 된다.

(A) 좋은 차 .... 너무 표괄적인 표현
(B) 차를 얼마나 많이 쓸 것인가 .... 너무 지엽적인 표현
(C) 좋은 차를 만드는 방법 .... 적절한 표현

【정답】 C

[Question Type 2]

[5] 미국사람들은 영국사람들과 같은 말을 쓴다. 그러나 미국인들은 영국인들과 여러 면에서 다르다. 첫째, 미국인들의 발음이 영국인들과는 다르다. 예를 들어, 대부분의 미국인들은 'car'라는 단어의 'r'자를 발음하지만 영국인들 대부분은 하지 않는다. 미국인들은 'dictionary'란 단어를 'dik-shun-ar-y'라고 발음하지만 영국인들은 'dik-shun-ry'라고 발음한다. 일부의 철자 또한 다르다. 영국사람들은 'colour', 'centre'라고 쓰지만 미국인들은 'color', 'center'라고 쓴다. 마지막으로, 어떤 단어들은 다르다. 미국사람들은 자동차에 'gasoline'을 사용하지만, 영국인들은 'petrol'을 쓴다. 가솔린과 페트롤은 같은 것인데도 미국인들과 영국인들은 그것에 대해 다른 말을 사용한다.

(A) 미국영어

(B) 영어

(C) 미국영어와 영국영어의 발음차

(D) 미국영어와 영국영어의 차이

【정답】D

[6] 영어로 새로운 단어를 암기하는 데 어려움을 가지고 있습니까? 많은 사람들이 이 문제를 안고 있습니다. 이 방법은 새로운 단어들을 암기하는 데 도움을 줄 수 있습니다. (1) 새로운 단어를 본다. 단어의 철자와 모양을 본다. 눈을 감는다. 단어가 보입니까? (2) 단어를 듣는다. 단어의 사운드를 듣는다. 들은 단어를 본다. (3) 단어를 큰소리로 말한다. 책을 덮는다. 단어를 보지 않는다. 그 단어를 말할 수 있습니까? (4) 단어를 쓴다. 그 단어를 서너 번 쓴다. 쓴 단어를 말한다. (5) 새로운 단어를 사용한다. 오늘 수업시간에 그 단어를 사용하고, 오늘밤 집에서 사용한다. 내일이나 다음 주에 사용한다. 신문에서 그 새로운 단어를 찾아보고, 라디오나 TV에서 그 단어를 새겨듣는다. 어떤 새로운 단어를 암기하기 위해서는 그것을 사용해야만 한다.

(A) 새로운 단어를 암기하는 방법

(B) 영어의 새로운 단어들

(C) 새로운 단어들 보기

(D) 영어의 새로운 단어들 사용

【정답】A

[7] 컴퓨터 칩은 우리의 생활양식을 변화시켰다. 컴퓨터 칩으로 아주 작은 컴퓨터를 만들 수 있다. 우주 과학자들은 이 소형 컴퓨터들을 위성이나 우주선에 사용한다. 대기업들은 이런 소형 컴퓨터들을 사업에 이용한다. 우리는 컴퓨터 칩으로 아주 작은 계산기를 만들 수 있다. 어떤 계산기는 신용카드만큼 작고, 그렇게 비싸지도 않다. 컴퓨터 칩은 디지털 시계를 만드는 데 사용되기도 한다. 일반시계는 스프링이나 움직이는 바늘이 있으나, 디지털 시계는 움직이는 부품이 없다. 디지털 시계는 숫자로 시간과 날짜를 보여주고, 심지어 어떤 디지털 시계는 알람과 스톱위치도 있다. 컴퓨터 칩은 이 모든 것을 가능하게 한다.

(A) 소형 컴퓨터

(B) 컴퓨터 칩의 사용

(C) 디지털 시계

(D) 컴퓨터의 사용

【정답】B

[8] 오늘날 대부분의 자동차가 가솔린을 사용하지만, 미래에는 많은 사람들이 전기자동차를 운전할 것 같다. 전기자동차는 대기를 오염시키지 않는다. 배터리에서 나온 전력이 전기자동차의 모터에 동력을 건다. 전기자동차의 운전자들은 자동차에 가솔린을 주유하지 않아도 된다. 대신, 전력으로 배터리를 충전할 수 있도록 자동차를 전력단자에 연결한다. 전기자동차 운전자는 밤에 자동차를 전력단자에 연결한다. 아침이면 배터리는 하루종일 운행할 수 있는 충분한 전력이 충전된다. 전기자동차는 가솔린 동력자동차만큼 빠르지는 않으며, 150마일(270킬로미터)이상 여행할 수 없다. 150마일 후에는 운전자가 배터리를 재충전해야 한다. 그러나 전기자동차는 오염이나 비싼 가솔린 가격 문제들에 대한 한 가지 해답이 될 수 있다.

(A) 오염과 비싼 가솔린

(B) 전기자동차의 배터리

(C) 가솔린자동차

(D) 전기자동차

【정답】D

[9] 존과 마샤는 미국 남서부의 한 주, 뉴멕시코에 있는 태양열 주택에 살고 있다. 주택의 남쪽 벽에 15개의 창이 있고, 지붕에 4개의 집광판이 있다. 두 개의 집광판은 생활용수를 데우고, 두 개는 주택난방을 보조한다. 겨울에 존과 마샤는 매일 아침 집의 남쪽 커튼을 열어 젖혔다가 매일 저녁에 내린다. 태양광이 낮동안 집을 덥게 하고, 밤에는 커튼이 집안의 열을 보존한다. 더운 여름철에는 존과 마샤는 낮동안에 커튼을 내려두고, 집광판 두 개를 끈다.

(A) 존과 마샤

(B) 뉴멕시코

(C) 태양열 주택

(D) 집광판

【정답】C

[10] 대부분의 미국인들은 고양이를 애완동물로 생각한다. 그러나 모든 고양이가 애완동물은 아니다. 어떤 고양이들은 인간을 돕기도 하지만, 다른 고양이들은 문제이다. 예를 들면, 농장에서나 오래된 주택에서는 고양이들이 이롭다. 들쥐나 생쥐 같은 작은 동물들을 잡는다. 그러나 어떤 경우, 사람들은 고양이가 주위에 있는 것을 원치 않는다. 어떤 사람들은 뜰에서 새들을 구경하길 원한다. 고양이들이 새들을 죽이거나 쫓아버리는 것이다. 고양이들은 도시에서도 문제다. 예를 들어, 로마에서는 고양이 수천 마리가 길거리나 낡은 건물에서 살고 있다. 그들이 내는 소음이 매우 시끄러운데, 더럽고 위험하다.

  (A) 고양이들은 문제가 될 수 있다.
  (B) 대부분의 미국인들은 고양이를 애완동물로 생각한다.
  (C) 고양이들은 단순한 애완동물이 아니다.
  (D) 고양이들은 언제나 사람들에게 이롭다.

【정답】 A

[11] 지구는 늘 변한다. 변하는 방식 중에 한 가지가 침식이다. 어떤 침식은 날씨에 기인한다. 예를 들면, 바람이 침식을 일으킨다. 사막에서 바람은 모래를 휘몰아 간다. 비도 침식을 일으킨다. 대지를 씻어 내리고, 바위 모양을 변화시키기도 한다. 또 다른 침식은 강물에 의해서다. 강물이 산을 통과할 때, 산을 깎아들어 간다. 오랜 시간이 지나면 산은 낮아지고 땅은 평평해진다.

  (A) 비가 침식을 일으킨다.
  (B) 산은 오랜 시간이 지나면서 변한다.
  (C) 침식은 지구를 변화시킨다.
  (D) 침식은 강물에 기인한다.

【정답】 C

[12] 영어로 어휘력을 향상시키는 많은 방법이 있습니다. 한 가지 방법이 영문소설을 읽는 것입니다. 소설들은 흔히 새로운 단어들을 담고 있습니다. 여러분들은 늘 의미를 추측할 수 있기 때문에 이 새로운 단어들을 이해하는 것이 어렵지 않습니다. 문장의 다른 단어들은 여러분에게 도움이 될 것이고 스토리도 역시 도움이 될 것입니다. 새로운 단어들의 의미가 스토리 의미의 일부이기 때문에 재미있는 스토리는 여러분이 새로운 단어를 이해하는 데 도움을 줄 것입니다.

  (A) 어휘력을 향상시키는 많은 방법이 있다.
  (B) 어휘력을 향상시키는 한 가지 방법은 소설을 읽는 것이다.
  (C) 새로운 단어들은 어휘력을 향상시키는 데 도움이 될 것이다.
  (D) 재미있는 스토리는 새로운 단어들을 이해하는 데 도움이 될 것이다.

【정답】 B

[13] 당신의 가족사에 대해 좀더 알기를 원하십니까? 족보학자가 도움이 될 것입니다. 족보학자는 많은 근거자료에서 가족사에 관한 정보를 찾도록 특별히 교육받습니다. 이 정보의 일부는 출생증명서, 결혼증명서, 사망증명서들과 같은 오래된 기록에서 나옵니다. 흔히 족보학자들은 오래된 신문이나 세금기록, 이민기록 등에서 정보를 찾습니다. 심지어 멀리 떨어진 도시나 마을을 찾아가 그곳에 살고 있는 사람들에게서 정보를 수집하는 일도 필요합니다. 일단 정보가 완벽하다면, 족보학자는 가족사를 기술하는 족보를 작성합니다.

  (A) 족보는 가족사를 기술한다.
  (B) 족보학자는 여러 곳에서 정보를 찾는다.
  (C) 족보학자는 가족사에 관한 정보를 찾을 수 있다.
  (D) 가족사에 관한 정보는 많은 근거자료에서 나온다.

【정답】 C

[14] 어린이들 대부분은 뛰어난 언어학습자들이다. 어린이들은 제2언어를 신속하고 쉽게 배울 수 있다. 반면에, 대부분의 어른들은 제2언어를 배우는 것이 어렵다는 것을 알게된다. 어른들은 열심히 공부해야 되고, 언어를 마스터하는 데는 항상 오랜 시간이 걸린다. 어른들은 늘 제2언어를 수학이나 과학, 역사 등 다른 과목들을 공부하는 방식으로 학습하려고 애쓴다. 그러나 어린이들은 모국어를 배운 방식으로 제2언어를 배운다. 어린이 언어학습자는 또다른 언어를 배우는 데 필요한 모든 기술을 가지고

있지만, 성인 언어학습자는 제2언어를 배우기 위해 이 기술들을 다시 배워야 한다.

(A) 어린이들은 뛰어난 언어학습자들이다.
(B) 어른들은 언어학습이 어렵다는 것을 발견한다.
(C) 어린이들은 어른보다는 더 훌륭한 언어학습자들이다.
(D) 어린이들은 어른보다는 더 빠르고 쉽게 배울 수 있다.

【정답】 C

[15] '플라톤'은 내가 가장 좋아하는 선생님이다. 그는 나에게 인내심을 가지고 대한다. 내가 아주 많은 실수를 해도 결코 지치거나 화내지 않는다. 그는 항상 모든 것을 아주 조심스럽게 설명하고 내가 모든 질문에 정확히 대답할 수 있도록 해준다. 수업이 끝나고 과외도움이 필요할 때, 그는 항상 자기 '사무실' 에—늦은 밤에도—있다. 내게 영어를 가르칠 뿐만 아니라, 타자를 가르치기도 한다. 그러나 '플라톤'은 진짜 우리 선생님들만큼은 친근하지가 않다. 그는 결코 미소를 띄거나 웃지도 않는다. 우리 가족에 대해서 묻는다거나, 다음 주말에 무엇을 할 것인지도 묻는 일이 없다. 사실이지, 그는 전혀 말을 하지 않는다. 알다시피, '플라톤'은 컴퓨터다. 내게 영어를 가르쳐주는 특별한 컴퓨터다.

(A) '플라톤'은 내가 가장 좋아하는 선생님이다.
(B) 컴퓨터는 진짜 선생님보다 더 낫다.
(C) '플라톤'은 영어를 가르치는 특별한 컴퓨터다.
(D) 진짜 선생님은 컴퓨터보다 더 친근하다.

【정답】 C

[16] 인도정부는 결혼한 남녀들에게 더 많은 자녀를 갖지 않도록 불임하기를 권한다. 중국에서는 한 자녀 이상 가지는 가정은 처벌을 받을 수 있다. 이 두 나라는 인구가 너무 많아서 사람수가 계속 증가하면, 그들을 위한 식량이나 주택, 일자리가 모자랄 것이다. 그 결론으로 인도와 중국, 그리고 인구가 많은 다른 나라들은 가족계획 정책을 따르고 있다. 그들은 각 가정에서 자녀수를 제한하기 원한다. 교사, 의사, 사회사업가들은 왜 피임이나 불임 같은 출산통제 방법을 써서 자녀를 적게 가져야 하는지를 사람들에게 설명한다.

(A) 일부 인구가 많은 국가들은 가족계획 정책을 따르고 있다.
(B) 인도와 중국은 인구가 매우 많다.
(C) 인도정부는 불임을 권한다.
(D) 중국에서는 한 자녀 이상 가질 경우 처벌을 받을 수도 있다.

【정답】 A

[17] 컴퓨터 검색이 소개되기 이전에 자료조사는 길고 지루한 일이었다. 이제, 주제별 도서나 논문의 카드 카탈로그나 시대별 목차를 찾는 데 긴 시간을 보내는 대신, 컴퓨터를 시켜서 검색을 하도록 할 수 있다. 찾는 주제만 컴퓨터에 입력하면 된다. 그러나 주제가 무엇인지를 정확히 알아야 하기 때문에 이 일이 생각만큼 쉽지는 않으며, 그 주제를 컴퓨터가 이해할 수 있는 용어로 표현해주어야 한다. 그래야 컴퓨터가 자기 메모리에서 주제에 관한 도서나 논문을 검색한다. 컴퓨터가 자기검색을 하는 데는 1초가 걸리지 않는다. 마지막으로 스스로 찾은 책이나 논문들의 제목과 저자들의 명단—해당 주제에 대한 참고문헌—을 인쇄한다.

(A) 자료조사는 길고 지루한 일이다.
(B) 참고문헌은 도서나 논문자료들의 제목이나 저자들의 명단이다.
(C) 컴퓨터는 도서나 논문자료들을 찾아줄 수 있다.
(D) 컴퓨터 검색은 자료조사에서 시간을 절약할 수 있다.

【정답】 D

[Question Type 4]

[18] 인구증가는 지구상의 심각한 문제이다. 20세기가 시작할 때 세계에는 약 15억의 인구가 있었다. 1984년에는 세계인구가 48억이었다. 2,000년까지는 약 61억이 될 것이다.

【주제문】 Population growth is a serious problem around the world.

[19] 도시는 많은 심각한 문제를 갖기 시작했다. 부자들과 기업들은 시의 세금을 더 이상 내지 않았다. 가난한 사람들은 세금으로 많은 돈을 낼 수 없었다. 그래서 도시들은 학교와 주택을 위해서 많은 돈을 갖지 못했다. 간혹 경찰이나 소방관들에게 봉급을 주지도 못한다. 그리고 도로나 공원을 잘 관리할 수도 없다.

【주제문】Cities began to have many serious problems.

[20] 제품가격의 변화가 생산과 소비의 변화를 일으킬 수 있다. 가격이 높을 때 생산은 증가된다. 제품의 가격이 올라갈 때, 생산자는 제품을 더 많이 만드는데, 이유는 그 제품을 판매할 때 더 많은 돈을 벌기 때문이다. 반면에 가격이 낮을 때는 소비가 증가한다. 제품가격이 내려갈 때, 소비자들은 저렴한 가격 때문에 제품을 더 많이 산다.

【주제문】Changes in the prices of goods can cause changes in production and consumption.

[21] 의복은 사람에 대해 많은 것을 말해준다. 어떤 사람들은 화려한 색상의 옷을 좋아한다. 그들은 모든 사람이 자기들을 쳐다보기를 바란다. 그들은 사물의 중심이 되고자 한다. 다른 사람들은 멋진 옷을 입고 싶어한다. 그렇지만 그 옷이 화려한 색상이거나 환상적이지는 않다. 그들은 사람들이 자기들을 쳐다보는 것을 원치 않는다. 또 늘 같은 것을 입는 사람들도 있다. 그들은 누가 자기들을 쳐다보든지 상관하지 않는다. 그들은 자기들에 대해 누가 어떻게 생각하든지 상관하지 않는다.

【주제문】Clothes can tell a lot about a person.

[22] 과학자들은 지구에 대해 많은 것을 알고 있다. 예를 들어, 산이 어떻게 만들어지는지 화산이란 무엇인지를 이해하고 있다. 그러나 화산이 언제 뜨거운 용암을 공기중으로 내보낼지는 모른다. 그들이 지구 외부에 대해서는 알고 있을 지 모른다. 하지만 내부에 대해서는 아직 확신하지 못한다. 그리고 과학자들은 지구가 어떻게 만들어졌는지에 대해서는 잘 모른다. 그들은 여기에 대해 많은 다른 생각을 가지고 있다. 지구를 연구하는 과학자들에게는 아직 많은 다른 의문점들이 있다.

【주제문】Scientists know a lot about the earth.

[23] 아파트를 임대할 때, 임대계약서를 가지는 것이 중요하다. 임대계약이란 아파트 소유주와 임차인 사이에 하는 합의이다. 그것은 아파트 임대의 액수를 말해주고, 임대료를 언제, 어디에 납부해야 하는지에 대한 정보를 준다. 또한 그 아파트에 얼마나 살 수 있는지를 말해준다. 임대계약은 아파트 소유주에게 이롭지만, 임차인에게도 이롭다. 임대계약에 서명하면, 소유주는 임대료를 올릴 수 없고 적절한 사유 없이 아파트를 나가라고 말할 수 없다.

【주제문】When you rent an apartment, it is important to have an apartment lease.

[24] 1930년대 초기의 경제 대공황은 많은 사람들을 놀라게 했다. 그들은 미국기업이 그런 무서운 문제점들을 안고 있으리라고는 생각도 못했다. 오랫동안 그들은 그 문제점들이 심각하다고 믿지를 않았다. 많은 기업인들이 곧 호경기가 오리라 희망했다. 심지어 후버 대통령도 대공황을 심각하게 생각하지 않았다. 그는 1930년에 미국인들에게 문제점들은 이미 사라지고 있다고 말했다. 그러나 이것은 사실이 아니었다. 수백만의 미국인들이 직업을 갖지 못했다. 이중 많은 사람들이 집이 없거나 식량이 없었다. 많은 미국인들이 살기가 힘들었다. 그리고 수년 간 나아지지 않았다.

【주제문】The Great Depression of the early 1930s surprised many people.

[25] 우리는 '개인적인' 광고를 보고 한 나라에 대해 많은 것을 배울 수 있다. 이런 광고는 사람들과 그들이 안고 있는 문제에 대해 우리에게 말해준다. 이 문제의 한 가지 예는 스페인에서 나온다. 스페인의 한 작은 도시에 마흔두 명의 남자들이 있었다. 그런데 거기에는 여자들이 많지 않았다. 그 남자들은 아내를 얻고 싶었다. 그래서 시의 한 신문에다 개인적인 광고를 실었다. 도시의 일부 여자들은 혼자 사는 것이 행복하지 않았다. 그래서 그들은 전화로 그 광고에 답했다. 그들은 그 도시와 남자들에 대해서 좀더 알고 싶었다. 그러나 여자들은 그 도시에 가서 살지를 않았다. 사실 농장에서 일하고 싶지 않았던 것이다.

그들은 작은 도시의 남자들 하고는 사실은 결혼하고 싶지 않았다. 그래서 남자들은 아내를 구할 수가 없었다. 여자들은 여전히 혼자였다. 스페인의 모든 남자 여자들이 이 사람들 같지는 않다. 그러나 이 광고는 스페인의 커다란 문제들에 관한 어떤 것을 우리에게 말해줄 수가 있다.

【주제문】 We can learn a lot about a country from the "personal" ads. These ads tell us about people and their problems.

[Question Type 5]

[26] 보호무역주의자들은 수입 대비 수출 초과가 유익한 무역수지균형을 유지하는 데 필수라고 주장한다. 이때 초과란 귀금속으로써 '현금보유액'이 될 수 있다. 그러나 이것은 어떤 나라가 총 국가생산물을 수출하고 그 대가로 금이나 은만을 수입할 때 모든 무역균형 중 가장 유리한 것이 발생한다는 것을 의미한다. 사람이 금이나 은을 먹을 수는 없으므로 분명 보호무역주의자들이 잘못 생각하고 있는 것이다.

【결론】 Since one cannot eat gold and silver, the protectionists must surely be wrong.

[27] 행정부 관리들은 석유세, 수입수수료, 대체연료를 위한 정부보조금 등을 없앤다고 한다. 자유시장체계가 적정한 가격에 적정한 양의 석유를 생산한다는 것이다. 그것은 늘 그럴싸한 분석이었다. 지금, 페르시아 만으로부터 석유를 보호하려고 행정부가 기꺼이 생명과 돈을 걸고 있는 점에 비춰 볼 때, 그것은 완전히 불합리해 보인다. 석유의 실질 비용은 공급을 보호하고 있는 군대의 비용을 포함해야 한다.

【결론】 The real cost of oil should include the cost of military forces protecting supplies.

[28] 제품의 가격을 알기는 쉽다. 하지만 그 제품의 비용은 얼마일까? 많은 소비자들이 가격(price)과 비용(cost)을 같은 것으로 생각하지만 그것은 오해다. 가격은 소비자가 제품을 사기 위해 지불하는 돈의 액수를 말하고, 비용은 생산자가 제품을 만들기 위해 지출하는 돈의 액수를 말한다. 예를 들어, 생산자가 신발을 만들 경우, 생산자는 신발을 만들기 위해 가죽과 실, 풀, 재봉틀을 구입해야 한다. 신발을 만드는 노동자들에게 임금도 지불해야 한다. 가죽과 실, 풀, 재봉틀, 노동자들을 위한 돈이 신발을 만드는 비용이다. 그런 다음 생산자는 신발의 가격을 결정한다. 돈의 일부가 신발을 만들기 위해 생산자에게로 가야 하기 때문에 가격은 항상 비용보다 높다.

【결론】 The price is always higher than the cost because some money must go to the producer for making the shoes.

[29] 1814년에 조지랩은 인디애나주 하모니에서 이상 공동체를 시작했다. 1824년에 랩은 공동체를 로버트 오웬에게 팔았는데, 그는 거기서 새로운 이상 공동체를 시작했다. 그는 새 공동체를 '뉴 하모니'라 이름 붙인다. '뉴 하모니'는 겨우 2년 지속된다. 1825년에 프랜시스 라이트가 테네시주 멤피스 근처에서 '내쇼바' 공동체를 시작한다. 내쇼바 공동체는 1830년에 끝난다. 이상적인 농업 공동체인 '브룩크 농장'이 1841년에서 1847년까지 존속한다. 뉴욕시 인근의 무정부주의 공동체인 '모던 타임즈'는 1851년 조시아 워런이 시작했는데, 1857년에 끝난다. 우리는 1800년대에 시작된 이 이상 공동체들이 단기간에 끝난 것을 알 수 있다.

【결론】 We can see that these utopian communities that started in the 1800s lasted only a short time.

[30] 대학교육을 받기 위한 수강료와 기타 비용이 계속 치솟고 있고, 최근 학생들에 대한 정부의 보조금 삭감은 일반가정의 자녀 교육비 감당을 아주 어렵게 했다. 우리는 곧 다시 한번 대학교육이 부자들만의 특권인 그날을 보게 될 것이다.

【결론】 We may soon see the day when a college education is once again the privilege of only the very rich.

[31] 띠톱이 왕복운동 톱보다 더 효과적이다. 띠톱의 날

은 분당 8,000에서 10,000피트 속도로 움직이는 반면, 매분 18인치를 200번 타격하는 왕복운동 톱은 분당 겨우 300피트의 절단속도를 가지고 있다.

【결론】 A band saw is more efficient than a reciprocating saw.

[32] 찰스 디킨스의 두번째 소설, 『니콜라스 니클바이』는 일부 비평가들에 의해 낭만주의적이라고 언급되어 왔는데, 그러나 그 소설은 실제로 대단히 사실주의적이다. 디킨스는 요크셔를 여행하였을 때, 소설을 쓰기 위한 자료를 수집하였는데, 교육이라는 미명하에 어린 학생들을 학대한 싸구려 기숙학교의 비참한 여건을 직접 조사하였다.

【결론】 Nicholas Nickleby, the second novel of Charles Dickens, has been referred to by some commentators as romantic, but the novel is actually highly realistic.

[33] 미연방 지불준비위원회는 지난달 통화공급상승을 늦추는 데 동의한 것이 분명하다. 한 달 뒤 물가가 한 달 전보다 더 오르고, 이자율도 눈에 띄게 올랐다. 과거에도 비슷한 상황에서 위원회는 인플레션 억제에 동의했다.

【결론】 The Federal Reserve Board must have moved last month to slow the growth of the money supply.

[34] 가격이 높을 때 생산자는 물건을 더 많이 만들고, 가격이 낮을 때 소비자는 물건을 더 많이 구입한다. 가격이 올라가면 그 물건에 대해 돈을 더 많이 벌기 때문에 생산자는 물건을 더 많이 만든다. 가격이 내려가면 낮은 가격 때문에 소비자는 물건을 더 많이 구입한다. 이것은 제품가격의 변화가 생산과 소비에서 어떻게 변화를 일으키는지를 우리에게 보여준다.

【결론】 This shows us how changes in the prices of goods can cause changes in production and consumption.

[35] 가격이 높을 때 생산자는 자신의 제품으로 더 많은

돈을 벌 수 있다. 가격이 낮을 때 소비자는 자신의 돈으로 더 많은 제품을 구입할 수 있다. 제품가격에서의 이런 변화는 생산과 소비에서의 변화를 일으킨다. 제품가격이 올라갈 때 생산자는 더 많은 돈을 벌기 위해 더 많은 물건을 만들 것이다. 가격이 내려가면 소비자는 낮은 가격 때문에 물건을 더 많이 살 것이다.

【결론】 These changes in the prices of goods can cause changes in production and consumption.

Focus 2. 제목(Title) 고르기

[1] 컴퓨터는 매우 유용하다. 그러나 문제를 일으킬 수 있다. 문제점 하나가 컴퓨터의 메모리다. 완전하지 않기 때문에 가끔 컴퓨터는 중요한 정보를 잃어버린다. 또 다른 문제는 기계다. 컴퓨터는 기계이고, 기계는 부서질 수 있다. 컴퓨터가 부서지면 칠판의 분필글씨처럼 모든 정보가 지워질 수 있다.

【정답】 B

[2] 과학으로서 또는 지식의 한 분야로서 화학은 물질의 행위와 관련된 사고나 개념에 대한 관심이다. 이 개념들이 비록 추상적일지라도 그 응용은 인류문화에 구체적인 영향을 주었다. 이 영향은 현대의 기술공학에 기인하는데, 약 200년 전에 시작된 것으로 보이며 이후 급속히 성장하였다.

【정답】 C

[3] 니키는 병원의 어린이 부서 확대를 위한 모금을 하기 위해 9월 초에 있을 후원회 등반에 참가한다. 그녀와 다른 아홉 사람들은 에베레스트산을 오르내리는 데 한 달을 보낼 것이다. 이번이 병원에서 아픈 어린이들을 위한 시설을 건립하는 데 필요로 하는 기금을 모으기 위한 마지막 시도이다. 그들은 5년 간이나 모금을 위해 애썼다.

【정답】 D

[4] 영국은 네 나라로 구성되어 있다 : 잉글랜드, 스코트랜드, 웨일즈 그리고 북아일랜드이다. 수도인 런던은 영국

정부의 중심지이다. 그러나 지역당국이 교육, 보건, 도로 등에 일부 책임을 지고 있다. 법률은 의회가 만든다. 의원들은 특정지역의 국민들에 의해 선출된다.

【정답】B

[5] 지구상에서 가장 낮은 기온은 1960년 8월 26일 남극 대륙의 소련과학기지 보스톡에서 기록되었다. 그러나 보스톡은 사람들이 잠시 머무는 곳이다. 사람들이 일년 내내 살 곳으로 선택한 가장 추운 곳은 해발 700미터의 산골짜기에 600명이 사는 한 마을이다. 오이미야콘이다.

【정답】D

[6] 마가렛 미드에 따르면, 젊은 세대는 기성세대와 본질적으로 다르다고 한다. 어른들의 세상은 사라졌고, 그들은 현대 세계의 모든 문제를 이해하지 못한다. 한편, 젊은 사람들은 이런 문제들과 함께 성장했고, 그 문제들에 깊이 관심을 가진다. 기성세대는 기업조직, 정부, 교육에 여전히 힘을 행사하고 있다. 젊은 사람들은 현대사회의 요구에 맞추어 이런 분야에서 변화를 주고싶어 한다. 그들의 차이를 조화시키기 위해 두 세대는 세상이 변했다는 것과 사회의 많은 문제들을 해결하는 데 새로운 해결책이 필요하다는 사실을 깨달아야 한다.

【정답】B

[7] 먼저, 월세나 식량 등 매달 지출해야 하는 돈인 고정비용부터 리스트를 작성하라. 일부 비용을 추정한다면 낮게 보다는 높이 잡아라. 그 다음 보험 같은 큰 비용을 기술하고, 그 월 비용을 뽑는다. 이제 의료비 같은 비상 지출을 기술한다. 나머지는 오락이나 여행 등 '용돈'이다. 리스트를 작성하고 그대로 따라 하면, 매달 돈이 떨어지는 염려는 안해도 된다.

【정답】A

[8] 제임스는 파키스탄에서 영국으로 온 이민가족과 그들이 영국에 정착한 문제들에 관한 텔레비전 극을 썼다. 그 극은 놀랄 만큼 성공적이었고, 미국 텔레비전 방송사에 팔렸다.

제임스는 제작 협조차 뉴욕에 초청되었다. 그는 공항에서 한 시간 거리에 있는 둘위치에 살았다. 비행기가 8시 30분에 떠나기로 되어 있었으므로, 그는 아침 7시30분경에는 공항에 가야 했다. 그는 6시30분에 오라고 택시를 예약하고, 알람시계를 5시45분으로 맞춰놓고, 잠자리에 들었다. 불행히도 시계 태엽 감는 것을 잊어버렸기에 자정이 조금 지나서 멈췄다. 택시운전사 역시 그날 밤 늦게까지 근무하고서 늦잠을 잤다.

【정답】A

[9] 우리가 텔레비전에서 보는 시츄에이션코메디(시트콤)는 아주 긴 역사를 가지고 있다. 첫 시트콤은 기원전 4세기로 거슬러 올라간다. 그 당시에는 사람들이 활동적인 사회활동을 했고 여흥을 즐겼다. 이런 많은 것들이 극형태로 나왔다. 메넌더라는 사람은 가벼운 희곡과 시트콤을 많이 썼다. 그의 최고작은 돈이 많은 불평꾼에 관한 것이다. 많은 사람들이 그를 싫어하지만 그를 골탕먹이는 것은 좋아한다. 장난은 그를 화나게 하지만, 그것은 청중들을 웃게 했다. 이것이 바로 오늘날 시츄에이션코메디가 우리에게 주는 것이다.

【정답】C

[10] 지난 가을, 필라델피아시(市)가 쓰레기 11톤을 비행기에 실어 스위스로 보냈다. 2주일 후에 배가 돌아 왔다. 플라스틱, 종이, 금속, 연료용 유기물질 등 재활용 제품들로 분리된, 건조하고 화학적으로 안정된 것들이었다. 쓰레기 운반비행은 단 17분 만에 쓰레기가 원료로 전환되는 스위스제 재활용시스템을 거치도록 되어 있었다. 이 공장은 쓰레기 재활용이 가능한 자동화로 고안된 시스템 중의 하나이다. 점차 쓰레기는 자원으로 여겨지고 있다. 기하학적인 증가율로 고갈되고 있는 자연자원을 보존하려면 우리는 재활용할 수밖에 없다.

【정답】A

Focus 3. 문장의 전개순서 찾기

[1]

(A) 임대관리는 미국에서 최근 공정하게 시작되었다.

(B) 세계 2차대전 중에 미국정부는 미국의 모든 도시에 임대관리를 강제 실시하였다.

(C) 1980년대 초에는 미국인들의 거의 1/4이 도시에서 임대관리로 살았다.

(D) 2차대전 이전에는 임대관리를 하는 미국도시가 거의 없었다.

(E) 2차대전 이후에 오직 한 도시—뉴욕—만이 임대관리를 계속하였다.

【정답】 A - D - B - E - C

[2]

(A) 다음, 유리창 세척액에 부동액을 첨가하라. 그렇지 않으면, 세척액이 얼어서 용기가 깨질 수도 있다.

(B) 첫째, 눈 내린 빙판길을 자주 운전할 생각이라면 스노우타이어를 장착하라.

(C) 겨울에, 특히 눈내린 빙판길 운전은 몇 가지 간단한 주의사항만 갖추면 고생을 덜 할 수 있다.

(D) 마지막으로, 겨울날씨에 운전할 때, 바퀴체인이나 언 잠금장치를 녹이는 스프레이 한 통, 유리창 긁개 등을 자동차에 싣고 가는 것도 좋은 생각이다.

(E) 둘째, 라디에이터에 부동액의 양을 점검하고 필요하면 더 첨가하라.

【정답】 C - B - E - A - D

[3]

(A) 그러나, 소비자들은 신발이 비싸서 많이 사지 않았다.

(B) 결과적으로, 신발 생산자들은 소비자들이 신발을 많이 살 수 있도록 신발가격을 내렸다.

(C) 신발가격은 생산자들이 만드는 신발 수량과 관계가 있다.

(D) 동시에, 신발 생산자들은 가격이 내려갔기 때문에 신발생산을 줄였다.

(E) 예를 들어, 지난달 신발가격이 높았다. 그래서 신발생산자들은 신발을 더 많이 만들었다.

【정답】 C - E - A - B - D

[4]

(A) 대부분의 도시에서 원룸아파트의 임대료가 한 달에 $250 이상이다.

(B) 예를 들어, 로스엔젤레스에 살면, 원룸아파트 하나를 임대하는 데 $400 이상 주어야 하고, 시카고에서는 같은 아파트 임대에 $650 넘게 지불하여야 한다.

(C) 켄터키주의 루이스빌이나 플로리다주의 잭슨빌 같은 작은 도시에는 임대료가 더 적지만, 큰 도시에서는 임대료가 더 많다.

(D) 미국에서 가장 비싼 임대료는 뉴욕에서인데, 거기서는 시내 전 지역에서 원룸아파트 하나를 임대하는 데 적어도 월 $700는 지불하여야 한다.

(E) 아파트 임대료는 미국 도시마다 다르다.

【정답】 E - A - C - B - D

[5]

(A) 나중에 사람들은 두루마리로 감기는 가죽조각에 글을 쓰기 시작하였다.

(B) 원시시대에 사람들은 바위에 메시지를 새기거나 그림으로 그렸다.

(C) 중세에는 양피지라고 불리는 무거운 종이가 글쓰기에 사용되었다. 책은 힘들게 손으로 필사되었다.

(D) 15세기 중엽에 인쇄기의 발명으로 현대 인쇄산업이 탄생하였다.

(E) 문자매체의 일부형태는 수세기를 걸쳐서 사용되었다.

【정답】 E - B - A - C - D

[6]

(A) 만약 아기 탄생일에 큰 폭풍이 있었다면 그 아기는 번개구름이라고 이름지어졌을 것이다.

(B) 미국 인디언 이름은 매우 설명적이다. 왜냐하면, 인디언들은 흔히 물리적인 속성이나 자연발생적인 사건이나 동물 등의 이름을 따서 이름지어졌다.

(C) 회색 독수리, 붉은 개, 큰 곰, 점박이 늑대 등은 동물들의 이름을 따서 지은 이름들의 예다.

(D) 눈에 띄는 물리적인 특징을 가진 인디언들은 큰 발이

나 꼬부라진 다리와 같은 이름들이 주어졌을 것이다.

【정답】 B - D - A - C

[7]
(A) 한 가지, 개인의 I.Q. 점수는 상당히 변한다.
(B) 많은 전문가들도 I.Q. 점수가 지능과 관련이 있는지 의문을 갖는다.
(C) 게다가, 대부분의 심리학자들은 지능검사가 중산층의 어린이들에게 유리하게 치우쳐 있다는 데 동의한다.
(D) 표준화된 지능검사의 타당성은 교육자나 심리학자들에게서 심각하게 의문시되고 있다.
(E) 사실, 성취동기는 어떤 사람의 학습능력을 결정하는 데 지능만큼이나 매우 중요해 보인다.

【정답】 D - B - A - C - E

[8]
(A) 게다가, 연구원들은 효율적인 전기자동차의 개발작업을 계속하고 있다.
(B) 자동차산업에서의 연구원들은 전통적인 가솔린엔진을 대체할 여러 형태의 엔진과 대체 연료를 실험하고 있다.
(C) 한 가지 새로운 형태의 엔진은 가솔린 대신에 디젤유를 연소하는 데, 수년간 유용하였다.
(D) 마지막으로, 몇몇 자동차 메이커들은 가솔린과 알코올의 혼합인 메탄올을 자동차연료로 실험하고 있다.
(E) 둘째 형태는 가솔린, 디젤유, 등유, 다른 추출물 또는 메탄올 등으로 만든 연료를 사용할 수 있는 가스터빈엔진이다.

【정답】 B - C - E - D - A

Focus 4. 문장 연결하기

[Question Type 1]

[1] 그들이 부딪친 많은 난관에도 불구하고 열기구 비행사들은 가까스로 목적지에 도착하였다.

【정답】 A

[2] 그 후보는 대학에서 정한 모든 자격요건에 부합하였다. 그래서 이 대학원은 그녀에게 석사학위를 수여하였다.

【정답】 C

[3] 첫눈에 그 아이디어는 매력이 있어 보인다. 그러나 정리되어야 할 많은 사항들이 있다.

【정답】 B

[4] 문제는 태어날 때부터 우유를 먹어온 어린이들이 바로 우유로부터 크게 혜택을 입는 데 비해, 어떤 나이가 될 때까지 우유를 전혀 마셔보지 않은 사람들은 우유가 몸에 받지 않는다.

【정답】 C

[5] 15세기 전에 다른 유럽인들이 신세계를 다녀갔다는 것은 사실이다. 그러나 콜럼버스는 자기 항해의 궁극적인 결과로 인해 그가 신세계를 발견한 것으로 믿어진다.

【정답】 C

[6] 분명 NASA의 우주계획이 대단히 비용이 많이 드는 것으로 인정이 되지만, 우주공학의 새로운 상업적 활용이라는 측면에서 볼 때는 상당한 이익이 있었다.

【정답】 D

[7] 특별히 좋은 결과를 낳은 것으로 보아, 내년에도 같은 접근을 시도하기로 결정되었다.

【정답】 B

[8] 상호 수용가능한 아무런 의제가 도출되지 않아서, 회담은 결국 취소되었다.

【정답】 A

[9] 10여 년이 넘게 수면 연구가들은 일상적으로 소모되고 밤사이에 보충되는 어떤 특별한 효소를 찾았었다. 그래서 실제로 어떤 것이 존재한다면 그런 물질이 발견되지 않은 것이 놀랍다.

【정답】 A

[10] 그 증거는 나르휠 고래의 엄니가 유니콘의 신화적인 뿔과 놀랄 만큼 닮았다는 사실과 또한 15세기의 북유럽 어부들이 신비한 효험이 있다고 알려진 나르휠 고래의 엄니를 약제상들에게 팔았다는 사실을 내포하고 있다.

【정답】 D

[11] 췌장암은 치명적인 결과를 가져다주면서 번지고 있다. 즉, 미국의 환자수는 지난 20년 동안 두 배로 증가하였으며 이 병은 이제 미국에서만 연간 2만명의 목숨을 앗아가고 있다. 그것은 또한 치료하기 가장 어려운 암 중의 하나다. 그 희생자들은 거의 3년 이상을 살지 못한다.

【정답】 B

[12] 반 고흐의 초기 그림들은 어두었으나, 1886년에 파리로 이주한 후, 그곳에서 피사로, 드가, 고갱 등을 만났고, 나중에 그를 유명하게 만드는 밝은 색채의 힘찬 그림을 그리기 시작하였다. 주기적인 광기의 발작에도 불구하고, 그는 오늘날 널리 알려진 수많은 작품들을 성공적으로 제작하였다.

【정답】 A

[13] 그 도시는 신생국가가 '외부'세계와 접촉하는 주요 거점이 되는 경향이 있다. 그 신생국가는 다른 나라의 정치적 대표들을 끌어들이고 있다. 따라서, 떠오르는 나라의 수도인 그 도시는 이 신생국가의 적절한 이미지를 외부세계에 제공하는 데 매우 중요한 역할을 한다.

【정답】 A

[14] 모든 사람은 두 개의 영역, 즉 내면세계와 외면세계에 살고 있다. 내면세계란 예술, 문학, 도덕, 종교 등으로 표현되는 정신적인 목적의 세계이다. 외면세계란 우리가 살아가는 방편인 고안장치, 기술공학, 기계적인 체계, 도구체계 등의 영역이다.

【정답】 D

[15] 현대공학에서 가장 위대한 진보의 하나는 컴퓨터의 발명이다. 그것들은 이미 산업분야와 대학에서 널리 사용되고 있으며, 일반인들 역시 사용가능한 때가 올 것이다.

【정답】 B

Focus 5. 핵심어(key word) 넣기

[Question Type I]

[1] 하키는 한쪽이 50-60야드, 한쪽이 90-100야드가 되는 평지에서 각기 11명씩 두 팀이 펼치는 경기이다.

【정답】 A

[2] 레이온이나 나일론 등 합성섬유로 만들어진 직물의 등장은 우리 문명에 많은 변화를 주었다.

【정답】 D

[3] 스위스의 다보스는 많은 결핵환자들에게 꽤 잘 알려져 있다. 그들은 높은 산의 공기를 마시기 위하여 그곳에 갔다. 그곳은 좋은 휴양지였다.

【정답】 B

[4] 사람들에게 부(富)나 권력을 부여한다고 해서 우리가 그들을 자동적으로 훌륭하고 덕망있는 사람으로 만들지는 못한다. 참으로 진실은 흔히 그 반대인 것 같다.

【정답】 B

[5] 국제적인 시각에서 볼 때, 한국전쟁의 성과는 매우 중요하였다. 그러나 미국 대중에게 준 영향은 압도적으로 부정적이었다.

【정답】 C

[6] 악(惡)이 될 힘이 결핍되어 있는 사람이라면 누구든 자신의 선(善)으로 칭찬받을 수 없다. 그런 경우, 일반적으로 선은 나태와 의지부족의 결과일 뿐이다.

【정답】 C

[7] 미국 흑인들의 발호는 자유와 평등을 '지금' 그리고 '당장' 현실로 실현시키려는 깊고도 열렬한 결의에서 성장

한다.

【정답】A

[8] 전체주의국가들의 역사책 대부분은 민족주의적이고 감상적이며, 특정국가의 완전한 우월성에 대한 민족적 자부심과 환상으로 가득차 있다.

【정답】B

[9] 1940년대에 한국은 미국외교정책의 극히 변방에 있었을 뿐만 아니라, 대부분의 아시아 국가들처럼, 미국 국민들에게도 거의 알려지지 않았다.

【정답】A

[10] 잠이 필요한 이유는 여전히 연구가들을 당황하게 하고 있다. 잠이 건강에 필수적인 것 같지는 않다. 장기간의 수면 부족은 일시적인 방향감각 상실을 초래하지만, 그 효과가 영구적이지는 않다.

【정답】A

[11] 대부분의 집주인들은 주택이나 차고 옆에 서 있는 죽은 나무는 제거되어야 하는 것으로 생각한다. 썩어가는 가지나 나무 전체가 넘어져서 건물에 심한 손상을 줄 수도 있다고 알고 있다.

【정답】B

[12] 과학의 발견은 흔히 복합적인 은총이다. 한편으로 귀중한 살충제를 주어서 농부들이 훨씬 많은 농산물을 거둘 수 있게 하지만, 한편으로는 자연의 균형을 파괴하여 그 혜택을 상쇄시켜 버린다.

【정답】D

[13] 사람은 모든 동물 가운데 가장 무서운 존재 중의 하나이고, 끊임없이 자기와 같은 종족을 공격하는 유일한 존재이다. 역사를 통해서 볼 때, 짧은 기간을 제외하고 지독한 전쟁이 없이 살아온 적이 결코 없다.

【정답】D

[14] 그 나라의 천연자원 덕분에, 아주 최근까지 모든 미국인들은 당연히 조상들보다는 돈을 많이 벌 것으로 기대할 수 있었다. 그래서 만일 그가 돈을 적게 벌었다면, 그가 게으르고 무능했기 때문으로 그 잘못은 분명 자신의 것이었다.

【정답】D

[15] 산업혁명 이후 대량실업의 공포가 공학기술의 변화를 초래하였다. 그러나 일자리를 파괴하기는커녕 신속한 공학기술의 진보는 높은 비율의 직업창출을 수반하였다.

【정답】B

[16] 19세기는 스트라우스와 말러 같은 작곡가들에 의해서 상당히 향상된 현대적인 교향악단의 완성을 보았다. 현대 오케스트라에 자주 등장하는 악기들은 현악기로서 바이올린, 비올라, 첼로, 콘드라베이스, 하프 등이다.

【정답】D

[17] 발전하는 과학에서 변화란 것이 새건물에 자리를 내주기 위해 낡은 건물을 파괴하는 것에 비유되어서는 안되고, 오히려 어떤 동물유형의 점진적인 진화에 비유되어야 한다. 우리는 낡은 이론이 무익하고 헛된 것이라고 믿어서는 안된다.

【정답】D

[18] 외모로 판단할 수는 없다. 볼품없는 외모와 느리고 육중한 동작 때문에 곰은 어리석다는 평판을 받아왔다. 그러나 동물원 사육사들은 자신들이 다루는 모든 동물들 가운데 곰이 가장 영리한 축에 속한다는 데 동의한다.

【정답】D

[19] 하나의 공동체란 한 가족처럼 작을 수도 있고, 인류만큼이나 클 수도 있다. 각각의 작은 공동체는 하나의 큰 공동체의 일부분이고, 각각의 큰 공동체는 더 작은 공동체들로 구성된다. 공동체를 결정하는 유일한 중요한 요소는 사람들이다.

【정답】A

[20] 인류의 여러 종족들이 서로 충분한 성적인 매력을 가지고 있다. 그래서 유전적 혼합에 있어 어떤 지리적 또는 문화적 장애가 없는 경우, 수천 년이 지나면 인류는 인종적으로 단일화될 것이다.

【정답】 C

[21] 어떤 역사가는 '역사는 현재를 삼킨다'라고 역사를 말하였다. 나는 그가 말하고자 하는 것을 완전히 이해하지는 못하지만, 과학에서는 분명히 그 정반대이다. 즉, 현재가 과거를 삼키는 것이다. 이것은 사상사에 대한 과학자의 오도된 무관심을 보여준다.

【정답】 B

[22] 인간, 컴퓨터, 동물은 어떤 의미에서 사고한다고 말할 수 있다. 이들 각자의 사고과정은 다를 것이다. 각자 자신만의 강점과 약점을 가지고 있을 것이다. 강약의 특별한 조화의 이점은 해야 할 일에 달려 있을 것이다.

【정답】 B

[Question Type 2]

[23] 많은 음식은 건조함으로써 온전히 보존될 수 있다. 음식에서 부패를 일으키는 박테리아와 곰팡이는 습기 없이는 번성할 수가 없다.

【정답】 A

[24] 취미란 사람이 생계비를 벌기 위한 수단보다는 개인적인 흥미 때문에 시간과 정력을 규칙적으로 바치는 어떤 것이다.

【정답】 D

[25] 어떤 고대 종교는 인간이 악을 무시하지 말고, 세상에서 선을 따라야 한다고 가르쳤다. 다시 말해서, 선을 구하되 세상에는 악도 역시 존재한다는 것을 명심하라.

【정답】 A

[26] 서양문명의 두 가지 기본목표는 인간의 삶을 보존하는 것과 경제적 안정을 주는 것이다. 건강과 부(富)를 위한 공동노력이다.

【정답】 D

[27] 그 동물의 입은 그의 좁은 목구멍과 비교할 때 너무 크다. 음식을 입에 가득 넣었을 때, 삼키기 전에 오랫동안 씹어야 한다.

【정답】 D

[28] 드라마는 오래전에 인도에서 번성하였다. 그곳에서 공연된 연극은 항상 해피엔딩이었기 때문에 힌두 관객들은 비극에 낯설었다.

【정답】 D

[29] 국제연합은 문제를 만들기 위해서가 아니라 해결하기 위해, 갈등을 심화시키기보다는 평화를 증진시키기 위해, 발전을 가로막는 장애를 만드는 것이 아니라 격려하기 위해, 속박에 기여하는 게 아니라 자유를 양육하기 위해 만들어졌다.

【정답】 C

[30] 위기의 시대에는 '좋았던 옛날'을 그리워하듯이 생각하는 경향이 있는데, 그래서 과거의 장점은 더 커보이고 그 결점들은 감소된다.

【정답】 A

[31] 언어는 사회적 행동의 한 형태이므로 우리는 어떤 사람의 행위에 대해 반응을 일으키듯이 그 사람의 언어양식에 대해 반응을 한다.

【정답】 D

[32] 도둑은 어떤 집을 털기 위해 경비견의 주의를 딴데로 돌리려 하였다. 짖어서 집주인에게 알리는 대신에 고기를 먹을 것이라 기대하면서 그는 개에게 고기 한 덩이를 던졌다. 그러나 그 개는 음식제공을 거절하였고, 집주인에게 알렸다. 그 개에게서 교훈을 얻건데, 현명한 이는 뇌물을 주의해야 한다.

【정답】 D

[33] 우리 정부의 민주제도는 대의제도에 바탕을 두고 있고, 그리고 효과적인 대의제도는 후보와 유권자간의 의사소통에 있으므로, 우리 정부형태의 성공은 언어의 사용에 크게 의존하고 있음이 분명하다.

【정답】 A

[34] 가난과 불행이 다가오지만, 미신은 지식에 의해서만 극복될 수 있다.

【정답】 D

[35] 사람들은 돈에 대한 그들의 태도에 따라 두 부류로 나뉜다. 하나는 돈을 가지려 하고, 다른 하나는 쓰려고 한다.

【정답】 B

Focus 6. 문장 완성하기

[Question Type I]

[1] 상상의 자유에도 불구하고 당신은 언제나 인과의 법칙에 묶여 있다. 고층건물에서 뛰어내리는 것도 자유이고, 일주일 동안 식사를 안하는 것도 자유이다. 그러나 그 결과를 모면할 자유는 없다.

【정답】 C

[2] 우리는 매일 수입된 원료를 가지고 국내에서 만들어진 많은 것을 사용한다. 다른 나라들은 우리가 가지지 못한 광물과 채소들을 가졌고, 우리는 그들이 자급할 수 없는 어떤 것을 가지고 있다. 만약 우리가 국제교역을 할 수 없다면 우리나라의 일부 공장들이 문을 닫아야 했을 것이다.

【정답】 B

[3] 미국혁명 중에 봉기한 식민지들이 독립전쟁에 참가할 것을 계속 설득하였는데도, 캐나다 국민들은 영국에 계속 충성하였다.

【정답】 D

[4] 고정수입을 가진 사람들은 물가가 하락할 때 다행이다. 물가가 비쌀 때보다 달러로 더 많은 상품과 서비스를 살 것이기 때문에 실질수입은 증가한다.

【정답】 D

[5] 여러분이 처음 대학에 올 때 여러분은 지적으로 아주 어리고, 자신의 지적 능력만으로 안전하게 나아갈 만큼 배우지 못했습니다. 여러분의 사상은 아직 여러분 자신의 것이 되질 못합니다. 그러므로 여러분이 대학에서 배워야 할 첫째 것은 여러분 자신의 사상 위에 서는 것입니다.

【정답】 A

[6] 한국경제체제는 고립되어 존재하지 않고, 세계경제체제의 일부분이다. 이렇듯 한국 국민의 경제생활은 모든 다른 민족들의 경제생활에 대단히 영향을 받는다.

【정답】 D

[7] 많은 사람들이 자신의 재능, 정력이나 창조적인 능력들을 파괴하는 부분적인 자살을 하면서 인생을 살아간다. 자신에게 선(善)하기를 배우는 것이 타인들에게 선하기를 배우는 것보다 종종 더 어렵다. 이 글에 따르면, 우리는 자신의 능력을 소홀히 하지 않도록 유의해야 한다는 것이다.

【정답】 D

[8] 좋은 영어를 사용하는 능력은 동의어를 사용하면서 차이를 주의 깊게 관찰함으로써 향상된다. 말과 노새를 구별할 수 없는 사람은 탈 것을 선택함에 있어 실수를 범하기 쉽다. 우리가 단어를 선택할 때 실수를 피하려면 밀접하게 관련된 단어들의 의미 차이를 공부하는 것이 필요하다.

【정답】 B

[9] 우리가 우리의 적을 증오할 때, 우리는 그들에게 우리를 지배하는 힘, 즉 우리의 잠, 식욕과 행복을 지배하는

TOEFL Beginner's Reading Comprehension

(빼앗을) 힘을 부여하게 된다. 그들이 얼마나 우리에게 근심을 주고 있는지 안다면, 그들은 아마 즐겁게 춤을 출 것이다. 우리의 증오는 결코 그들을 다치게 하는 게 아니고, 우리의 밤낮을 지옥과 같은 혼란 속으로 빠뜨린다. 이 글에서 제기된 도덕은 '당신의 증오로 자신을 불행하게 하지말라' 이다.

【정답】 B

[10] 한 집단의 사람들이 어떤 나라에 정복당하여, 정복국가의 언어와 관습을 배우도록 강요받을 때, 그렇게 하는데는 피정복민들 쪽의 많은 저항이 있기 마련이다. 그러나 사람들이 자발적으로 자신들의 조국을 떠나 새로운 나라에 갈 때는 새로운 나라의 관습과 언어를 배우는 데 주저하지 않아야 한다.

【정답】 A

[Question Type 2]

[11] 중국의 자이언트 팬더곰이 생존을 위해 의지하는 대나무는 80년에서 100년마다 겨우 한 번 꽃을 피우기 때문에, 그 동물이 계속해서 생존할 수 있다는 것이 놀랍다.

【정답】 D

[12] 비록 여러 제작자들이 히틀러의 종말을 바탕으로 한 영화 지원에 관심을 가졌지만, 그런 영화를 만드는 데 필요한 기록은 발견되지 않았다.

【정답】 D

[13] 조면기의 발명은 섬유질을 손상하지 않고 목화의 파란 씨를 채취하는 단순한 방법 그 이상을 의미하였다.

【정답】 B

[14] 우주비행사 프로그램에 선발되는 남녀에게 어떤 일이 일어나고 있는데, 단순히 향상된 신체조건이나 기술적 능력 이상의 어떤 것이다.

【정답】 C

[15] 30년 전에는 그가 시애틀에서 클리브랜드까지 여행하는데 4일이 걸렸다.

【정답】 D

[16] 그 학생은 강의내용 때문이 아니라 강사의 전달방식 때문에 혼동되었다.

【정답】 A

[17] 형태보다는 기능에 대한 연구가 어떤 다른 체계를 생산한다.

【정답】 C

[18] 중세 사람들은 지구가 우주의 중심이라는 관념이 너무도 확고해서 사람들은 새로운 발견이나 이론의 관점에서 그 관념을 생각해보는 것을 꺼려하였다.

【정답】 C

[19] 최근까지, 서로 다른 계층의 사람들이 서로에 대해 알게 되는 유일한 방법은 직접 접촉을 통해서였다.

【정답】 B

[20] 그러나 이 자동차회사에는 내년도 모델보다 더 기대를 걸고 있는 많은 것들이 있다.

【정답】 D

[21] 완벽한 시설이 갖추어진 교실과 유능한 교사들이 있는 웨스트레이크 고등학교에서조차 대학 입학시험에 실패하는 학생들이 많이 있다.

【정답】 C

[22] 어쩌면 우리는 어떤 대가를 치르고서라도 인플레이션과 싸운다는 생각보다는 오히려 실업률을 끌어내리는 관점에서 생각해야 한다.

【정답】 D

[23] 그 회사의 회장은 시카고에서 주주들에게 행한 연설에서 장래 임금인상은 5% 이내로 유지되어야 한다고

말하고 싶어하였다.

【정답】 C

[24] 관광을 탈출이나 휴일행락과 동일시하는 경향이 너무나 확고해서, 우리는 관광을 순례와 같은 관점에서 생각하기를 꺼린다.

【정답】 D

[25] 순례자들은 인도의 거의 모든 열차, 버스, 산길 등에서 만날 수 있다. 그러나 우리는 그들을 순례자로 인식하지 못하기도 한다.

【정답】 C

Focus 7. 지칭어 찾기

[Question Type 1]

[1] 행정부는 일반학생들에게 재정지원을 더 하겠다고 결정하였다. 이번주 행정부는 내년에 35% 필요하다는 근거를 바탕으로 장학생 수를 늘리겠다고 밝혔다.

【정답】 it—The administration

[2] 비록 엘킨스 교수가 최근에 다니엘 부교수와 타일러 교수에게서 도전을 받고 있지만, 그녀는 5년을 한길로 훌륭히 가르쳐온 공로로 황금사과상을 받았다.

【정답】 she—Professor Elkins

[3] 그녀는 종종 자기 어머니 주디 갈렌드에 비유되었으나, 그러나 리자 미넬리 자신은 스스로의 힘으로 스타가 된 것으로 밝혀졌다.

【정답】 She—Liza Minelli

[4] 구명정에 타고 있던 한 여인이 그녀에게 뛰어내리라고 소리를 쳤지만, 배의 난간에 서 있던 그 여자는 자신이 구조될 기회가 전혀 없다고 깨달은 것 같았다.

【정답】 she—the woman standing at the rail of the ship

[5] 듀런이 자신들의 첫 대전에서 레너드에 관해 증명한 한 가지 사실은 그가 벌점을 많이 받을 수 있다는 것이었다.

【정답】 he—Leonard

[6] 그 영화사의 대변인은 최근의 자사 서부서사물의 실패에 대해 기자들과 논의하였다. 회사는 그 영화를 만드는데 비용으로 들인 15,000,000달러 이상 손실을 입을 것이라고 말했다.

【정답】 He—A spokesman of the film company

[7] 크리스 크리스토퍼슨을 주연으로 한 「천국의 문」의 감독인 마이클 키미노는 최근 올해 안에 또 다른 영화를 시작할 것이라고 보고하였다.

【정답】 he—Michael Cimino

[8] 비록 최근 몇 해 더욱 어려운 처지에 놓여 있었지만, 중소 은행들은 자신들 지역사회의 개발방향에 계속해서 영향을 미칠 수 있다.

【정답】 they—small bankers

[9] 위원회는 물품을 구매하기 전에 모든 적용 가능한 법률을 연구할 것을 모든 외국인 투자자들에게 제안했다.

【정답】 they—all foreign investors

[10] 그 농구팀은 시끄러운 지지자들이 없지 않았으나, 그들은 이 열광의 쇼에 좀처럼 반응하지 않았다.

【정답】 they—The basketball team

[Question Type 2]

[11] 그를 처음으로 출판사에 소개한 스콧 핏제럴드는 헤밍웨이가 대립하지 않은 몇 안되는 동시대 작가 중에 한 사람이었다고 말했다.

【정답】 him—Hemingway

[12] 하루는 슈퍼마켓에서 그를 발견하고서, 아처는 황량

한 이웃동네의 한 아파트까지 절뚝거리는 그 남자를 따라 갔다.

【정답】 him – the man with the limp

[13] 그 상(賞)은 위원장에 의해 그 극작가에게 수여되었 는데, 그는 그를 일러 말 그대로 수백만의 관객들과 텔레 비전 시청자들에게 즐거움을 가져다 주었다고 말하였다.

【정답】 him – the playwright

[14] 그녀에게 가서 자동차 열쇠를 얻어오라고 제인이 메리를 설득하고 있는데, 존스부인이 우연히 방문에서 엿 듣고 있다가 재빨리 아래층으로 내려가서는 집을 나갔다.

【정답】 her – Mrs. Jones

[15] 몇 달 만에 처음으로 그녀를 가까이서 보자, 엘리자 베드는 그녀가 정말로 늙어가기 시작했다는 것을 쓸쓸히 깨달았다.

【정답】 her – the woman

[16] 라이언 부인은 저녁에 캘리를 여기 데려와 옷을 골 라주고 싶었기에, 그러리라 마음먹었다.

【정답】 her – Kelly

[17] 그들을 잘 알기 때문에, 해먼드씨 가족은 셰퍼드씨 가족이 그들의 손님을 맞으러 제시간에 나올 것 같지 않 음을 깨달았다.

【정답】 them – the Shepherds

[18] 다이어트 약으로 환자들를 치료하는 의사들은 중독 의 위험성을 그들에게 경고한다.

【정답】 them – patients

[19] 그들을 이해하는 것이 흔히 어렵지만은 않지만, 말 더듬이들은 종종 부모들에게 많은 걱정을 끼치기도 한다.

【정답】 them – stutters

[20] 모든 종류의 곤충에 빠져서, 어린이들은 그것들을

채집하고 연구하느라 시간을 보냈다.

【정답】 them – insects of all kinds

[Question Type 3]

[21] 1977년에 존 스프렉클씨의 옛집이 역사적인 기념 가옥의 지위를 획득하였다. 그 집의 역사는 1908년으로 거슬러 올라가는데, 그때 스펙클씨에 의해 지어졌다.

【정답】 Its – the former home of John D. Speckels

[22] 연중 온화한 기후, 해변, 해양공원 등 때문에 많은 사람들이 매년 샌디애고를 찾는다. 그러나 그곳의 가장 유명한 곳은 아마도 예외적으로 훌륭한 샌디애고 동물원 일 것이다.

【정답】 its – San Diego

[23] 그것의 효용성은 과거의 것이지만, 그의 첫번째 자 전거는 그의 침실 구석에 계속해서 세워져 있었다.

【정답】 Its – his first bicycle

[24] 음악선생님은 최근 새로온 자신의 제자 도나 윈터 가 지금까지 자신이 받아본 학생 중에 가장 위대한 잠재 성을 가졌다고 보고하였다.

【정답】 her – The music teacher

[25] 경제학자인 바바라 워드와 아파트를 함께 쓴 몇 년 의 경험을 근거로 엘리자베드 먼로는 그녀를 이른 아침에 글을 쓰는 비범한 재능을 소유한 작가라고 묘사하였다.

【정답】 her – Elizabeth Monroe

[26] 스턴이 자기 고향 출신의 젊은 변호사와 함께 조직 에 합류하고서 그의 사업은 성장하기 시작하였다.

【정답】 His – Sterne

[27] 500여 종의 갖가지 라일락으로 뒤덮인 자신의 60에 이커의 땅을 가지고 있어서, 메인주 케니분크의 켄 버딘씨 가 어째서 라일락맨으로 알려져 있는지를 쉽게 이해할 수 있다.

【정답】 his – Ken Berdeen

[28] 그들의 이웃인 반투족은 부시맨들이 살아가는 방식에 어떤 영향을 끼치기 시작하였다.

【정답】 Their – the Bushmen

[29] 셰익스피어 연극에서 우리에게 흥미를 주는 것은, 그 극의 플롯보다는 오히려 아이디어와 무엇보다도 그것들이 표현된 방식들이기 때문에, 그 극들을 보고 또 보아도 즐겁다.

【정답】 their – Shakespeare's plays

[30] 피고인들은 그들의 변호사들의 충고를 무시한 채 배심원들의 해임을 주장하였다.

【정답】 their – The defendants

[Question Type 4]

[31] 그녀의 자매들인 도리스와 메이와 함께 진은 카운티 바자회에서 있을 연례 콘테스트용 케익을 구웠다. 진은 자기 것은 안타깝게도 놓쳤지만, 도리스가 참가자격 리본을 따서 기뻤다.

【정답】 hers – Jean, cakes

[32] 댄스교습에 관한 그녀의 논문에서 캐롤린은 마리온 라이스의 교습법을 묘사하고 그녀의 교습법이 이웃의 야심찬 춤꾼들에게 어떤 지방 댄스교사의 그것보다도 더 영향을 미쳤다고 지적하였다.

【정답】 hers – the methods of Marion Rice

[33] 그 비평가는 그녀의 것을 전혀 언급하지 않았지만, 샐리는 그가 메리의 그림에 관해 무엇을 말해야 했는지를 들었을 때, 실망보다는 안도감을 느꼈다.

【정답】 hers – Sally, paintings

[34] 반 클리번은 그들의 콘서트 활동을 막 시작하는 많은 젊은 피아니스트들에게 충고와 격려를 해주었다. 그의 콘서트 활동은 그가 모스크바의 제1회 차이코프스키 경연대회에서 대상을 받았던 1958년에 시작되었다.

【정답】 His – Van Cliburn, concert careers

[35] 피에르 가르뎅은 자신의 관심을 확대하여 식당주인이 되었다. 그의 식당은 1893년에 세워진 유명한 '파리의 맥심'이다.

【정답】 His – Pierre Cardin, a restaurant

[36] 빌은 톰 번의 기사를 읽고 난 후, 같은 주제를 훨씬 더 표면적으로 자세히 다룬 자신의 것이 상(賞)을 받으리라고 그는 확신하였다.

【정답】 his – Bill, article

[37] 자신들의 것이 군중으로부터 좋은 반응을 불러 일으킨 차였기에, 소년클럽의 회원들은 그 차가 겨우 2등을 차지하자 실망하였다.

【정답】 theirs – float, the members of the boy's club

[38] 데이비드와 록사나는 로스와 찰리의 아파트가 매우 호화롭게 꾸며져 있지만, 자신들의 아파트가 전망은 더 좋을 것이라고 생각하였다.

【정답】 theirs – David and Roxanna, apartment

[39] 영국인들은 1415년 에진코트의 전투에서 놀랍게도 프랑스인들을 물리쳤는데, 그것은 그들의 사수들이 더 훈련이 잘된 사수들이었기 때문이었다.

【정답】 theirs – The English, archers

[40] 존은 성공하지도 못한 채 아주 많은 지방 요리대회에 참가하였기에, 그의 요리가 전국대회에서 우승 참가품목이라는 데에 그는 놀랐다.

【정답】 his – John, recipes

[Question Type 5]

[41] 스미스 앤 필립스 연구원은 타일러재단에서 수여하는 2백만 달러 지원금의 수혜자로 지정되었다. 이것은 사마귀 원인 연구를 계속하는 데 사용하기로 되어 있다.

【정답】 This – a grant of two million dollars

[42] 뉴저지의 원예학자들 그룹이 새로운 프로젝트에서 일하고 있다. 이것은 완전히 다른 종류의 장미를 개발하는 것을 포함하고 있다.

【정답】 This—a new project

[43] 매일하는 운동프로그램은 대부분의 사람들에게 수면시간을 줄이는 결과를 낳는다. 이것은 규칙적으로 운동하지 않는 사람들보다 운동을 하는 사람들이 더 숙면을 취한다는 사실에 부분적으로 원인이 있다.

【정답】 This—the need for less sleep

[44] 그는 자기사업의 실패를 술 때문이라고 했다. 그것은 결국 간경화로 병원신세를 지게 된 원인이기도 했다.

【정답】 That—drink

[45] 많은 사람들이 음주를 알코올 중독과 연결짓는다. 그러나 그것이 지나친 과음의 유일한 결과는 결코 아니다.

【정답】 that—drunkenness

[46] 그는 자기들의 신혼여행으로 바하마 군도에 가겠다고 주장하였다. 다행히도, 그것은 그녀가 가고 싶어한 바로 그곳이었다.

【정답】 that—the Bahamas

[47] 많은 뚱뚱한 사람들이 자신들의 상태를 신체 이상 탓으로 돌리지만, 의사들은 이런 것이 결코 비만의 원인은 아니라고 주장한다.

【정답】 these—physical disorder

[48] 펜실바니아에서 복권이 당첨된 뒤, 그녀는 메르스데스 자동차 한 대와 콘도 한 채를 구입하였다. 이것들은 그녀가 이제까지 현금으로 지불할 수 있었던 최초의 두 가지 큰 구매였다.

【정답】 These—a Mercedes and a condominium

[49] 좋은 포도주를 마시고 이태리 음식을 먹는 것이 젊은 시절 그가 가장 즐기던 오락이었다. 나중에 이런 점이 그의 돈을 작은 이태리 식당에 몽땅 투자하도록 하였다.

【정답】 these—his favorite pastimes

[50] 결함 있는 장비가 때때로 롤러스케이팅 사고에 책임이 있다. 그러나 균형의 문제가 대부분의 추락을 일으키는 점들이다.

【정답】 those—problems with balance

[51] 새로운 이주민들이 결정하려고 애썼던 첫번째 것이 국기와 국가로, 그것들은 국가 정체성의 가장 중요한 상징이 되는 것들이다.

【정답】 those—a flag and a national anthem

[52] 오렌지와 보라색이 그해에 유행이었으나, 그것들이 모든 사람들에게 가장 잘 어울리는 색상은 결코 아니었다.

【정답】 those—Orange and purple

[53] 린든 존슨은 1963년에서 1968까지 대통령이었는데, 이때는 베트남전이 처음으로 미국 국민들의 관심이 된 때였다.

【정답】 those—1963 to 1968

[54] 노화의 표시는 피할 수 없다. 그러나 감출 수 있는 것들이 화장품 회사들에는 특별한 관심사이다.

【정답】 those—Signs of aging

[Question Type 6]

[55] 1954년, 로저 배니스터는 처음으로 1마일을 4분에 달렸다. 오늘날 기준으로 보면 이 시간은 엄청나게 느려 보인다.

【정답】 This time—four minutes

[56] 결국 두 과학자는 독자노선을 따르기로 채택하였다. 이 선택은 옳은 것으로 판명되었고, 10년이 지나 그들은

노벨화학상을 수상하였다.

【정답】 This choice – to follow their original line

[57] 그 여객차장은 자신의 기념연회에서 황금시계를 선물받았다. 이 선물은 그가 철도에 봉직한 50년을 기리기 위해서였다.

【정답】 This gift – a gold watch

[58] 많은 교육자들은 학생들이 선생님에게서 공식적으로 설명듣는 것보다 그들이 스스로 학습하는 정보를 더 잘 기억든다는 사실을 이제 믿고 있다. 이 사실은 많은 학급에서 방법론적인 변화를 몰고왔다.

【정답】 This fact – 앞 문장 전체

[59] 의사는 소년의 맹장을 제거하기로 결심하였다. 이 수술은 섬이라는 상황에서 매우 어렵게 이루어졌다.

【정답】 This operation – to take out the boy's appendix

[60] 썬더버드는 50년대 미국에서 가장 인기가 있었던 스포츠카였다. 그러나 그 특별했던 제품이 너무도 변해서 대부분의 미국인들은 이제 더 이상 그 차를 스포츠카로 여기지 않는다.

【정답】 That particular make – The Thunderbird

[61] 다소 내키지 않았지만, 이사벨과 페르디난드는 인도를 찾아나서는 콜럼부스의 항해에 자금을 제공하기로 동의하였다. 그 결정은 지난 수천 년 가운데 아마 가장 중요한 발견으로 이어졌다.

【정답】 That decision – to fund Columbus's voyage in search of Indies.

[62] 알버트 아인슈타인은 어려서 읽고 쓰는 데 느렸다. 그 놀라운 사실은 모든 어린이가 같은 나이에 같은 것을 배워야 할 필요는 없다는 생각에 신뢰를 주었다.

【정답】 That surprising fact – 앞 문장 전체

[63] 웰링턴은 1815년 워털루에서 나폴레옹을 물리쳤다. 그 전투는 한 시대의 종말과 또 다른 시대의 시작을 기록하였다.

【정답】 That battle – Waterloo

[64] 존 케네디는 1963년 11월 22일 치명적으로 총탄을 맞았다. 그 비극은 어느 정도 화려한 시대로 묘사되던 것을 끝냈다.

【정답】 That tragedy – 앞 문장 전체

[65] 곤충들을 보고서 그는 눈을 감고 가만히 신음소리를 냈다. 비록 이런 반응들이 이성적이지 않음을 알고 있었지만, 그는 그것들을 통제할 수가 없었다.

【정답】 these reactions – covered his eyes and moaned softly

[66] 우리 지방의 도서관은 매달 10권 정도의 베스트셀러를 수령한다. 이 책들은 출입구 근처에 있는 특별 서가에 두고 있다.

【정답】 These books – best sellers

[67] 새로운 쇼핑몰의 지도에 식당 5개가 나와 있다. 붉은 글씨로 표시된 이곳들은 업무상 만남이나 사적인 연회 장소로 유용하다.

【정답】 Those facilities – five restaurants

[68] 그는 지나치게 과음과 과식을 하였는데, 그 문제들이 결국 회사의 부사장이 되는 길을 막았다.

【정답】 those problems – He drank and ate to excess

[69] 어릴 때, 그는 테니스와 수영 레슨을 받았고, 스포츠 캠프에서 여름을 보냈으며, 어린이야구연맹에서 활동하였다. 프로 선수로서, 그는 자신의 예의바른 태도는 그런 경험들의 덕분이라고 지적하였다.

【정답】 those experiences – 앞 문장 전체

[Question Type 7]

[70] 가게의 모든 코너마다 모든 종류의 시계들이 있었지만, 존은 결국 그가 처음 보았던 것을 골랐다.

【정답】 one-clock

[71] 방문객들이 뉴욕에 있는 동안 수많은 쇼를 관람했지만, 그것들 중에 정말로 재미있는 것은 하나뿐이었다.

【정답】 one-show

[72] 그 제안들은 위원회의 위원들 간에 충분히 논의되었는데, 그중에 하나만 원안대로 상정되었다.

【정답】 one-proposal

[73] 그랜트, 심킨스와 몇몇 다른 유명작가들의 조각작품들이 개막전에 전시중이다. 그러나 비평가들로부터 호평을 얻은 유일한 작품들은 비교적 알려지지 않은 작가에 의한 것이었다.

【정답】 ones-Sculptures

[74] 문제에 앞서 나오는 지시사항이 학생들로 하여금 자신들이 이해하고 있다고 느끼는 것들에 집중하도록 도와준다는 점을 주목하라.

【정답】 ones-questions

[75] 명백히 이익이 없는 것들을 제거한 후에, 그 위원회 위원들은 심사를 위해 남아있는 신청서들을 통과시켰다.

【정답】 ones-applications

[76] 미국과 유럽의 여행자들은 고고학적인 장소와 해변 휴양지로써 유카탄을 찾는데, 전자로서는 세계에서 가장 다양하고 가장 매력적인 곳이다.

【정답】 the former-archeological sites

[77] 대학원생이나 학부생이나 두 가지 선택에 관심을 가져야 한다. 그러나 비록 후자가 선택될지라도 교과과정이 끝나고 이어지는 두 학기 내에 마쳐야 한다.

【정답】 the latter-alternatives

[78] 로스엔젤레스와 미니에폴리스는 방문객들에게 많은 메이저리그 스포츠행사와 다양한 문화적 볼거리를 제공한다. 그러나 전자의 기후는 1년 내내 매력을 발휘한다.

【정답】 the former-Los Angeles

[79] NASA의 과학자들과 우주비행사들은 앨 셰퍼드의 첫 궤도내 비행과 존 글렌의 궤도여행에 다같이 흥분하였다. 그러나 미국국민들의 관심을 사로잡은 것은 후자였다.

【정답】 the latter-John Glenn's orbital journey

[80] 정부와 개인적인 영역 둘 다 기초와 응용 연구에 자금을 지원하고 있다. 그러나 전자를 위한 지원금은 경제적으로 어려운 시기에는 비교적 제한되는 경향이 있다.

【정답】 the former-basic research

Part 3. 독해기초연습 2

Group 1. 사실적 이유를 묻는 문제

[1] 의복화재는 말 그대로 부엌의 위험이다. 길고 휘날리는 소매는 부엌에서 있을 곳이 없다.—그런 소매는 후라이팬 손잡이에 너무 잘 걸리고, 레인지 버너에 불붙기 쉽고, 일반적으로 거치적거린다. 인화성이 강한 합성섬유가 가장 불안하다. 만약 레인지가 창가에 있다면, 레인지 위로 휘날려 불이 붙을 수 있는 긴 커튼은 피해야 한다.

【정답】 1. C 2. D

[2] 방울뱀이 자기의 존재를 알리는 수단인 이 음향기관은 단단한 껍질이 느슨하게 연결되는 속 빈 고리들로 형성된다. 꼬리를 흔들 때 이것들이 붕붕거리는 소리를 낸다. 어릴 때부터 방울뱀은 그 꼬리의 끝 부분에 있는 단추에서 그 기관들을 형성하기 시작한다. 그래서 매번 껍질을 벗을 때마다 새로운 고리가 형성된다. 보통 사람들은 그 고리를 세면 뱀의 나이를 알 수 있다고 믿지만, 이 생

각은 틀렸다. 사실은 뱀은 1년에 4번이나 껍질(허물)을 벗는다. 또한 방울뱀들은 시간이 지나면서 새로운 피부를 입기도 하고 버리기도 한다.

【정답】1. A 2. C

[3] 윌리엄스버그는 요크와 제임스 두 강 사이에 있는 반도에 자리잡고 있는 버지니아의 역사적인 도시이다. 이 도시는 미국에 영국의 첫 영구식민지가 제임스타운에 정착되고서 26년이 지난 1633년에 영국의 식민지 주민들에 의해 정착이 되었다. 처음에는 윌리엄스버그의 식민지는 반도의 한가운데 위치해 있다고 하여 미들 플랜테이션이라 불렸다. 윌리엄스버그의 위치가 식민지 주민들에게 뽑힌 것은 땅의 배수가 제임스타운 자리보다 그곳이 더 좋았고, 모기도 적었기 때문이었다.

【정답】1. D 2. B

[4] 마리앤 무어는 1887년 세인트루이스에서 태어나서 1909년 브라이언모어 대학을 졸업하였다. 그녀는 몇 년간 속기를 가르쳤고, 그후 뉴욕에서 도서관 사서로 일했다. 1925년에서 1929년까지를 유명한 문학잡지 『다이얼』의 편집직원이었다. 『관찰』이라는 제목의 그녀의 시집이 1924년에 미국에서 출간되었지만, 무어양은 최근에야 유일하게 큰 갈채를 받았다. 받을 만하였다.

【정답】1. B 2. C

[5] 지구의 광범위한 지역이 얼음으로 덮여 있던 빙하시대는 적어도 여섯 번 정도 발생한 것으로 알려져 있다. 과거의 빙하시대는 움직이는 얼음벽이나 녹는 빙하들에 의해 묻혀진 외부물질의 증거를 보여주는 암반층에서 알 수 있다. 또 U자형 계곡, 조각된 풍경, 매끄러운 바위표면 등과 같이 움직이는 얼음벽으로부터 만들어진 육지의 형태에서도 알 수 있다.

【정답】1. C 2. B 3. D

[6] 존 듀이의 철학에서는 지성과 이성 사이에 뚜렷한 차이가 생긴다. 듀이에 따르면, 지성은 유일한 삶의 실용성과 지혜의 관계인, 사실주의와 이상주의의 균형을 이루

는 절대적인 방법이다. 지성은 다른 것들과의 상호작용과 그것들을 아는 것을 포함한다. 반면에 이성은 단지 관찰자의 행위로서, 사물 세계의 밖에 있는 대상을 바라보거나 부여잡는 마음이다. 이성이 있으면 일정 수준의 정신적 확실성이 이루어진다. 그러나 우리의 삶을 형성하는 사건들을 통제하는 것은 지성을 통해서다.

【정답】1. D

[7] 질소고정은 부가적인 질소가 끊임없이 생물학적 순환 속에 공급되는 과정이다. 이 과정에서 어떤 박테리아가 질소를 암모니아로 전환시킨다. 그리고 새로 생성된 이 암모니아는 대부분 식물들에 의해 흡수된다.

반대과정인 탈 질소작용은 질소를 공기 중으로 되돌려 보낸다. 탈 질소작용 과정에는 박테리아가 흙 속의 질산염 일부를 기체상태의 질소나 질소산화물로 변화시키는 원인이 된다. 이 가스형태로 질소는 공기 중으로 돌아간다.

【정답】1. B

[8] 켄터키주 포트녹스는 미 육군부대 주둔지인데, 미국 연방정부 금 보유량의 대부분을 보관하는 대단위 저장소인 '포트녹스 금괴보관처'로 더 유명하다. 1936년에 완성된 보관실은 화강암, 철구조, 콘크리트로 건설된 2층 건물에 들어 있는데, 보관실 자체는 철골과 콘크리트로 만들어졌고, 무게가 20톤이 넘는 문이 있다. 자연히 최신의 보안장치가 포트녹스에 설치되고, 근처 주둔 육군부대는 심도있는 보호를 제공한다.

【정답】1. B 2. C

[9] 광물을 확인하는 한 가지 특징은 한 광물을 다른 광물로 긁어 봄으로써 결정할 수 있는 상대적인 경도이다. 이런 테스트에서 단단한 광물은 약간 부드러운 광물을 긁을 수 있지만, 부드러운 광물은 더 단단한 광물을 긁을 수가 없다. 모스경도 기준은 경도에 따라 광물의 등급을 결정하는 데 쓰인다. 경도 1의 활석에서 경도 10의 다이아몬드에 이르기까지 10가지 광물이 이 기준에 올라 있다. 이 기준에서 보면, 석영(7번)은 장석(6번)보다 단단하기 때문에 긁을 수 있다. 그러나 장석은 석영에다 표시를 할 수가

없다.

【정답】 1. B 2. A

[10] 일반적으로 허리케인은 5월에서 11월까지 북대서양에서 발생한다. 9월이 허리케인 시즌의 절정이다. 아주 드물게는 그곳에서 10월에서부터 이듬해 4월까지 발생하기도 한다. 이 시기에 허리케인이 발생하는 주 요인은 바다표면의 온도가 가장 따뜻하고, 대기 중의 습도가 가장 높다는 것이다.

북대서양에서 매년 발생하는 열대성 태풍 가운데, 평균 5개 정도만이 허리케인이라 할 수 있을 정도로 강하다. 허리케인이라고 분류되려면, 열대성 폭풍이 적어도 시속 117 킬로미터에 이르는 풍속의 바람을 가져야 한다. 그러나 흔히 바람은 그보다 더 강하다. 강력한 허리케인의 바람은 시속 240 킬로미터를 쉽게 넘어간다.

【정답】 1. D 2. B

[11] 인간의 심장은 4개의 방으로 나뉘어져 있다. 혈액을 펌프질하는 주기에 따라 각각의 기능을 수행한다. 심방은 위쪽에 있는 벽이 얇은 방으로, 심장 박동 사이사이 혈관에서 흘러나오는 피를 모아 담는다. 심실은 아래쪽에 있는 두꺼운 벽의 방으로, 심방으로부터 피를 받아 매번 심장이 수축할 때, 동맥으로 밀어 넣는다. 좌심방과 좌심실은 오른쪽의 것들과 따로 작동한다. 심장의 오른쪽에 있는 방들의 역할은 신체조직으로부터 산소가 고갈된 피를 받아 허파로 보내는 것인 한편, 심장의 왼쪽에 있는 방들은 허파로부터 산소가 풍부한 피를 받아 신체조직으로 돌려보낸다.

【정답】 1. B 2. A 3. C

[12] 철도의 황금시대란 철도가 번성하여 미국의 대중교통에서 사실상 거의 독점을 유지한 남북전쟁이 끝나고부터 제1차 세계대전이 시작될 때까지의 기간을 말한다. 이 기간의 중요한 발전 가운데 하나는 획일성의 현저한 성장이었다. 특히 선로 폭과 시간의 표준화를 통해서였다.

남북전쟁 말기에는 미국철도의 약 절반만이 1.4미터의 현재의 선로 폭으로 깔렸고, 나머지 많은 곳, 특히 남부의 주에서는 1.5미터의 선로를 가지고 있었다. 전쟁이 끝난 뒤 몇 년 간 트랙은 1.4미터 선로로 바뀌었고, 1886년 6월 1일까지는 트랙의 표준화가 완성되어 철도체계의 효율성과 경제성이 향상된 결과를 낳았다.

철도 효율성의 또 다른 이점은 1883년에 표준시각의 시작이었다. 표준시 채택으로서 4개 시간권역이 전국에 확립되었고, 철도시간표를 단순화하고 철도서비스의 경제성을 향상시키게 되었다.

【정답】 1. C 2. B 3. D

[13] 지금은 유명한 링컨의 게티스버그 연설이 발표 당시에는 오늘날과 같이 걸작으로 인식되지 않았다. 심지어 링컨은 1863년 남북전쟁이 절정일 때, 게티스버그 전장에 헌정하는 그 행사에 기조 연설자가 아니었다. 기조 연설자는 연설가 에드워드 에버레트로서 링컨의 짧은 소견은 그의 2시간 연설 뒤에 이어진 것이었다. 링컨은 오늘날 대부분의 미국인들이 즉시 알 수 있는 다음의 말로 자기에게 할당된 짧은 행사시간을 시작했다. "87년 전 우리의 조상들은 이 대륙 위에 자유를 이념으로 품은 나라, 모든 인간이 평등하게 창조되었다는 명제를 헌정 받은 새 나라를 탄생시켰습니다." 연설을 할 당시에는, 링컨이 한 말에 거의 관심이 주어지지 않았고, 링컨도 자신이 행사에 참석한 것이 그렇게 성공적이지는 않았다고 생각하였다. 오늘날 그 연설이 모든 시대를 통틀어 가장 위대한 연설의 반열에 놓이는 상승 인지도를 얻기 시작한 것은 그 연설이 출간되어 등장한 이후였다.

【정답】 1. C 2. B 3. A

[14] hay fever는 꽃가루에 대한 계절적인 알레르기이다. 그러나, 이 알레르기의 침투가 발열의 원인이 되는 것도 아니고, 또 그런 발병이 꽃가루를 생산하는 풀보다는 다른 식물에서 생길 수 있기 때문에 hay fever(건초 알레르기)라는 용어는 적절한 묘사라기엔 부족하다. hay fever는 흔히 바람에 날리는 꽃가루, 특히 돼지풀 꽃가루가 원인이 된다. 공기 중의 꽃가루 양은 크게 지리적 위치와 날씨, 계절에 따라 결정된다. 예를 들어, 미국 동부에서는 일반적으로 여러 식물에서 생긴 꽃가루에 의해 심한 알레르기 고통을 일으키는 세 번의 시기가 있는데, 나무에서 생긴 꽃가루가 널리 퍼지는 3 · 4월의 봄, 들풀 꽃가

루가 공기 가운데 퍼지는 6 · 7월의 하절기, 돼지풀 꽃가루가 가장 농도 짙게 퍼지는 8월 말이다.

【정답】 1. B 2. C 3. D

[15] 대륙이동설에 따르면, 대륙들은 제자리에 고정되어 있지 않고, 대신 지구표면을 천천히 움직여 서로서로 상대적인 위치가 끊임없이 변하고 있다. 이 이론은 지도제작자들이 지구의 대륙들을 서로 끼워 맞췄을 때 얼마나 딱 맞게 떨어지는지를 발견한 18세기에 처음 제기되었다. 오늘날의 대륙들은 한때 하나의 커다란 대륙이었던 것이 여러 개로 쪼개져서 따로 떨어졌다는 제안이었다.

오늘날 지각표층 구조학 이론은 대륙이동설에서 발전하였다. 표층구조학 이론은 지구표면이 여섯 개의 대륙과 많은 작은 암반으로 나뉘어진다고 한다. 이 암반들은 지구의 내부 핵을 구성하고 있는 용암 위에 떠있다. 이 암반들은 대양 바닥과 대륙으로 구성되어 있는데, 2억년 전부터 서로 쪼개지고 이동하기 시작했을 것이다.

【정답】 1. C 2. B 3. D 4. D

Group 2. 추론적 이해를 묻는 문제

[1] 메논교회 가운데 가장 보수적인 교파는 암만종파로서, 33,000명의 회원들이 오늘날 주로 펜실바니아, 오하이오, 인디애나 주 등지에 살고 있다. 그들의 생활양식은 세상과의 분리와 생활의 단순성을 교리로 하는 믿음을 반영하고 있다. 그들은 300년 전에 일어난 사회변화를 단호히 거부하고, 대신 17세기 생활양식에 근거하여 안전하게 남아 있기를 택하였다. 라디오, 텔레비전, 전화, 전등, 자동차도 없이 산다. 소박한 스타일과 색깔에 옛날식 옷을 입는다. 현대식 농사장비 대신에 말이나 연장으로 땅을 경작한다. 그들은 평범한 활동으로 헛간 상량식이나 누비이불 모임 등 매우 공동체적인 삶의 형태를 가지고 있다.

【정답】 1. A 2. D

[2] 많은 종의 조류들이 현대인들에 의해 의심의 여지없이 가속적으로 멸종되고 있다. 1600년 이래 전세계적으로 대략 100여 종의 조류들이 멸종되고 있는 것으로 평가

되었다. 북미에서 처음 멸종된 것으로 알려진 새는 19세기 초까지만 해도 대서양 어민들의 식량과 미끼의 손쉬운 원천으로 역할을 해온 날지 못하는 새, 바다쇠오리였다.

바다쇠오리가 멸종된 후 곧, 두 종의 북미 종인 캐롤라인 앵무새와 여행비둘기가 수적으로 눈에 띄게 멸종해가기 시작하였다. 최후의 캐롤라인 앵무새와 여행비둘기가 1914년 9월에 보호상태에서 죽었다. 이 멸종된 종족 외에도, 흰머리수리, 송골매, 캐롤라인 콘도르 같은 몇 종이 오늘날 위태로운 상태인 것으로 알려져 있다. 그들의 멸종을 막으려는 조치가 진행되고 있다.

【정답】 1. C 2. B 3. A

[3] 미국인들이 흔히 남부와 북부의 경계가 된다고 생각하는 메이슨―딕슨라인은 실제로는 메릴랜드와 웨스트버지니아 일부지방으로부터 펜실바니아 주를 구별하는 주경계이다. 남북전쟁 전에 펜실바니아의 이 남쪽경계선은 남부노예주와 북부 노예폐지주를 분리해 주었다.

메이슨―딕슨라인은 남북전쟁이 일어나기 전에 펜실바니아와 메릴랜드의 주경계분쟁 결과로 생겼다. 두 영국인 천문학자 찰스메이슨과 제르미야딕슨이 그 지역을 조사하기 위해 초빙되어 두 주 사이의 경계를 공식적으로 표시해주었다. 그 조사는 1767년에 끝나고, 주경계는 돌로 표시되었다.

【정답】 1. D 2. B 3. A 4. A

[4] 조울증은 주로 감정에 영향을 미치는 또 다른 정신의학적 질병이다. 이 질병을 앓고 있는 환자는 일정 기간 흥분증세와 극도의 우울증의 사이를 번갈아가며, 비교적 정상적인 주기로 또는 비정상적인 주기로 왔다갔다 한다. 조울증 환자가 겪는 감정의 변화는 일반인들이 경험하는 매일의 감정변화를 훨씬 넘어간다. 흥분증세를 보이는 기간에 감정상승은 아주 심해서 광범위한 불면증, 극도의 과민성, 상승된 공격성 등의 결과를 낳을 수도 있다. 우울증의 기간은 몇 주일 또는 몇 달간 지속되는데, 환자는 일반적인 피로감, 무력감, 절망감 등을 경험하고, 심한 경우에는 자살을 생각할 수도 있다.

【정답】 1. B 2. A 3. B 4. C

[5] 과학 대중화의 도구역할을 한 또 다른 프로그램은 「코스모스」였다. 공영 텔레비전에 방송된, 이 시리즈는 과학의 여러 분야의 주제와 쟁점을 다루었다. 그 프로그램의 주요 작가이자 나레이터는 유명한 천문학자이자 퓰리처상 수상 작가인 칼 세이건이었다.

【정답】 1. A

[6] 1960년 미국 대통령 선거운동은 공화당과 민주당 간의 경쟁에서 정치적으로 혁신적이며 대단한 영향력을 미친 TV토론 시리즈를 특징으로 한다. 상원의원이던 존 케네디는 민주당 예비주자들 가운데 일찌감치 선두에 섰고, 로스앤젤레스 전당대회에서의 첫 투표에서 대통령선거의 민주당 대표자로 지명되었다. 당시 아이젠하워 대통령 아래서 부통령직을 수행하고 있던 리차드 닉슨은 공화당의 지명을 받았다. 닉슨과 케네디 두 사람 모두 전국에 걸쳐 활발하게 운동을 하였고, 텔레비전의 직접토론에 모습을 나타내는 전례 없는 진보를 하였다. 정치전문가들은 그 토론이 선거에 결정적인 영향력이 되었다고 주장한다. 1억이 넘는 시청자들 앞에서 케네디는 잘 알려지고 경험이 풍부한 후보라는 닉슨의 이점을 훌륭하게 극복하였고, 대통령직을 수행하기에는 경험이 너무 부족하고 성숙하지 못하다는 그에 대한 대중인식을 뒤집었다.

【정답】 1. B 2. B 3. D 4. A

[7] 20세기 미국음악에서 눈에 띄는 또 다른 경향은 더 진지한 작곡을 위한 어떤 기초로 민속음악과 팝음악을 이용해왔다는 것이다. 전통적인 소재에서 이렇게 차용한 동기는 좀더 단순한 형식으로 돌아가고자, 애국적인 감정을 고양하고자, 청중들과 신속하게 공감대를 수립하고자 하는 작곡가 측의 욕구일 수 있다. 이유야 어떻든, 찰스 아이브스, 아론 코플랜드 등의 작곡가들은 미국의 전통적인 후렴구들의 취향을 풍기는 새로운 음악형식의 곡들을 내놓았다. 아이브스는 작곡을 할 때, 애국가와 찬송가, 재즈, 팝송 등을 활용하였고, 반면에 코플랜드는 특별히 자신의 발레곡 「꼬마 빌리」 「로데오」 「아팔라치아의 봄」 등의 소재로 민속음악을 이용하였다.

【정답】 1. B 2. A 3. C 4. D 5. C

Group 3. 종합적 판단을 묻는 문제

[1] 군사포상은 오랫동안 충성의 상징으로 여겨왔으나, 미국이 막 혁명을 끝낸 젊은 국가로서 군주제의 냄새가 나는 것으로부터 거리를 두었을 때는 군사적인 장식에 대한 강한 거부감이 있었다. 독립전쟁 말기부터 남북전쟁 때까지 1세기 동안 미국은 어떤 군사훈장도 수여하지 않았다. 1861년에 훈장기관이 대단한 논의와 관심의 대상이 되었다. 남북전쟁에서 1차 세계대전까지 훈장이라고는 미국정부에서 수여된 군사포상뿐이었고, 오늘날에도 지극히 영웅적인 경우에만 수여된다. 비록 미국이 아직 군사포상 수여를 다소 경계하고 있지만, 1차 세계대전 이후에 몇 차례의 수상이 실시되어 왔다.

【정답】 1. D 2. B 3. C

[2] *In Cold Blood*(1966)은 논픽션 소설의 유명한 표본이다. 사실에 입각한 사건을 기초로 쓰는 최근에 유행하는 형태로서 저자는 실제 사건으로 이끌어가는 기초적인 힘과 생각, 감정 등을 묘사하려고 한다. 트루먼 카포티의 책에서 저자는 캔사스 농장에 사는 한 가족의 가학적인 살해를 살인자의 관점에서 묘사하고 있다. 책을 연구하기 위해 카포티는 살인자들을 인터뷰하였고 자신의 책이 사건의 충실한 재건을 보여준다고 그는 주장한다.

【정답】 1. A 2. D

[3] 지금까지 최면상태에서 피고로부터 얻어진 자백은 미국의 법원에서 증거로 받아들여지지 않았다. 최면분야의 전문가들은 그런 자백이 완전히 신뢰할 수 있는 것이 아니라는 사실을 발견하였다. 최면상태의 조사 대상자들은 두 가지 이유 중 하나 때문에 자기들이 저지르지 않은 범죄를 자백할 수가 있다. 자신들이 그 범죄를 저질렀다고 상상하거나 또는 자기들이 자백하기를 다른 사람들이 원한다고 믿는 것이다.

최면상태에서 얻어진 자백에 관련된 획기적인 사건이 모처럼 연방대법원까지 갔다. '레이라 대 디노' 사건에서 혐의자는 지방검사를 위해서 정신과의사에 의해 최면에 걸렸다. 그리고 최면 후의 상태에서 그 혐의자는 살인에 대한 3가지 자백에 서명하였다. 그것들을 얻기 위해 사용된 정신적인 협박 때문에 그 자백들은 부당하다고 대법원이 판결하였다. 그 자백들이 그 혐의자에게 불리한 유일한 증거였기 때문에 그는 바로 석방되었다.

【정답】 1. D 2. D

[4] 세계의 산림채벌이 진행되는 비율은 놀랄 정도이다. 1950년에는 지구 육지표면의 약 25%가 산림으로 덮여 있었는데, 25년이 지나서는 삼림의 양이 20%까지 줄었다. 1950년에서 1973년까지 25%에서 20%로 감소된 것은 2천만 평방 킬로미터의 삼림을 잃는 놀라운 손실을 보여준다. 2020년까지는 육지산림의 2천만 평방 킬로미터를 더 잃을 것이라는 예측들이 있다.

산림채벌의 대부분은 개발도상국의 열대림에서 발생하는데, 이는 증가한 농업용지를 위한 개발도상국들의 요구와, 목재나 목재품을 수입하려는 선진국들 쪽의 욕구를 충족시키게 된다. 예를 들어, 미국에서 소비되는 합판의 90% 이상이 열대림을 가지고 있는 개발도상국들로부터 수입된다. 1980년대 중반까지는 열대림의 이용을 감시하기 위한 국제적인 규제기구를 설립하려는 시도의 형태로, 확대되는 이 문제에 대한 해답들을 찾고 있을 것이다.

【정답】 1. C 2. A 3. B

[5] 방울뱀은 인간에게는 지독히도 혐오스러운, 위험하고도 치명적인 뱀이라는 명성을 지니고 있다. 비록 방울뱀이 실제로 인간을 죽일 수 있는 유독성 뱀이지만, 그 본성이 신화나 민속에서는 다소 과장되어온 것 같다.

방울뱀은 본래 공격적이지 않고 일반적으로 방어를 취할 때만 공격한다. 방어자세에서 방울뱀은 몸체의 앞부분을 땅에서 들어올려서 앞으로 찌르기 위한 준비자세로 S자 모양을 취한다. 정면을 찌른 끝에, 방울뱀은 독니를 적에게 찔러 넣고 독을 주사한다.

방울뱀의 종류는 30가지가 넘는데, 20인치에서 6피트까지의 길이와 독성에 따라 다양하다. 미국에서는 방울뱀에 물려 죽는 경우가 아주 적은데, 물린자들의 사망률이 2%도 안된다.

【정답】 1. A 2. D 3. C 4. B

[6] 1933년에 미국에서 대단위 금융위기가 일어났다. 2년 전에 많은 은행들이 도산했고, 예금을 잃게 될 두려움이 많은 예금주들을 자극하여 은행에서 자신들의 자금을 빼내게 하였다. 문제는 미시건 주에서 더욱 심각하였는데, 주지사인 윌리엄 컴스톡이 1933년 2월 14일자로 주의 모든 은행활동에서 지불중지를 선언하기에 이른다. 미시건 주의 금융공황은 재빨리 다른 주에 퍼졌고, 3월 6일까지는 프랭클린 루스벨트 대통령이 미국전역에 예금지불중지를 선언하였고, 전국이 은행활동을 하지 않은 채 남아 있었다. 의회는 금융위기를 해결하기 위해 즉시 특별회기를 열었고, 3월 9일에는 재무구조가 건강한 은행들이 업무재개를 할 수 있도록 지원하는 1933년 비상금융조례를 통과시켰다. 3월15일까지는 전국재정비축의 90%를 관리하는 은행들이 사업을 재개하였다.

【정답】 1. A 2. C 3. D 4. C

Part 4 독해종합연습

Step 1

[1] 성적표는 매 학기가 끝날 때 학생에게 우송된다. 학생부라는 이 누계기록이 전학증명이나 확인목적으로는 적당하지 않다. 추가되는 학생부 사본은 매 3달러에 발급 받을 수 있다.

a grade repórt : 성적표 seméster [siméstər] *n.* 학기, 특히 2학기제의 학기를 말한다. cúmulative [kjú:mjəleitv] *adj.* 누적되는, 점증하는(*cf.* cúmulate [kjú:mjəlit] *v.* 축적하다) student copy : 학생부 válid [vǽlid] *adj.* 타당한 transfér [trænsfɚ:r] *n.* 이송, 전출, 전학(증명서) certificátion púrpose : 확인목적 addítional [ədíʃənəl] *adj.* 추가되는, 가외의

이 단락은 사실 나열식의 글이다. 핵심어 : student copy

1. 문제의 핵심어 : receive his grades, how
   본문의 정답찾기 : 1행('A grade report is mailed …')
2. 문제의 핵심어 : student's copy
   본문의 정답찾기 : 2~3행(' … "student copy," is not valid for ….')
3. 본문의 정답찾기 : 첫 문장(' … at the end of each semester.')
4. 글의 종류, 용도를 묻고 있다.

【정답】 1. A 2. D 3. B 4. C

[2] 로봇이 미래에 어떤 중요한 위치를 차지하려면, 달빛 특급이라고 불리는 '마이크로마우스'에 작은 감사라도 표해야 할 것이다. 마이크로마우스는 미로를 통해 길을 '감지'하고 두 번 지나간 후에는 정확한 길을 기억할 수 있는 로봇 쥐다. 미로를 세번째 달릴 때는, 달빛특급은 벽에 부딪치지 않고 길을 잘못 드는 일도 없이 처음부터 끝까지 기어갈 수 있다.

prominent [prámənənt] *adj.* 탁월한, 출중한 a prominent place : 중요한 위치 owe [ou] *v.* 빚지다 gratitude [grǽtətjuːd] *n.* 감사 moonlight special : 달빛특급 rodent [róudənt] *n.* 쥐 maze [meiz] *n.* 미로 path [pæθ] *n.* 길, 통로 crawl [krɔːl] *v.* 기어가다 bump into ~ : ~에 부딪히다 make a (wrong) turn : 방향을 (잘못) 잡다

주제문 : 첫 문장 핵심어 : micromouse, a robot rodent

1. 문제의 핵심어 : Moonlight Special
   본문의 정답찾기 : 3~4행
2. 문제의 핵심어 : micromouse can do
   본문의 정답찾기 : 셋째 문장('can feel … and memorize …')
3. 문제의 핵심어 : after two runs through a maze
   본문의 정답찾기 : 4~6행

【정답】 1. C 2. A 3. D

[3] 학습과 기억에 관한 연구를 할 때는 오징어보다 문어가 더 흥미로운 소재이다. 맛있는 물고기나 게가 있는 곳으로 안내하는데 오로지 눈에만 의존하여 자유롭게 헤엄치는 오징어와는 달리, 문어는 해저의 바닥에서 먹이를 먹는다. 문어는 먹이를 확인하기 위하여 눈만 아니라 촉수도 사용한다. 문어의 두뇌는 두 가지 다른 기억 저장영역을 가지고 있는데, 하나는 시각기억이고 하나는 촉감기억이다.

octopus [áktəpəs] *n.* 문어 squid [skwid] *n.* 오징어 rely on ~ : ~에 의존하다 a tasty fish : 맛있는 물고기 crab [kræb] *n.* 게 tentacle [téntəkəl] *n.* 촉수 storage area : 저장영역 visual memories : 시각기억 tactile memories : 촉감기억

주제문 : 첫 문장 핵심어 : octopus

1. 문제의 핵심어 : the squid find its food
   본문의 정답찾기 : 2~4행(Unlike the free swimming squid, which relies exclusively on its eyes to guide it to a tasty fish or crab, octopus …)
2. 본문의 정답찾기 : 주제나 요지는 글의 첫 문장을 읽으면 보인다.(1~2행)
3. 문제의 핵심어 : can describe the octopus
   본문의 정답찾기 : octopus를 찾아 해당 문장을 읽는다.(4~7행)

【정답】 1. A 2. B 3. D

[4] 경제팽창은 5월에도 계속되었다. 정부의 발표는 산업생산, 개인소득, 주택건설시공에서 이익을 남겨주었다. 그러나 주택건설은 부진한 상태로 있었다. 주로 새로운 가정의 비용이 평균소득보다 훨씬 더 빨리 상승했기 때문인데, 그래도 주택시공은 4월보다 작은 상승을 보여주었다.

expansion [ikspǽnʃən] *n.* 팽창, 확대 gain [gein] *n.* 이익, 취득 housing starts : 주택건설 시공 sluggish [slʌ́giʃ] *adj.* 부진한, 활기없는

주제문 : 첫 문장 핵심어 : economic expansion

1. 문제의 핵심어 : economic expansion
   본문의 정답찾기 : 둘째 문장(Government reports shows …)
2. 문제의 핵심어 : housing starts
   본문의 정답찾기 : 5~6행(but housing starts did show a small increase over those of April.)
3. 문제의 핵심어 : housing construction is recovering slowly because
   본문의 정답찾기 : 3~5행(Housing construction, however, remained sluggish, mainly because the cost of new homes has risen much faster than average incomes)

【정답】 1. A 2. C 3. C

[5] 어떤 특정한 일을 할 수 있는 능력과 그 일에 대한 실행이 반드시 병행하는 것이 아님은 상식이다. 간혹 훌륭한 잠재력을 가진 사람들이 게으름이나 그 일에 대한 흥미부족 때문에 간혹 일에 실패한다. 반면에 평범한 재주를 가진 사람들이 노력과 고용주들의 이익에 대한 충성심을 통해서 간혹 훌륭한 결과를 성취한다. 그러므로 직원에 대한 최종 테스트는 일에 대한 그의 실행력임이 명백하다.

cómmon knówledge : 상식(= cómmon sénse) performance on the job : 그 일에 대한 실천력 not always : 언제나 ~하지는 않는다 go hand in hand : 병행하다, 같이 가다 poténtial [pouténʃəl] *adj.* 잠재하는(= latent), 가능한 fall down on ~ : ~에 실패하다(= fail in) lack of ~ : ~의 부족 índustry [índəstri] *n.* 근면, 노력 ínterests : 이익

주제문 : 첫 문장 결론문 : 마지막 문장
핵심어 : performance on the job

1. 문제의 핵심어 : The most accurate statement
   본문의 정답찾기 : 주제문과 결론문을 읽고 추론할 수 있다.
2. 문제의 핵심어 : The employee of most value
   본문의 정답찾기 : 2~6행 (서술문)
3. 문제의 핵심어 : an employee's efficiency
   본문의 정답찾기 : 마지막 문장(It is clear, therefore, that the final test of any employee is his performance on the job.)

【정답】 1. B 2. C 3. B

[6] 대부분의 학생들은 자기 선생님들이 인간적인 약점을 지닌 인간이라는 것을 믿으려하지 않는다. 그러나 학생이 어떤 선생님을 잘 알게 되면, 그는 반드시 이 권위적인 인물이 많은 종류의 결점과 나쁜 습관—과음에서부터 약속에 늦는 것까지—을 가지고 있다는 사실을 발견하게 된다. 그의 사무실은 깔끔하지 못하거나, 그의 자녀들이 버릇없기도 하고, 심지어 소득세 납부에 관하여 거짓말을 하기도 한다. 간단히 말해서, 이 증거들은 선생님들이 학생들과 똑같은 인간이라는 사실을 말해주고 있다.

be unwilling to do :~하기를 꺼린다 húman wéakness : 인간적인 약점 get to know : 알게되다 inváriably : 반드시, 언제나 authority fígure : 권위적인 인물 posséss [pəzés] *v.* 소유하다(= have) flaw [flɔː] *n.* 결함(= weakness) untídy [ʌntáidi] *adj.* 깔끔하지 못한 íll-mánnered : 버릇없는 íncome tax retúrn : 소득세 납부 in short : 간단히 말해서 just as ~ as … : …처럼 꼭 같이 ~한

주제문 : 첫 문장 핵심어 : teachers, human beings, human weaknesses

1. 문제의 핵심어 : students think
   본문의 정답찾기 : 첫 문장, 1~2행
2. 문제의 핵심어 : The passage states
   본문의 정답찾기 : 마지막 문장(In short, the evidence suggests that …)

【정답】 1. C 2. D

[7] 유행성독감 바이러스는 수백만 개의 개별 원자들로 구성된 단일 분자생물이다. 박테리아가 유독성 물질들을 그들이 공격하는 유기물체 속에 숨기는 식물의 한 형태로 여겨지는 반면에, 유행성독감 바이러스와 같은 바이러스들은 그 스스로 살아있는 유기체이다. 그것들이 엄격히 규정된 원자구조들을 가지고 있기 때문에, 우리는 그것들은 규칙적인 화학적 분자라고 생각할 수도 있다. 그러나 한편, 그것들이 무한한 양으로 증식할 수 있기 때문에 우리는 그것들을 살아있다고도 생각해야 한다.

influénza [influénzə] *n.* 유행성 독감 mólecule [máləkjuːl] *n.* 분자 compósed of ~ : ~로 구성되다 átom [ǽtəm] *n.* 원자 secrete ~ into … : ~을 …에 숨기다 póisonous súbstance : 유독성 물질 body of the organism (that) thay attack : 그들이 공격하는 유기체 on the other hand : 한편 múltiply [mʌ́ltəplai] *v.* 증식하다, 곱하다 unlímited quántities : 무한한 양으로

주제문 : 첫 문장 핵심어 : virus, molecule, atom

1. 문제의 핵심어 : bacteria
   본문의 정답찾기 : 2~4행
2. 문제의 핵심어 : Viruses are alike because …
   본문의 정답찾기 : 5~8행
3. 문제의 핵심어 : atomic structures of virus
   본문의 정답찾기 : 5~6행

【정답】 1. D 2. C 3. B

[8] 인격은 인간에 대한 존경이며, 경험을 다르게 해석할 수 있는 권리이다. 인격은 이기심을 천부적인 특징으로 인정하지만, 그러나 인간은 비록 망설이긴 하지만 고무적인 협동본능에 신뢰를 두고 있다. 인격은 폭정을 싫어하고, 무지를 참지 못하며, 늘 개선을 지향한다. 인격은 마음껏 웃고, 부끄럼 없이 눈물을 흘릴 수 있는 능력을 내포한다. 더구나, 인격은 사실 앞의 엄청난 겸손으로써, 그 진실이 쓴 약이 될 때라도 진리와 금방 동맹을 맺는다.

cháracter [kǽriktər] *n.* 인격(= personálity) respéct [rispékt] *n.* 존경 intérpret [intɔ́ːrprit] *v.* 해석하다 sélf-ínterest : 이기심, 이기주의 a nátural trait : 천부적인 특성 hésitant but héartening ínstinct to coóperate : 망설이지만 고무적인 협동본능 allérgic to ~ : ~에 신경과민을 보이는, 싫어하는 týranny [tírəni] *n.* 폭정, 전제정치 írritable [írətəbəl] *adj.* 화를 잘 내는 írritable with ígnorance

: 무지를 참지 못하는 open to impróvement : 개선의 여지가 있는 implý [implái] v. 내포하다, 암시하다 whole-héartedly : 마음껏, 온 마음으로 weep [wi:p] v. 울다, 눈물을 흘리다 unashámedly [ʌnəʃéimdli] adv. 부끄러워하지 않고 treméndous humílity : 엄청난 겸손 an automátic allíance : 자동적인 동맹 bítter médicine : 쓴 약

주제문 : 첫 문장   핵심어 : character

1. 문제의 핵심어 : title
   본문의 정답찾기 : 첫 문장(주제문)을 읽으면 제목을 알 수 있다. 인격의 정의이다.
3. 문제의 핵심어 : the man of character
   본문의 정답찾기 : 2~6행(서술문인 둘째 문장부터 하나 씩 살핀다.)

【정답】 1. D 2. D 3. C

[9] 미국에 있는 대부분의 대학이 비록 가을과 봄에 수업이 진행되는 2학기 제도이지만, 일부 학교는 가을, 겨울, 봄, 여름 분기로 구성되는 4학기제를 시행하고 있다. 9월에서 6월까지의 학년도는 각각 9월, 1월, 3월에 시작하는 11주의 3학기로 나뉘어져 있다. 6월에서 8월까지의 여름 학기는 다양한 기간의 짧은 학기로 구성되어 있다. 학생들은 전체 4학기에 등록을 함으로써 1년 내내 공부하는 기회로 이용할 수 있다. 대부분의 학생들은 가을학기에 수업을 시작하지만, 다른 학기가 시작될 때 들어갈 수도 있다.

a seméster sýstem : 2학기제 óffer [ɔ́fər] v. 주다 (= províde) obsérve [əbzɔ́:rv] v. 시행하다, 관찰하다 a quárter sýstem : 4학기제 quárter [kwɔ́:rtər] n. 분기, 학기 comprísed of ~ : ~로 구성되다 (= compósed of) acádemic year : 학년도 be divíded into ~ : ~로 나뉘다 séssion [séʃən] n. 학기, 회기 váring : 다양한 (= changing) length : 길이(cf. long take advántage of~ : ~을 이용하다) opportúnity [ɑpərtjú:nəti] n. 기회 (= chance) year round : 1년 내내, 연중 enróll in~ : ~에 등록하다

주제문 : 첫 문장   핵심어 : a quarter system

1. 문제의 핵심어 : academic year
   본문의 정답찾기 : 4~5행
2. 문제의 핵심어 : semester system
   본문의 정답찾기 : 2행
3. 문제의 핵심어 : title
   본문의 정답찾기 : 첫 문장 또는 핵심어

【정답】 1. D 2. D 3. C

[10] 플루타크는 위대한 목적을 위해 인생을 사용하고, 거기서부터 크게 출발할 수 있었던 사람들을 좋아하였다. 그러나 그 위대함을 손상하는 결함이나 악행을 간과하지 않았다. 그의 영웅 중의 영웅은 알렉산더 대왕이었다. 그는 어떤 사람보다도 알렉산더를 좋아하였다. 반면에, 그의 혐오 중의 혐오는 그릇된 신념, 명예롭지 못한 행위였다. 그럼에도 불구하고 그는 어떻게 알렉산더가 용감한 페르시아 군대에게 그들이 항복할 경우, 안전한 인도를 약속하고도, "심지어 그들이 행군을 할 때, 그가 그들을 쓰러뜨려 학살하였는지"를 전혀 경감하려는 의도없이 말한다. 플루타크는 "약속위반은 그의 업적에 길이 남을 오점이다"라고 슬프게 말한다. 그는 애처롭게 덧붙였다. "그러나 그것 하나뿐이다." 그는 그 이야기를 말하기 싫어하였다.

grand púrpose : 위대한 목적 pass over : 간과하다, 무시하다 vice [vais] n. 악(opp. vírtue [vɔ́:rtʃu:] n. 덕) mar [ma:r] v. 손상시키다 the grándeur : 위대성 abominátion [əbɑmənéiʃən] n. 혐오 bad faith : 그릇된 신념 dishónorable [disánərəbəl] adj. 불명예스런 exténuate[iksténjueit] v. 경감하다 cónduct [kándʌkt] n. 처신, 인도, 안내 a safe cónduct : 안전한 인도 surrénder [sərénder] v. 항복하다 fall upon : 쓰러뜨리다 put (them all) to the sword : (그들 모두)를 베어죽이다, 처형하다, 학살하다 breach [bri:tʃ] n. 위반, 파기 a breach of his word : 약속위반 a lásting blémish : 길이 남을 오점 píteously[pítiəsli] adj. 애처롭게

주제문 : 첫 문장   핵심어 : Plutarch, grand purposes, weakness and vices, Alexander

1. 문제의 핵심어 : Plutarch feel about Alexander
   본문의 정답찾기 : 1~5행
2. 문제의 핵심어 : Plutarch hate, human failure
   본문의 정답찾기 : 3~5행
3. 문제의 핵심어 : Plutarch, Alexanders's treatment of the Persians
   본문의 정답찾기 : 5~11행, 특히 마지막 문장

【정답】 1. B 2. A 3. C

[11] 흔히 강우량으로 일컬어지는 강수량은 비, 우박, 눈의 형태로 지상에 도착하는 물의 양의 측정치이다. 미국 전역의 연평균 강수량은 36인치이다. 그러나, 눈 1피트가 강수량 1피트와 동일하지 않다는 사실을 이해해야 한다. 강설량을 계산하는 일반적인 공식은 눈 38인치가 강수량 1인치와 같다. 예를 들어, 뉴욕에서 1년에 눈이 76

인치 내리면 강수량 2인치로만 기록된다. 비 40인치는 강수량 40인치로 기록된다. 연간 총 강수량은 42인치로 기록된다.

precipitátion [prisipətéiʃən] *n.* 강수량 ráinfall : 강우 referréd to ~ : ~로 일컬어지는 méasure [méʒər] *n.* 측정 quántity [kwántəti] *n.* 양(*opp.* quálity [kwáləti] *n.* 질) hail [heil] *n.* 싸락눈, 우박 fórmula [fɔ́ːrmjələ] *n.* 공식 compúting [kəmpjúːtiŋ] *n.* 계산, 산정 snówfall : 강설

주제문 : 첫 문장 핵심어 : precipitation, rain, hail, snow

1. 문제의 핵심어 : precipitation
   본문의 정답찾기 : 1~3행
2. 문제의 핵심어 : average annual rainfall in inches in of the United States
   본문의 정답찾기 : 3~4행
3. 문제의 핵심어 : 152 inches of snow in a year, annual precipitation
   본문의 정답찾기 : 6~7행에 공식이 나와 있다.(formula : thirty-eight inches of snow — one inch of precipitation) 즉, 38 : 1 = 152 : X
4. 문제의 핵심어 : precipitation, another word
   본문의 정답찾기 : 1행

【정답】 1. B 2. A 3. B 4. C

[12] 오네이다 족은 이로쿼이 연맹의 다섯 국가 중의 하나로, 이로쿼이어(語)를 말하는 북미 인디언 부족이었다. 다른 이로쿼이 족들처럼, 오네이다 족도 옥수수 농업에 종사하였다. 그들은 동맹 안에 각각 3명의 대표자를 두고 있는 세 씨족으로 나뉘었다. 각 공동체는 추장 또는 여러 추장들에게 조언을 하는 지역협의체를 두고 있었다. 오네이다 족은 미국독립전쟁에 식민지의 명분을 지원하였는데, 결과적으로 조셉 브란트 추장이 이끄는 친 영국 이로쿼이 족들의 약탈을 경험하였다. 그들은 미국 영토 안으로 물러나, 정찰대로 봉사하였다. 전쟁이 끝난 후에는 고향으로 돌아갔고, 그들의 피해에 대해서는 미국정부의 보상을 받았다.

the Onéida : 오네이다 족 tribe [traib] *n.* 부족, 종족 league [liːg] *n.* 연맹, 동맹 práctice [práktis] *v.* 종사하다 ágriculture [ǽgrikʌltʃər] *n.* 농업 clan [klæn] *n.* 씨족 represéntative [reprizéntətiv] *n.* 대표자, 대의원 confederátion [kənfedəréiʃən] *n.* 연합, 동맹 a lócal cóuncil : 지역협의회 chief [tʃiːf] *n.* 추장, 촌장 the cólonist cause :

식민지 명분(근거) the Américan Revolútion : 미국독립전쟁 róbbery [rɑ́bəri] *n.* 강도, 약탈(= ravage) the pro-Brítish Iróquois : 친 영국 이로쿼 족들 (*cf.* pro-(친-) ↔ anti-(반-)) retíre [ritáiər] *v.* 은퇴하다 American line : 미국 국경 scout [skaut] *n.* 정찰대, 스카우트 cómpensate [kámpənseit] *v.* 보상하다

주제문 : 첫 문장 핵심어 : the Oneida

1. 문제의 핵심어 : the way of life of the Oneida Indians
   본문의 정답찾기 : 3행
2. 문제의 핵심어 : they retired
3. 문제의 핵심어 : after the American Revolution what happened to the Oneida
   본문의 정답찾기 : 마지막 문장

【정답】 1. B 2. C 3. A

[13] 해와 달은 둘 다 지구로부터의 거리에는 아무런 차이가 없는데도, 뜨고 질 때 더 커 보인다. '달의 환상'이라고 알려진 이 지각현상은 오랫동안 연구되어 왔다. 달을 쳐다보는 사람의 근육의 긴장과 달을 더 크게 보이게 하는 지평선상의 다른 것들과 달을 비교하는 등 많은 설명들이 과학자들 사이에 논쟁이 되어왔지만, 그 현상에 대해 널리 받아들여지는 설명이 지금까지는 없다.

percéptual [pərséptʃuəl] *adj.* 지각(력)의 illúsion [ilúːʒən] *n.* 환상 múscle stráin : 근육의 긴장 compárison [kəmpǽrisən] *n.* 비교 (*cf.* compáre [kəmpέər] *v.* 비교하다) dispúte [dispjúːt] *v.* 논쟁하다 thus far : 지금까지는, 여기까지는

주제문 : 첫 문장
핵심어 : the Sun, the Moon, Moon illusion

1. 문제의 핵심어 : title
   본문의 정답찾기 : 첫 문장(주제문)을 읽고 제목들을 다시 본다.
2. 문제의 핵심어 : Moon illusion
   본문의 정답찾기 : 1~4행(Both the Sun and the Moon appear larger when they are rising or setting, although … are from the Earth. This perceptual phenomenon, known as the "Moon illusion," …)
3. 문제의 핵심어 : Moon illusion
   본문의 정답찾기 : 3~8행("Moon illusion," has been studied over the years. … but thus for there is no widely accepted explannation of the phenomenon.)

【정답】 1. A 2. B 3. D

[14] 가끔 우리 과거의 어떤 시대나 사건들이 주목을 거의 또는 전혀 받지 못한다. 이유는 이런 주제들에는 쓸만한 정보가 거의 없거나, 아니면 이 주제들이 논쟁의 여지가 있거나 부끄러운 것이라서 우리가 그것들을 만나기가 꺼려지기 때문이다. 그러나 우리가 과거의 일부를 무시하거나 부인할 때, 우리는 역사가 우리에게 가르쳐줄 수 있는 교훈을 배울 수 없고, 그 역사의 일부인 사람들을 소홀히 하게 된다. 이 분들은—또 그들의 역사는—보이지 않게 될 수도 있고, 조만간 이들이 우리가 역사로 생각하는 것의 일부가 되어야 한다는 사실을 우리가 잊어버릴 수가 있다.

éra [íərə] *n.* (역사나 정치적인) 시대 **éras or evénts from our past** : 과거의 시대들이나 사건들 (= history) **aváilable** [əvéiləbəl] *adj.* 유용한 **controvérsial** [kàntrəvə́:rʃəl] *adj.* 논쟁의, 논쟁의 여지가 있는 **shámeful** [ʃéimfəl] *adj.* 부끄러운 **be relúctant to do** :~하기를 꺼려하는 **fail to do** : cannot do **lésson** [lésn] *n.* 교훈 **in time** : 조만간, 시간이 지나면

주제문 : 첫 문장
핵심어 : eras or events from our past, history

1. 문제의 핵심어 : main point
   본문의 정답찾기 : 주제문을 통해서 알 수 있다.
2. 문제의 핵심어 : motivation for studying history
   본문의 정답찾기 : 5~6행(··· learn the lessons that history can teach us)
3. 문제의 핵심어 : the work of historians, valuable
   본문의 정답찾기 : 주제문의 의미와 같은 맥락이다.

【정답】 1. D 2. A 3. B

[15] 몇 가지 발견과 새로운 기술과 장비 개발의 결과로, 조개류 산업의 중요성이 1950년 이후 증가하였다. 조개류인 굴이 새로운 기술을 이용하여 대량으로 양식되었다. 해양생물학자들은 화학약품을 이용하여 수온을 높임으로써 굴이 여름뿐만 아니라 가을, 겨울, 봄에도 알을 낳도록 유도할 수 있다는 것을 알아냈다. 또한 질병에 저항력이 강하고, 빨리 성장하고 더 큰, 새로운 배종의 굴을 부화시키는 데도 성공하였다. 게다가 양식굴은 맛도 더 좋다!

as the resúlt of ~ : ~의 결과 **discóvery** [diskʌ́vəri] *n.* 발견(*cf.* **discóver** [diskʌ́vər] *v.* 발견하다) **equípment** [ikwípmənt] *n.* 장비 **shéllfish** [ʃélfiʃ] *n.* 조개류 **óyster** [ɔ́istər] *n.* 굴, 조개 **cúltivate** [kʌ́ltəveit] *v.* 경작하다, 재배하다, 양식하다 **by means of ~** : ~에 의하여,~을 이용하여 **maríne biólogist** : 해양 생물학자

chémicals [kémikəls] *n.* 화학약품 **raise-raised-raised** (*vt.* 올리다) : **rise-rose-risen** (*vi.* 오르다) **indúce** [indjú:s] *v.* 유도하다, 야기하다 **lay** [lei] *vt.* 놓다, 낳다 (lay-laid-laid) (*cf.* lie-lay-lain (*vi.* 눕다, lying)) **breed** [bri:d] *v.* (알을) 까다, (새끼를) 낳다 **strain** [strein] *n.* 변종 **be resístant to ~** : ~에 저항하는 **grow-grew-grown** (자라다)

주제문 : 첫 문장 핵심어 : shellfish industry

1. 문제의 핵심어 : main topic
   본문의 정답찾기 : 주제문 속에서 찾는다.
2. 문제의 핵심어 : before the use of the new technology
   본문의 정답찾기 : 6~7행(··· oysters to lay eggs not only in the summer, but also in the fall, winter, and spring.)
3. 문제의 핵심어 : new strains of oysters
   본문의 정답찾기 : 7~9행(···new strains of oysters that were resistant to diseases and grew faster and larger.)

【정답】 1. C 2. A 3. D

[16] 유럽과 아시아의 새로운 사람들을 지구의 끝으로 이동시킨 것은 새로운 종류의 도구들을 발명하고, 사냥꾼, 어부, 채집가, 여행가로서의 그들의 효율성을 향상시키는 새로운 방법으로 그것들을 사용한 능력이었다. 이 발명품들 중에 첫번째 것은 다른 도구를 만들기 위해 디자인된 도구들을 포함하고 있다. 부싯돌 정은 뿔이나, 상아, 뼈, 나무 등으로 멋진 작품을 만드는 데 사용될 수 있었다. 직물은 골풀이나 나무껍질로 직조될 수 있었다. 바구니는 곡식 보관용으로 만들어졌고, 호리병박은 물을 담아두기 위해 수집되었다. 작살이나 창과 기타 던지는 무기들은 인간이 죽일 수 있는 동물의 범위를 넓혔다. 아마도 가장 중요한 발명은 인간이 자신을 물위로 데려다 주는 데 사용한 것들이었다. 그들은 자신의 능력과 생존수단을 향상시켰을 뿐 아니라, 인구를 강이나 바다로 퍼뜨렸다.

invént [invént] *v.* 발명하다 **invéntion** *n.* 발명 **efficiency** [ifíʃənsi] *n.* 효율성 **colléct** [kəlékt] *v.* 수집하다 **colléctor** *n.* 수집가 **ímplement** [ímpləmənt] *n.* 도구(= tool) **flint chísels** : 부싯돌 끌(정) **fábric** [fǽbrik] *n.* 직물 **weave** [wi:v] *v.* 짜다, 직조하다 (weave-wove-woven) **rush** [rʌʃ] *n.* 골풀 **bark** [ba:rk] *n.* 나무껍질 **store** [stɔ:r] *v.* 보관하다 **gráin** [gréin] *n.* 곡식 **gourd** [guərd] *n.* 호리병박(호박류) **harpóon** [ha:rpún] *n.* 작살 **spear** [spiər] *n.* 창 **míssle** [mísəl] *n.* 던지는 무기 **exténd** [iksténd] *v.* 확장하다 **range** [reindʒ] *n.* 영역 **... the animals (that) man could kill.** **signíficant** [signífikənt] *adj.* 중요한

(= important) those (which) man used to carry him over the water. means [mi:nz] *n.* 수단 subsístence[səbsístəns] *n.* 생존 spread [spred] *v.* 퍼뜨리다 populátion [pɑpjəléiʃən] *n.* 인구

주제문 : 첫 문장 핵심어 : ability to invent and use tools

1. 문제의 핵심어 : 주제(topic)
   본문의 정답찾기 : 주제문(1~4행)
2. 문제의 핵심어 : device used for fashioning other materials
   본문의 정답찾기 : 4~6행
3. 문제의 핵심어 : missile
   본문의 정답찾기 : 8~9행

【정답】 1. D 2. B 3. C

[17] 언어를 사용하지 않고 의사전달을 하는 많은 방법이 있다. 신호, 부호, 상징, 제스처 등은 기존의 모든 문화에서 발견될 수 있다. 신호(signals)의 기본적인 기능은 예를 들어, 전신회로의 점이나 선과 같이 주의를 끄는 방식으로 주위환경과 충돌을 하는 것이다. 언어를 표현하도록 부호화되어서 의사전달의 잠재력은 매우 크다. 한편, 언어의 부호화에 적응력이 덜한 부호(signs)는 그 자체로 큰 의미를 담고 있다. 멈춤 표시나 이발소 네온기둥은 의미를 빠르고 편리하게 전달한다. 상징(symbols)은 수용자의 문화적 인식정도와 관계가 복잡하게 얽혀 있기 때문에, 신호(signals)나 부호(signs)보다는 묘사하기 더 어렵다. 어떤 문화에서는 극장에서의 갈채가 연주자들에게 인정한다는 청각적인 상징을 보내는 것이다. 손 흔들기나 악수 같은 제스처는 어떤 문화적인 메시지를 전달한다.

sígnal [sígnl] *n.* 신호 sign [sain] *n.* 부호, 표시 sýmbol [símbəl] *n.* 상징 impínge upon :~와 충돌하다 envíronment [inváiərənmənt] *n.* 환경 in such a way : 그런 식으로 attráct [ətrǽkt] *v.* 끌다 atténtion [əténʃən] *n.* 주의 dot [dɑt] *n.* 점 dash [dæʃ] *n.* 선 télegraph círcuit : 전신회로 code [koud] *v.* 부호화하다 codificátion [kɑdəfikéiʃən] *n.* 부호화 poténtial [poutén∫əl] *n.* 잠재성 adáptable [ədǽptəbəl] *adj.* 적응(순응)할 수 있는 a bárber pole : 이발소 네온기둥 convéy [kənvéi] *v.* 전달하다 (= cárry, commúnicate) convéniently [kənvíːnjəntli] *adv.* 편리하게 íntricate [íntrəkit] *adj.* 복잡한, 뒤얽힌 recéiver : 수용자 percéption [pərsépʃən] *n.* 인식, 감지 applauding [əplɔ́ːdiŋ] *n.* 갈채 perfórmer [pərfɔ́ːrmər] *n.* 연주자, 연기자 áuditory [ɔ́ːditɔːri] *adj.* 청각의 appróval [əprúːvəl] *n.* 인정, 승인 such as ~ : ~와 같은 (= like) wave [weiv] *v.* 흔들다 cúltural méssage : 문화적인 메시지

주제문 : 첫 문장 핵심어 : ways of communication, signals, signs, symbols, gestures

1. 문제의 핵심어 : signal
   본문의 정답찾기 : 3~5행
2. 문제의 핵심어 : applauding
   본문의 정답찾기 : 11~12행
3. 문제의 핵심어 : conclude
   본문의 정답찾기 : 주제문(1~3행)

【정답】 1. B 2. C 3. A

[18] 사람들 사이에 거리가 없을 때, 자신의 거리를 유지할 수 있는 유일한 방법은 공동체에서 수용된 예절에 의해서이다. 예절은 집단으로 교정되는 촉매수단이다. 그것들은 개인적인 위엄을 상실하지 않고도 사회적 교류를 가능하게 한다. 그것들은 사생활의 침범에 대항하는 방호복이다. 물러나야 하는지 나아가서 친밀해도 되는지를 보고해 주는 선발정찰대이다. 그것들은 우호적이지만 모호한 문화인들의 제스처이다. 내 생각에, 인구가 많은 나라의 예절은 땅이 넓은 나라의 예절보다 (예를 들어, 유럽과 일본의 예절같이) 늘 더 형식적이다. 우리는 더 가까운 영역에서 이전보다 더 많은 사람을 만나게 되기 때문에 미국의 예절에 대한 점증하는 관심을 정밀하게 보고 있는 것이다. 우리는 교정의 소용돌이에 우리들의 사생활이나 개인성을 팔지 않고 집단의 일부가 되는 방법을 찾아야 할 필요성을 느낀다.

keep one's distance : (누구의) 거리를 유지하다 code [koud] *n.* 규범 étiquette [étiket] *n.* 예의범절 accéptance [ækséptəns] *n.* 수용 mánners [mǽnərz] *n.* 예절 ántidote [ǽntidout] *n.* 해독제, 교정수단 adjústment [ədʒʌ́stmənt] *n.* 조정 sócial intercóurse : 사회적 교류 fórfeit [fɔ́ːrfit] *v.* 상실, 몰수 dígnity [dígnəti] *n.* 위엄 ármor [áːrmər] *n.* 방호복, 갑옷투구 invásion [invéiʒən] *n.* 침략 advánce [ædvǽns] *adj.* 먼저의, 선발의 *v.* 나아가다 advánce patróls : 선발 정찰 withdráw [wiðdrɔ́ː] *v.* 물러나다, 후퇴하다 íntimacy [íntəməsi] *n.* 친밀 noncommíttal [nɑnkəmítl] *adj.* 애매한, 확실한 언질을 안주는 crowded country : 인구가 많은 나라 fórmal [fɔ́ːrml] *adj.* 형식적인 open country : 땅이 넓은 나라 rising concérn : 점증하는 관심 precísely [prisáisli] *adv.* 정밀하게, 정확하게 encóunter [enkáuntər] *v.* 만나다(= meet) individuálity [indəvidʒuǽləti] *n.* 개인성 mess [mes] *n.* 혼란, 소용돌이 a mess of adjústment : 조정의 소용돌이

주제문 : 첫 문장
핵심어 : distance between people, etiquette, manners

1. 문제의 핵심어 : manners in Europe
　　본문의 정답찾기 : 8~14행(특히, we feel the need to find ways …)
2. 문제의 핵심어 : manners
　　본문의 정답찾기 : 3~8행
3. 문제의 핵심어 : people cherish …
　　본문의 정답찾기 : 4~6행

【정답】**1. C 2. A 3. C**

[19] 역학의 일반적인 원칙은 물체의 움직임과 그런 움직임을 생성하는 힘의 관계를 설명해주는 규칙들이다. 선조들의 연구에 크게 기반을 두고 있는 아이작 뉴튼 경은 1687년에 출간된 자신의 유명한 *Principia*(원리)라는 책에서 세 가지 역학법칙을 추론해냈다.

　뉴튼 이전에 아리스토텔레스는 어떤 물체의 자연상태는 정지상태이며, 운동을 지속하기 위해 그것에 힘을 행사하지 않으면 움직이는 물체는 정지하게 된다는 사실을 수립하였다. 갈릴레오는 떨어지는 물체의 움직임을 정확히 설명하고, 물체를 계속 움직이도록 유지하는 데 아무런 힘도 필요하지 않다는 것을 기록하는 데 성공하였다. 힘의 효과는 운동을 변화시키는 것이라고 그는 지적했다. 휴젠은 운동방향의 변화는 속도변화가 그렇듯이 가속도를 가지며, 더 나아가 힘을 가할 필요가 있음을 확인하였다. 케플러는 태양주위를 도는 혹성들의 운동을 설명하는 법칙을 추론해냈다. 본래 뉴튼은 갈릴레오와 케플러에게서 빌어온 것이었다.

príncíple [prínsəpl] *n.* 원칙　dynámics [dainǽmiks] *n.* 역학　démonstrate [démənstrit] *v.* 시사하다, 나타내다　body : 물체　force [fɔːrs] *n.* 힘　in large part : 크게, 대부분　prédecessor [prédisesər] *n.* 조상, 선조　dedúce [didjúːs] *v.* (논리) 연역하다, 추론하다(*opp.* indúce [indjúːs] *v.* (논리) 귀납하다)　prior to :~전에 (= before)　estáblish [istǽbliʃ] *v.* 설립하다　the natural state : 자연상태　a state of rest : 정지상태　maintáin [meintéin] *v.* 유지하다, 지속하다　succéed in -ing :~에 성공하다　describe [diskráid] *v.* 묘사하다, 설명하다　behávior [bihéivjər] *n.* 움직임(= action, motion)　óbject [ábdʒikt] *n.* 물체(= body)　diréction [dirékʃən] *n.* 방향　invólve [inválv] *v.* 포함하다 (= contáin)　accelerátion [ækseləréiʃən] *n.* 가속도　just as ~ : ~와 꼭 같이　plánet [plǽnət] *n.* 혹성　primárily [praimárəli] *adv.* 본래

주제문 : 첫 문장　핵심어 : principles of dynamics

1. 문제의 핵심어 : the natural state of a body was a state of rest

**　본문의 정답찾기 : 6~8행**
2. 문제의 핵심어 : behavior of falling object , first scientist to correctly describe
　　본문의 정답찾기 : 8~10행
3. 문제의 핵심어 : Newton based his laws
　　본문의 정답찾기 : 마지막 문장(… that Newton borrowed.)
4. 문제의 핵심어 : purpose
　　본문의 정답찾기 : 첫 단락의 마지막 문장

【정답】**1. C 2. D 3. D 4. A**

[20] 옥스포드의 윌리엄 포크너는 옥스포드 토박이가 아닐 뿐더러, Faulkner라는 성으로 태어나지도 않았다. 그는 1897년 9월 25일, 미시시피주의 뉴 알바니에서 태어났고, 가족은 성을 Falkner라고 철자를 적었다. 그는 27살 때 첫번째 책을 출간하였다. 53살이던 해 그는 노벨문학상을 받았다. 1962년 7월 6일 그가 죽었을 때는 동시대 미국의 중요 작가로 널리 인정받았다. Faulkner 또는 Falkner인 그는 생의 거의 대부분을 미시시피 타운, 그의 작품을 읽은 수백만의 독자들이 옥스포드가 아닌 제퍼슨이라고 알고 있는 바로 그곳에서 보냈다. 심지어 옥스포드 사람들에게조차 포크너는 일평생 신화적인 존재였다. 예를 들면, 윌리엄의 성(姓)에 'u'자를 누가 첨가하였는가 하는 신화가 있었다. 오랫동안 일반적으로 받아들여진 이야기로는 작품 The Marble Faun (1924)을 조판하던 어느 부주의한 인쇄공이었다는 것이다. 포크너 전기작가 카블 콜린스는 작가 자신이 첨가하였다고 시사한다. 초기인 1918년에 적어도 가끔씩.

not A ; nor B : A도 아니고, B도 아니다　nátive [néitiv] *n.* 토박이　spell[spel] *v.*~라고 철자를 적다　acknowledge [æknálidʒ] *v.* 인정하다　a cáreless printer : 부주의한 인쇄공　setting type : 식자(조판)　démonstrate [démənstreit] *v.* 시사하다, 표명하다　occásionally [əkéiʒənəli] *adv.* 이따금

주제문 : 첫 문장　핵심어 : William Faulkner

1. 문제의 핵심어 : death
　　본문의 정답찾기 : 2~3행과 7행에서 각각 출생연도와 사망연도를 찾아 계산하면 쉽게 나온다.
2. 문제의 핵심어 : most of his life
　　본문의 정답찾기 : 7~9행(…he spent almost the

whole of his life in the Mississippi town which millions who read his works know not as Oxford but as Jefferson.)

3. 문제의 핵심어 : u

본문의 정답찾기 : 14행(the writer himself added it). 먼저, 본문에서 'u'자가 보이는 행을 찾으면 답이 쉽게 나온다. 11행(mystery of who put the "u" in William's last name).

【정답】 1. D 2. B 3. C

Step 2

[1] '위성도시'라는 용어는 대도시와 주변의 소도시들이나 경제적으로 대도시에 의존되어 있는 도시들과의 관계를 묘사하는 데 쓰인다. 위성도시는 거대교역도시와 상업적으로 연계하여 집결과 배포의 중심지가 되기도 하고, 또는 근처의 어느 중심지의 산물로서의 단일산업 경제로 존재하는 제조업이나 광공업의 중심지들이 될 수도 있다. 이 후자의 형태가 일반적으로 우리가 '위성도시'라는 용어를 사용할 때의 의미인 것이다. 이런 의미에서 볼 때, 19세기의 메사추세츠 주 치코피와 로웰은 보스턴의 위성이었다. 둘 다 뉴 잉글랜드라는 거대도시의 경제에 보탬이 되도록, 보스턴 투자가들이 만든 공업도시였다. 풍부한 노동력을 제공할 수 있는 농장지역의 한 가운데, 수력이 풍부한 지역에 접한 값싼 땅에 위치하여, 말 그대로 위성도시였다. 일리노이 주의 풀먼과 인디애나 주의 게리 또한 근처 시카고의 아주 광범위한 경제와 연계하여 생긴 단일산업 도시였다. 베라 슐라먼과 스텐리 브더가 자신들의 훌륭한 도시 역사서에서 지적한 대로, 그런 곳들은 1차원적인 특성을 가지고 있어서 사회적 활력이라고는 거의 없었다. 이 도시들은 혼자서는 설 수 없었으니, 어떤 의미에서는 다기능 모 도시의 식민지였다.

term [tə:rm] *n.* 용어, 말 sátellite city : 위성도시 be depéndent upon/on ~ : ~에 의존하는 colléction [kəlékʃən] *n.* 집합 distribútion [distrəbjú:ʃən] *n.* 배포, 출하 línkage [líŋkidʒ] *n.* 연결 a tráding metrópolis : 거대 교역 도시 manufácturing or míning center : 제조업 또는 광공업 중심지 one-índustry ecónomy : 단일산업 경제 créature [krí:tʃər] *n.* 피조물, 산물 néarby [níərbai] *adj.* 근처의 (= néighboring) latter : 후자의 mean-meant-meant (의미하다) mill town : 공업도시 invéstor

[invéstər] *n.* 투자자 lócate [lóukeit] *v.* 위치시키다, 두다 water-power site : 수력이 있는 곳 midst [midst] *n.* 가운데 ample [ǽmpl] *adj.* 풍부한 in conjúnction with ~ : ~와 연대하여, 공동으로 broad-broader-broadest (넓은, 광범위한) éxcellent úrban biógraphy : 뛰어난 도시 역사서 one-diménsional quálity : 1차원적인 성격 sócial vígor : 사회적인 활력 in a sénse : 어떤 의미에서 multifúnctional móther city : 다기능의 모 도시

주제문 : 첫 문장 핵심어 : satellite city

1. 문제의 핵심어 : a satellite city, characteristic
본문의 정답찾기 : 3~6행. 이런 유형의 문제는 4가지 답을 하나씩 차례로 읽으며 틀린 답을 숨아나간다.

2. 문제의 핵심어 : Chicopee and Lowell, development
본문의 정답찾기 : 8~13행. 9행의 Chicopee와 Lowell을 찾아 이하 문장과 답을 번갈아 읽으며 정답을 찾는다.

3. 문제의 핵심어 : being economically dependent on another city
본문의 정답찾기 : 본문에서 도시 이름을 모두 찾은 다음, 하나씩 확인한다.
· satellite city : Chicopee and Lowell, Massachusetts, Pullman, Illinois
· mother city : Chicago, Illinois

【정답】 1. C 2. B 3. D

[2] 영국령 온두라스의 수도인 벨라이즈는 언제나 식민지의 행정, 문화, 지리적 중심지였다. 차양이 쳐진 베란다가 있는 큰집들이 특징적인, 독특한 해변도시이다. 허리케인 지역의 가장자리, 해발 2피트의 평균고도에 자리잡고 있어서, 도시는 해일에 약하다. 그래서 대부분의 건물들은 버팀목 위에 세워졌고, 다른 많은 건물들도 도로 높이에 스파르타식 (간소한) 가구를 가지고 있다. 삼면이 바다로 둘러싸인 이 도시에 부는 부드러운 바다바람의 시원한 효과는 저 혹독한 기후를 누그러뜨려 준다. 뉴 올리언즈 남쪽으로 800마일 약간 더 되는 곳, 자마이카에서도 서쪽으로 거의 같은 거리에 있는 중남미의 카리브해안에 자리잡고 있어서, 벨라이즈는 1859년에 인구가 거의 6,000명이었고, 1900년에는 1만명, 1960년대에는 3만 명에 달하였다.

administrative [ædmínəstreitiv] *adj.* 행정의 uníque [ju:ní:k] *adj.* 특이한 wáterfront [wɔ́:tərfrʌnt] *n.* 해변, 강변 large frame house : 규모가 큰 집 screened : 차양이 쳐진 periphery [pərí:fəri] *n.* 주변, 가장자리 (= óutskirts, edge, bórder) an áverage elevátion : 평균고도 above sea lével : 해발 vúlnerable

[vʌ́lnərəbəl] *adj.*~에 취약한 tídal wave : 해일 hence [hens] *adv.* 그러므로 stilt [stilt] *n.* (건축물을 버티는) 지주 fúrnishings [fə́ːrniʃiŋs] *n.* 가구, 설비 breeze [briːz] *n.* 미풍 surróund [səráund] *v.* 에워싸다 relíeve [rilíːv] *v.* 누그러뜨리다, 완화시키다, 구원하다 ótherwise [ʌ́ðərwaiz] *adv.* 다른 oppréssive [əprésiv] *adj.* 억압하는, 혹독한 lócate [lóukeit] *v.* 위치시키다, 두다 slíghtly [sláitli] *adv.* 약간

주제문 : 첫 문장 핵심어 : Belize

1. 문제의 핵심어 : Jamaica, locate
   본문의 정답찾기 : 9~12행
2. 문제의 핵심어 : storms and waves, houses of Belize
   본문의 정답찾기 : 6~7행(Hence most buildings are on stilts…)
3. 문제의 핵심어 : 1900~1960, population
   본문의 정답찾기 : 11~13행(Belize had a population of … ten thousand in 1900, and reached thirty thousand in the 1960's.)

【정답】 1. B 2. D 3. C

[3] 2차 세계대전 기간에 사용된 가장 중요한 무기 중의 하나는 대인용 무기가 아니라, 질병치료에 쓴 의약품이었다. 페니실린의 전시사용은 수천 명의 목숨을 살렸다. 예를 들어, 1차 세계대전 때, 미국 육군의 전 사망자의 18%가 폐렴 때문이었다. 2차 대전 때는 그 비율이 1% 이하로 내려갔다. 게다가, 상처가 감염되는 것을 방지하고, 감염된 상처의 치료과정을 단축시키도록 도와주는 데는 페니실린이 유용하였다.

not A, but B : A가 아니고 B이다 rather [rǽðər] *adv.* 오히려 pneumónia [njumóunjə] *n.* 폐렴 be respónsible for ~ : ~에 책임이 있는 less than ~ : ~이하 in addition : 게다가 instruméntal [instrəméntl] *adj.* 도구적인, 유용한 wound [wuːnd] *n.* 상처 keep A from -ing : A가 ~하는 것을 막아주다 (= prevent A from -ing) get infécted : 감염되다 (= become infected) speed [spiːd] *v.* 촉진하다 the héaling prócess : 치료과정

주제문 : 첫 문장 핵심어 : a drug, penicillin

1. 문제의 핵심어 : title
   본문의 정답찾기 : 첫 문장, 제목은 주로 주제문에 들어 있다.
2. 문제의 핵심어 : First World War, cause of death
   본문의 정답찾기 : 4~5행
3. 문제의 핵심어 : the death from pneumonia, First World War, Second World War
   본문의 정답찾기 : 4~6행

4. 문제의 핵심어 : Second World War, penicillin, purpose
   본문의 정답찾기 : 마지막 문장(6~9행)

【정답】 1. D 2. C 3. D 4. D

[4] 오랜 기간 재즈가 변화하고 발전을 해왔지만, 기본적인 성격은 유지하고 있다. 재즈의 발달에 이바지한 음악형식 중의 하나는 블루스였다. 재즈음악의 약 1/3이 블루스 형식이다. 로큰롤 음악의 절반 이상이 그렇다. 심지어 미국의 컨트리 앤 웨스턴 음악의 일부도 블루스 형식이다.

재즈의 발달에는 뉴 올리언즈의 음악인들이 중요한 걸음을 내딛었다. 간혹, 딕시랜드라고 불리는 뉴 올리언즈 재즈는 래그타임이나 유럽 민속음악의 요소뿐만 아니라 블루스와 흑인영가의 깊이 있는 감정을 가지고 있다.

retáin [ritéin] *v.* 보유하다, 간직하다 contríbute [kəntríbjut] *v.* 공헌하다, 이바지하다 piece : (노래) 한 곡 So are over half of the popular rock 'n' roll pieces.(도치) → Over half of the popular rock 'n' roll pieces are so. take a step : 한 걸음 나가다

주제문 : 첫 문장 핵심어 : jazz music

1. 문제의 핵심어 : main purpose
   본문의 정답찾기 : 주제문 속에서 찾는다.
2. 문제의 핵심어 : rock 'n' roll
   본문의 정답찾기 : 3~4행(About a third of jazz music is in the blues form. So are over half of the popular rock 'n' roll pieces.)
3. 문제의 핵심어 : the blues
   본문의 정답찾기 : 3~6행, 8~9행
4. 문제의 핵심어 : Dixieland
   본문의 정답찾기 : 8~9행(New Orleans jazz, sometimes called Dixieland, had the deep emotion of the blues)

【정답】 1. A 2. D 3. C 4. D

[5] 비행위성용으로 개발되는 새로운 원자시계는 이전의 시계들보다 더 잘 작동된다. 수소메이저를 구체화하는 이 시계는 작고 가벼운 포장을 제공하려고 새로운 마이크로웨이브 공동(空洞) 디자인을 사용할 것이며, 장기간의 내구성을 유지하기 위해 새로운 전자기술을 사용할 것이다. 3백만 년에 1초 정도까지 신뢰할 수 있기 때문에 이 시계는 정밀한 비행정보를 제공할 수 있다. 4개의 위성에서

신호가 한 장소에 도달할 때의 시간차는 불과 몇 야드 이내까지의 그 위치를 계산하는 데 사용될 수 있다.

atómic clock : 원자시계 navigátion [nǽvəgéiʃən] n. 항해, 비행 sátellite [sǽtəlait] n. 위성 devíce [diváis] n. 기계장치, 고안물, 여기서는 시계 incórporate [inkɔ́:rpəreit] v.~을 포함하다, ~을 구체화하다 hýdrogen [háidrədʒən] n. 수소 máser [méizər] n. 메이저, 전기충격 증폭기 (Microware Amplification by Stimulated Emission of Radiation) cávity [kǽvəti] n. 공동, 구멍 compáct [kəmpǽkt] adj. 작은, 압축된 maintáin [meintéin] v. 유지하다 long-term stabílity : 장기 내구성 stable[stéibl] adj. 신뢰할 수 있는, 안정성이 있는 precíse [prisáis] adj. 정밀한 cálculate [kǽlkjəleit] v. 계산하다

주제문 : 첫 문장 핵심어 : a new atomic clock

1. 문제의 핵심어 : characteristics of the clock
   본문의 정답찾기 : 5~6행
2. 문제의 핵심어 : new clock
   본문의 정답찾기 : 2~5행
3. 문제의 핵심어 : signals
   본문의 정답찾기 : 7~9행. 본문에서 숫자를 찾는다.
4. 문제의 핵심어 : purpose
   본문의 정답찾기 : 윗글은 어떤 제품에 대한 설명문이다.

【정답】 1. C 2. A 3. D 4. D

[6] 20세기 초 25년 간, 배들이 항해하면서 바다 밑바닥을 기록할 수 있도록 음향측심이 발달되었을 때, 심해 생명에 관한 어떤 것을 배울 수 있는 방법을 제공할 것이라는 것에 대해 아무도 의심하지 않았다. 그러나 이 새기구의 조종사들은 음파가 광선처럼 배에서 아래로 곧장 내려가서, 만나게 되는 단단한 물체로부터 반사되어 온다는 것을 곧 발견하게 되었다. 반사음향은 중간 깊이에서 물고기떼나 고래, 잠수함으로부터 반사되어 되돌아왔다. 그러나 두번째 음향은 바다에서 되돌아왔다.

écho sounding : 음향측심 under way to do : ~하려고 항해중인 depth [depθ] n. 깊이 suspéct[səspékt] v. 의심하다 means [mi:nz] n. 수단, 방법 óperator [ápəreitor] n. 조종사 beam [bi:m] n. 광선 refléct [riflékt] v. 반사하다, 반영하다 sólid óbject : 단단한 물체 intermédiate [intərmí:diət] adj. 중간의 presúmably [prizú:məbli] adv. 추측컨대, 아마 schools of fish : 물고기 떼 súbmarine [sʌ́bməri:n] n. 잠수함

주제문 : 첫 문장
핵심어 : echo sounding, sound waves, ship

2. 문제의 핵심어 : send down into the water

본문의 정답찾기 : 5~7행(…the sound waves, directed downward from the ship …)

3. 문제의 핵심어 : enterprises, using the instruments mentioned
   본문의 정답찾기 : 수중 음향측심에 관한 내용이므로, 4가지 답을 읽고 가장 어울리는 것을 고른다.

4. 문제의 핵심어 : purpose, the instrument originally designed
   본문의 정답찾기 : 첫 문장

【정답】 1. C 2. D 3. B 4. A

[7] 고고학자들은 이집트에서 고대 피라미드를 발굴하였고, 중남미에서도 더 최근의 피라미드들을 발굴하였다. 수천마일 떨어진 곳에서 발견된 이 구조물들의 디자인과 건축법에 유사점들이 눈에 띄었다. 일부 연구가들은 이 피라미드 건설자들 사이에 접촉이 존재하였을지도 모른다고 생각하였다. 노르웨이 탐험가 도어 헤이어달은 고대 이집트 그림을 바탕으로 배를 건조하여 문화적 접촉이론에 힘을 실어주기 위해서 바르바도 섬을 향하여 항해를 떠났다. 바르바도에 다다르려던 첫 시도에서 헤이어달은 많은 어려움에 부닥쳐서 노력을 포기해야만 했다. 두번째 시도에서 그는 고대 이집트인들이 그랬을 것처럼, 바르바도에 도착하였다.

archaeólogist [ɑ:rkiálədʒist] n. 고고학자 archaeólogy [ɑ:rkiálədʒi] n. 고고학 éxcavate [ékskəveit] v. 발굴하다 récent ones = recent pyramids similárity [siməlǽrəti] n. 유사점 constrúction [kənstrʌ́kʃən] n. 건축(법) apárt [əpá:rt] adv. 떨어져서 reséarcher [risə́:rtʃər] n. 연구원 cóntact [kántækt] n. 접촉 explórer [iksplɔ́:rər] n. 탐험가 put together a ship : 배를 건조하다 set sáil for ~ : ~를 향하여 항해를 떠나다 lend suppórt to ~ : ~에 지지하다, 힘을 실어주다 run into várious problems : 여러 가지 문제에 부딪치다 abándon [əbǽndən] v. 포기하다, 버리다 Bárbados : 영연방 서인도 제도에 속하는 섬

주제문 : 3~6행(Similarities have been noted in the design and construction of these structures found thousands of miles apart. Some researchers have wondered if contact could have existed between these pyramid builders.)
핵심어 : similarities, cultural contact

1. 문제의 핵심어 : first pyramid builders
   본문의 정답찾기 : 1행(Archaeologists have excavated ancient pyramids in Egypt)

2. 문제의 핵심어 : Thor Heyerdahl
   본문의 정답찾기 : 5~8행(Thor Heyerdahl, … set sail for Barbados to lend support to the theory of cultural contact.)
3. 문제의 핵심어 : Thor Heyerdahl, finally reach
   본문의 정답찾기 : 8~10행(Heyerdahl … On a second try he did reach Barbados)
4. 문제의 핵심어 : Thor Heyerhahl's ship, built
   본문의 정답찾기 : 5~7행(Thor Heyerdahl … put together a ship based on ancient Egyptian drawings)

【정답】 1. D 2. A 3. C 4. D

[8] 게티스버그 전투에서 포토맥 지구 육군 사령관으로 후커 장군의 후임이 된 조지 G. 미드 장군은 리 장군의 공격을 물리쳐서 남부연합군에 크게 피해를 주었다. 미드 장군은 노련한 방어적 전략으로 싸웠으나, 그야말로 자기의 승리에 만족을 하였다. 그는 리 장군이 자신의 전선을 떠나는 것을 보고 만족하였다. 그의 주된 관심사는 리 장군을 포토맥 지구 저 너머로 몰아내는 것이었다. 다른 북부연방군 장군들처럼, 모든 대 전투의 장수들이 지니고 있던, 적을 완전히 섬멸하는 살인본능이 그에게는 없었다. 전투 후에 그는 자기 부대원들에게 승전축하 전문을 보내어, '우리의 땅'에서 적을 몰아낸 것을 치하하였다. 결국, 이것은 내전이었다! 전문을 받았을 때, 링컨은 고민스럽게 소리를 질렀다. "세상에! 이게 다야?"

succéed [səksíːd] v. (재산, 지위를) 잇다, 후임이 되다 throw back : 되돌아가게 하다, 후퇴시키다 (throw-threw-thrown) attáck [ətǽk] n. 공격 hurt-hurt-hurt (다치게 하다) the Conféderate army : 남부연합군, 미국 남북전쟁 때 남부 11개 주 연합 군대 the Féderal army : 북부연방군 fight-fought-fought a skíllful defénsive báttle : 노련한 방어적인 전투 be sátisfied with ~ : ~에 만족하다 be contént to do :~에 만족하다 front [frʌnt] n. 전선 príncipal [prínsəpəl] adj. 중요한(= important) n. 교장(cf. prínciple [prínsəpl] n. 원칙) concérn [kənsə́ːrn] n. 관심 herd [həːrd] v. 무리를 쫓다, 몰다 herd Lee back over the Potómac : 리 장군의 군대를 몰아 포토맥 지구 저 너머로 되돌려 보내다 the killer ínstinct : 살인본능 fínish off the énemy : 적을 완전히 섬멸하다 engágement [engéidʒmənt] n. 교전, 전투 íssue an (congratulátory) órder : (축하) 사령을 내리다 troop [truːp] n. 부대 drive : 몰아내다 our soil : 우리 땅 after all : 결국 a civil war : 내전 (미국 남북전쟁을 가리킴) in ánguish : 고민스럽게

주제문 : 첫 문장

핵심어 : battle of Gettysburg, George G. Meade

1. 문제의 핵심어 : the battle of Gettysburg
   본문의 정답찾기 : 첫 문장
2. 문제의 핵심어 : George G. Meade
   본문의 정답찾기 : 1~5행. Meade 장군이 주어인 문장을 찾아 차례로 확인한다.
3. 문제의 핵심어 : Lincoln heard of Meade's order
   본문의 정답찾기 : 11~12행(When Lincoln read the order, he exclaimed in anguish, "My God! Is that all?")
4. 문제의 핵심어 : implication
   본문의 정답찾기 : 결론에 해당되는 마지막 문장을 읽고 유추한다.

【정답】 1. D 2. D 3. C 4. C

[9] 미국의 좋은 면뿐만 아니라 추한 면까지도 구체화한 데오도르 루스벨트는 자신의 '더 훌륭한 장점'과 거의 똑같은 만큼의 단점 때문에 국민들에게 존경을 받았다. 그의 결점은 국민 대다수의 결점이었다. 해리 더스톤 펙은 다음과 같이 지적하였다. "그의 자의식, 거드름 피는 기질, 박수갈채와 떠벌리기 좋아하기, 가끔씩 저지르는 공식 석상의 사소한 과실, 심지어 거리낌없는 연설, 불필요한 솔직함 그리고 형식 무시 등 루스벨트를 묘사하는 이런 것들이 실제로는 국민적인 장점들이었다." 루스벨트의 가장 혹독한 비평가 한 사람은 다음과 같이 썼다. "루스벨트는 인기가 있었다. 역사상 여느 대통령만큼 인기가 있었다. 미국은 히스테리 요소를 가지고 있다. 공식적인 히스테리는 그들에게 받아들여진다. 국민들 일부에게 육체적인 덩치는 위대함을 의미한다. 루스벨트는 그들 속의 민감한 심금을 건드린다. 우리 국민들 중 많은 이들이 허세를 부리고 주제 넘는다. 루스벨트가 그들의 이상이었다. 뽐내고 시끄러움이 우리들 일부에게 받아들여지는 것이다. 루스벨트가 우리를 만족시키는 것이다."

embódy [embádi] v. 구체화하다, 구현하다 the bad : 나쁜 것, 추한 것 the good : 좋은 것, 선 admíre [ædmáiər] v. 존경하다 cóuntryman : 국민, 동포 as much … as ~ : ~처럼 똑같이 …도 failings : 결함 finer quálities : 더 훌륭한 장점 deféct [difékt] n. 결점 majórity [mədʒɔ́rəti] n. 다수 self-cónsciousness : 자의식 swágger [swǽgər] n. 뽐냄, 거드름 (= boast) touch of the swagger : 거드름 피는 기질 love of appláuse : 박수갈채를 좋아함 publícity [pʌblísəti] n. 홍보, 떠벌리기 lapse [læps] n. 사소한 과실

dígnity [dígnəti] *n.* 위엄 occásional [əkéiʒənəl] *adj.* 이따금 occásional lápse of official dígnity : 가끔 저지르는 공식 석상의 사소한 과실 réckless [réklis] *adj.* 앞뒤 안 가리는, 개의치 않는 reckless speech : 거리낌 없는 연설 disregárd of form : 형식을 무시함 in reality = really trait [treit] *n.* 장점 crític [krítik] *n.* 비평가 bítterest crítics : 가장 혹독한 비평가들 hystérical [histérikəl] *adj.* 히스테리의, 발작적인 hystérics [histériks] *n.* 히스테리 발작 respónsive [rispánsiv] *adj.* 민감한, 반응하는 chord [kɔːrd] *n.* 감정, 심금 self-assértive : 주제넘은 swággering [swǽgəriŋ] *n.* 허세, 뽐냄 clámorousness [klǽmərəsnis] *n.* 시끄러움

주제문 : 첫 문장 핵심어 : Theodore Roosevelt, fallings (= defects) and finer qualities

1. 문제의 핵심어 : Roosevelt, defects
   본문의 정답찾기 : 3~4행(His defects were those of a majority of the people.)
2. 문제의 핵심어 : Roosevelt, characteristics
   본문의 정답찾기 : 4~8행에 나열된 성격을 종합적으로 나타내는 어휘를 찾는다.("the self-consciousness, the touch of the swagger, the love of applause and of publicity, the occasional lapse of official dignity, even the reckless speech, the unnecessary frankness, and the disregard of form" which characterized Roosevelt)
3. 문제의 핵심어 : physically
   본문의 정답찾기 : 11~12행(With some of our people physical size means greatness.)
4. 문제의 핵심어 : unidentified critic
   본문의 정답찾기 : 8~15행. 여덟행 모두 읽고 비평가의 일관된 생각을 유추한다.
   단서(Clue) : One of Roosevelt's bitterest critics wrote (혹독한 비평가들이 좋게 평가할 리가 없을 것이다.)

【정답】 1. B 2. C 3. C 4. D

[10] 오늘날 세계에는 5종의 원숭이들이 있다. 그 중 2종 ―기번과 시아망― 이 진정한 그네타기의 명수들이다. 그들은 이 가지에서 저 가지로 시계추처럼 그네타기 하며 이동한다. 그들의 팔은 대단히 길고, 손과 손가락도 길게 늘어나 특별하게 되어있다. 신체는 키가 작고 가벼우며, 다리가 짧다. 시계추의 무게를 최소화한, 그러한 디자인으로 그들은 나무 사이를 놀랄 만큼 빠르게 이동할 수 있다. 분명하게 분간이 될 정도로 정확하고 부드럽게 이 가지에서 저 가지로 그네타며, 보통 10피트 이상 되는 간격을 뛰

어넘는다. 땅에 내려왔을 때, 그럴 일이 결코 없지만, 기번은 직립하며, 균형을 유지하려 긴팔로 양쪽을 붙잡고서, 짧고 약한 다리로 어기적어기적 걷는다. 어슬렁거리는 기번은 우리에게 줄타기 곡예사를 연상케 한다.

ape [eip] *n.* 원숭이 swing [swiŋ] *v.* 흔들다, 그네 타다 swingers : 그네 타기 명수들 péndulum [péndʒələm] *n.* (시계)추, 진자, 흔들이 branch [bræntʃ] *n.* 나뭇가지 exceedingly [iksíːdiŋli] *adv.* 대단히, 몹시 elóngate [ilɔ́ːŋgeit] *v.* 길게 늘이다, 연장하다 shrink [ʃriŋk] *v.* 줄다, 수축하다 (shrink-shrunk-shrunken) rápidly [rǽpidli] *adv.* 빠르게 with a súreness and smóothness : 정확하고 부드럽게 appréciate [əpríːʃieit] *v.* 식별하다, 분간하다 negótiate [nigóuʃieit] *v.* 교섭하다, (울타리 등을) 뛰어넘다, 빠져나가다 negóciate gaps of ten or more : 10피트 이상의 간격을 뛰어넘다 stand eréct : 직립하다 waddle [wádl] *v.* 어기적어기적 걷다 for bálance : 균형을 잡기 위해 stroll [stroul] *v.* 어슬렁거리다 remind A of B : A에게 B를 연상케하다 tíghtrope walker : 줄타기 곡예사

주제문 : 1~3행(There are five kinds of apes in the world today. Two of them—gibbons and siamangs— are true swingers. They move by swinging like pendulums from branch to branch.)
핵심어 : apes, true swingers, move by swinging

1. 문제의 핵심어 : brachiation
   본문의 정답찾기 : 1~2행(Two of them—gibbons and siamangs—are true swingers. They move by swinging …)
2. 문제의 핵심어 : the apes, travel
   본문의 정답찾기 : 2~3행(They move by swinging like pendulums from branch to branch.), 6~9행 (they can move remarkably rapidly through the trees, swinging from branch to branch with a sureness …)
3. 문제의 핵심어 : a gibbon's movement
   본문의 정답찾기 : 7~8행(… with a sureness and smoothness …)
4. 문제의 핵심어 : a strolling gibbon
   본문의 정답찾기 : 마지막 문장(A strolling gibbon reminds one of a tightrope walker.)

【정답】 1. A 2. C 3. B 4. B

[11] 모든 살아있는 언어들은 그들의 역사의 과정 속에서 발생하였고 계속해서 발생하게 될 음운변화에 의해 특징지어진다. 일부 언어학자들은 이 음운변화과정을 물리적 법칙의 규칙성을 가지고 작동하는 어떤 것으로 간주한

다. '음운법칙'이란 언어에 있는 이런 구조적 변화의 절대적 규칙성을 설명하기 위해 언어학자 오거스트 레스킨이 고안한 용어이다. '음운법칙'이란 말은 주어진 어떤 장소와 시기에 어떤 음운이 변할 경우, 그 변화는 보편적이 되고 예외란 없게 된다는 것을 뜻한다. 이 규칙은 겉으로 예외들이 드러나도, 그것들은 학문적 영향, 외국어나 사투리의 차용, 또는 유사어 같은 일부 외적인 요소 때문이라는 취지로 수정을 가함으로써 경직성을 일부 상실하게 된다.

sound change : 음운변화 their history = history of all living languages línguist [líŋgwist] n. 언어학자 óperate[ápəreit] v. 작동하다 regulárity [regjəlǽrəti] n. 규칙성 phýsical law : 물리적인 법칙 sound law : 음운법칙 term [təːrm] n. 용어 devíse [diváiz] v. 고안하다(cf. device [diváis] n. 고안(물)) ábsolute [ǽbsəluːt] adj. 절대적인 univérsal [juːnəvə́ːrsəl] adj. 보편적인 excéption[iksépʃən] n. 예외 inflexibílity [infleksəbíləti] n. 경직성, 유연하지 못함 améndment [əméndmənt] n. 개정, 수정 efféct [ifékt] n. 취지, 효과, 결과 appárent [əpǽrənt] adj. 외면적인, 겉으로 드러난 due to ~ : ~때문이다 extráneous [ikstréiniəs] adj. 외적인, 이질적인(= írrélevant) fáctor [fǽktər] n. 요소 díalect [dáiəlekt] n. 방언, 사투리 análogy [ənǽlədʒi] n. 유사관계, 상사관계

주제문 : 1~3행 핵심어 : sound changes, sound law

1. 문제의 핵심어 : main topic
   본문의 정답찾기 : 1~2행을 읽고 요지를 파악한 뒤, 4가지 답 중에서 가장 요지를 압축하고 있는 말을 찾는다.
2. 문제의 핵심어 : Leskien, sound law
   본문의 정답찾기 : 4~8행('Sound law' …devised by linguist August Leskien to describe …The term 'sound law' means …will be universal and will have no exceptions.)
3. 문제의 핵심어 : regular sound change
   본문의 정답찾기 : 4~6행('Sound law' … to describe the absolute regularity of this kind of structural change in language.)

【정답】 1. B 2. A 3. D

[12] 나무껍질에 있는 여러 다른 조직은 나무의 원둘레가 늘어날 때, 코르크 형성층이 변화하고 나무껍질이 팽창함으로써 비롯된 결과이다. 너도밤나무에서 형성층은 표면 가까이에 남아서, 필요할 때 확장하거나, 나무줄기 겉으로 단단히 팽창한 듯이 보이는 부드러운 회색의 코르크 조직을 생산한다. 그러나 대부분의 종에서 연속적인 코르크 형성층은 모종 밑에 형성된다. 즉, 새로 생기는 코르크층은 절개부위를 형성하고, 확장하는 나무줄기로부터 압력을 받아 바깥 형성층을 없애게 된다. 어떤 나무에는 조각들에서 생기는 2차 코르크 형성층이 있다. 시간이 지나면서 이 조각부분들은 소나무 껍질의 조각에서 쉽게 볼 수 있는 비늘 층이 된다. 소나무처럼, 물푸레나무도 많은 껍질 조각의 2차 코르크 형성층이 있다. 나무줄기가 팽창할 때, 섬유질이 떨어져나가며 그물 같은 다이아몬드 모양의 주름을 만든다. 그러나 나무껍질은 비늘에서 벗겨져 떨어지지 않는다.

téxture [tékstʃər] n. (나무나 피부의) 조직, 결 result in~: 결국~이 되다 strétching : 팽창 trunk [trʌŋk] n. 나무줄기, 둥치 spécies [spíːʃiz] n. 종(pl. species) succéssive cork cámbium : 연속적인 코르크 형성층 láyer [leiər] n. 층(層) cut off : 절단, 절개부위, 지름길 patch [pætʃ] n. 조각, 부분 scale [skeil] n. 비늘, 저울 frágment of pine bark : 소나무 껍질의 조각 tíssue [tíʃuː] n. (생물의) 조직, 종이 fíber [fáibər] n. 섬유 pull apart : (붙어있던 것이 따로) 떨어져 나가다, 잡아당겨 따로 떼어놓다 fúrrow [fə́ːrou] n. 골, 주름 flake off : 벗겨져 떨어지다

주제문 : 첫 문장 핵심어 : different textures in tree bark

1. 문제의 핵심어 : main topic
   본문의 정답찾기 : 첫 문장이 주제문이다.
2. 문제의 핵심어 : as a tree grows, cork cambium
   본문의 정답찾기 : 7~8행(the new layer of cork that … kills the outer cambium under pressure from the expanding trunk.)
3. 문제의 핵심어 : ash tree, pine tree, similar
   본문의 정답찾기 : 10~13행(Like pines, ash trees have patches of secondary cork cambium. … the bark does not flake off in scales.)

【정답】 1. B 2. D 3. D

[13] 우리 태양계의 중심에 태양이라는 별이 있다. 이것은 아주 뜨거운 가스의 둥근 덩어리이다. 직경이 지구의 100배가 넘는다. 강력한 광선을 복사에너지 형태로 발산한다. 이 에너지는 초속 약 30만 킬로미터의 속도로 지구로 여행한다. 이것은 햇빛이 지구에 도착하는 데 8분 33초 걸린다는 뜻이다.

태양 표면의 온도는 섭씨 약 5,520도인데, 내부는 훨씬 더 뜨겁다. 오늘날 과학자들은 태양열이 천연 원자에너지에서 나온다고 믿고 있다. 이 과정에서 수소가 엄청난 양의 에너지를 발산하며 헬륨으로 변하는 것으로 생각된다.

이 물질이 에너지로 변한다. 이 에너지는 열과 빛의 형태로, 그리고 복사의 여러 형태로 존재한다.

diámeter [daiǽmitər] *n.* 지름, 직경 100 times as big as that of the Earth : 지구 직경의 100배나 큰 give off : 발산하다 (= emit) rays of light : 광선 rádiant [réidiənt] *adj.* 빛을 발하는 radiátion[reidiéiʃən] *n.* 복사, 방사 get to ~ : ~에 도착하다 (= reach) Celsius : 셀시우스(1701~1744), 스웨덴 사람으로 섭씨 온도계의 창안자. 섭씨 온도를 말한다.(= Centigrade) hýdrogen [háidrədʒən] *n.* 수소 hélium [híːliəm] *n.* 헬륨 enórmous [inɔ́ːrməs] *adj.* 거대한, 엄청난

주제문 : 첫 단락(At the center of our solar system is a star called the Sun.) 둘째 단락(The temperature on the surface of the Sun is about 5,520 Celsius, and it is much hotter inside.

핵심어 : Sun, temperature on the surface of the Sun

1. 문제의 핵심어 : sun
   본문의 정답찾기 : 1~4행
2. 문제의 핵심어 : temperature of the outer rim of the Sun
   본문의 정답찾기 : 7~8행(…about 5,520 Celsius, and it is much hotter inside.)
3. 문제의 핵심어 : manner, the Sun, produce energy
   본문의 정답찾기 : 9~12행

【정답】 1. C 2. B 3. D

[14] 1825년까지 많은 동부의 대학들―하버드, 예일, 콜럼비아, 펜실바니아―이 대학으로서 필수요건들을 일부 지니고 있었으나, 아직은 거의 개념이 없었다. 그들은 학교와 학원의 소집단들이었다. 사실 미국독립전쟁이 막 끝났을 때는 펜실바니아와 하버드 등의 학교들이 다소 우월한 대학명칭을 상상할 수가 있었고, 그리고 곧 버지니아 대학이 토머스 제퍼슨의 지도아래 설립되었다. 남부에서는 조지아와 나중에 노스 캐롤라이나가 일어나기 시작하였다. 이름은 비록 영예로웠지만, 이 모든 것의 내용은 아주 부족하였다. 좀 허약했던 법대, 의대, 신학대학들이 있었는데, 다소 느슨하게나마 이 대학들에 소속되어 있었다. 그러나, 남북전쟁이 끝나고 10년, 즉 대략 1866년에서 1876 사이가 미국에서 초기 대학개념이 활짝 꽃피던 위대한 시기였다고 일반적으로 알려져 있다.

institútion [institjúːʃən] *n.* 기관, 단체 ínstitute [ínstətjuːt] *n.* 대학, 전문학원 ingrédient [ingríːdiənt] *n.* 구성성분, 요소 (=

compónent, élement) the Revolútion : 미국독립전쟁 assúme [əsjúːm] *v.* 상상하다, 가장하다, ~인 체하다 preténtious [priténʃəs] *adj.* 거만한, 우쭐대는 (= boastful) found [faund] *v.* 설립하다(*cf.* find-found-found) súbstance [sʌ́bstəns] *n.* 실질, 내용, 본질 hónor [ánər] *v.* 경의를 표하다, 영예를 주다 feeble [fíːbəl] *adj.* 나약한 divínity school : 신학교 attách to : ~에 소속되다 the close of the War Between the States : 남북전쟁의 끝 (= the end of the Civil War)

주제문 : 첫 문장 핵심어 : the necessary ingredients of a university, the university idea

1. 문제의 핵심어 : 1825
   본문의 정답찾기 : 1~4행(By the end of the first quarter of the nineteenth century … had some of the necessary ingredients of a university, but hardly yet the point of view.)
2. 문제의 핵심어 : Thomas Jefferson, found
   본문의 정답찾기 : 7~8행(the university of Virginia was founded under the guidance of Thomas Jefferson.)
3. 문제의 핵심어 : the war between the states, end
   본문의 정답찾기 : 12~13행(the first decade after the close of the War Between the States, that is, from about 1866 to 1876)
4. 문제의 핵심어 : university idea, really develop
   본문의 정답찾기 : 14행(… the great early flowering of the university idea in America.)

【정답】 1. C 2. C 3. A 4. D

[15] 19세기에는 많은 사람들이 관상보기 또는 관상학뿐만 아니라 골상보기 또는 골상학 역시 과학적으로 타당한 근거가 있는 것으로 받아들였다. 그들은 사람의 두개골에 있는 융기가 그 사람의 성격을 나타낸다고 생각하였다. 입 모양이 그랬고, 코의 경사도 마찬가지였다. 오늘날의 생각은 두뇌 속에서 일어나는 일이 얼굴에 의존하지 않는다는 것이다. 그런데도, 점성학이 과학세계에서 계속 번성하고 있는 것과 꼭같이, 콤비로 불리게 된 관/골상학은 1980년대에 우리와 함께 남아 있다.

válid [vǽlid] *adj.* 근거가 있는, 타당한 not only A, but also B : A뿐 아니라, B도 face-reading : 관상보기 physiógnomy [fiziágnəmi] *n.* 관상학 head-reading : 골상보기 phrenólogy [frinálədʒi] *n.* 골상학 bumps [bʌmps] *n.* (두개골의 두) 융기 cránium [kréiniəm] *n.* 두개골(= skull) revéal [rivíːl] *v.* 드러내다, 나타내다 tilt [tilt] *n.* 기울기, 경사 'so did (the shape) …'

:~도 그랬어 what goes on in the brain : 두뇌 속에서 일어나는 일 astrólogy [əstrálədʒi] *n.* 점성술(학)(*cf.* astronomy [əstránəmi] *n.* 천문학) flóurish [flɔ́ːris] *v.* 번성하다 so too does ("phys/phren") :~도 또한 그렇다 come to be called : 불리게 되다

주제문(결론) : and yet, just as astrology continues to flourish in a scientific world, so too does "phys/phren," …remain with us in the 1980's.

핵심어 : facereading (physiognomy), head-reading (phrenology)

1. 문제의 핵심어 : main topic
   본문의 정답찾기 : 7~8행(so too does "phys/phren," … remain with us in the 1980's.). 주제문인 결론문의 핵심어는 둘이다.
2. 문제의 핵심어 : idea, acceptance
   본문의 정답찾기 : 1~2행(In the nineteenth century many people accepted as scientifically valid)
3. 문제의 핵심어 : physiognomy
   본문의 정답찾기 : 4~5행
4. 문제의 핵심어 : phrenology
   본문의 정답찾기 : 3행
5. 문제의 핵심어 : tone
   본문의 정답찾기 : 윗글은 객관적인 사실을 서술하는 설명문이다.

【정답】1. D 2. A 3. D 4. D 5. B

[16] 선입관이란 증거를 검토하기 전에 즉각 논쟁을 거부해버리는, 글자 그대로 속단을 뜻한다. 선입관은 건전한 추론이 아닌 격렬한 감정의 결과이다. 우리가 만일 문제의 진실을 찾아내려고 한다면, 가능한 한 열린 마음으로, 우리 자신의 한계와 경향을 깊이 인식하고서 문제점에 접근해야 한다. 그러나, 신중하고도 열린 마음으로 증거를 검토한 끝에 그 제안을 기각한다면, 그것은 선입관이 아니다. '후판단'이라 부를 수 있겠다. 그것은 분명 지식의 선행조건이다.

préjudice [prédʒədis] *n.* 선입관, 편견 líterally [lítərəli] *adv.* 글자 그대로, 사실(*cf.* líteral [lítərəl] *adj.* 문자 그대로의 líterary[lítəreri] *adj.* 문학의 líterate [lítərit] *adj.* 학식 있는, 교양 있는 líterature [lítərətʃər] *n.* 문학) prejúdgement [pri:dʒʌ́dʒmənt] *n.* 속단 rejéction[ridʒékʃən] *n.* 거절 conténtion [kənténʃən] *n.* 논쟁 out of hand : 즉시 exámine [igzǽmin] *v.* 검토하다 évidence [évidəns] *n.* 증거 sound [saund] *adj.* 건전한 réasoning : 추론 the truth of a matter :

문제의 진실 appróach [əpróutʃ] *n.* 접근 with as nearly open a mind as we can : 우리가 할 수 있는 한 열린 마음으로 with a deep awáreness of ~ : ~을 깊이 인식하고서 limitátion [limətéiʃən] *n.* 한계 predisposítion [pri:dispəzíʃən] *n.* 경향, 소질 proposítion [prapəzíʃən] *n.* 제안, 계획 post-judice : 후판단, 사후(思後) 판단 preréquisite [pri:rékwəzit] *n.* 필수조건, 선행조건

주제문 : 첫 문장과 7~10행(결론문)
핵심어 : prejudice, a prerequisite for knowledge

1. 문제의 핵심어 : subject
   본문의 정답찾기 : 윗글은 판단(judgement)에 관한 문제를 다루고 있다. prejudice, prejudgement, postjudice 등.
2. 문제의 핵심어 : prejudice, cause
   본문의 정답찾기 : 3행
3. 문제의 핵심어 : imply
   본문의 정답찾기 : 1~6행
4. 문제의 핵심어 : on the other hand는 앞뒤 문장이 역접 관계일 때 쓰는 연결어
5. 문제의 핵심어 : maxim
   본문의 정답찾기 : "지식의 선결조건은 선입관을 버리고 증거를 세심하게 검토하여 결론을 내리는 건전한 추론이다." 가 윗글의 요지이다.

【정답】1. C 2. A 3. A 4. D 5. B

[17] 빙하시대부터 여러 다른 종류의 들소들이 북미대륙에 서식해오고 있었으나, 오늘날은 두 종류만 생존하고 있다. wood bison은 둘 중에 더 큰놈으로, 지금은 서부 캐나다에서 주로 발견된다. 미국에서는 Plains bison 또는 버팔로가 더 잘 알려져 있다. 한때는 이 동물의 수많은 떼를 동부의 아팔라치아산맥에서 서부에 있는 록키산맥까지 어디서든 볼 수가 있었다.

bíson [báisən] *n.* 들소 have p.p … since … : since가 시간을 나타낼 때는 완료형을 동반한다 only two (bison species) exist. Better known in the United States is the Plains bison, or buffalo.(도치) → The Plains bison, or buffalo is better known in the United States. at one time : 한 때는 herd [həːrd] *n.* 무리, 떼 sight [sait] *v.* 찾아내다, 목격하다 could be sighted : 눈에 띄었다, 볼 수 있었다

주제문 : 첫 문장
핵심어 : bison, wood bison, Plains bison

1. 문제의 핵심어 : mainly discuss
   본문의 정답찾기 : 주제문 1~2행(today only two exist.)

2. 문제의 핵심어 : several types of bison
   본문의 정답찾기 : 1~2행(주제문)
3. 문제의 핵심어 : United States, well known
   본문의 정답찾기 : 4행(Better known in the United States is the Plains bison, or buffalo.)
4. 문제의 핵심어 : Plains bison
   본문의 정답찾기 : 4~7행(…herds of these animals …)

【정답】 1. B 2. D 3. A 4. A 5. C

[18] 헌법을 제정할 당시에는 정당이 없었다. 그러나 얼마 안 가서 미국정부가 어떻게 운영되어야 하는가에 대한 서로 다른 의견들이 사람들로 하여금 당파를 가지게 하였다. 반대되는 두 정당―알렉산더 헤밀턴이 이끄는 연방주의자들과 토마스 제퍼슨이 이끄는 반 연방주의자들―이 곧 형성되었다. 연방주의자들은 개별 주들과 전체로서의 국가를 위한 중요한 결정을 행사할 수 있는 강력한 연방정부를 원했다. 반 연방주의자들은 연방정부의 간섭없이 개별 주들이 각자 자신들의 결정을 행사하기를 원했다. 오늘날까지도 공화당과 민주당은 주정부 또는 연방정부 어느쪽이 더 많은 통제력을 가져야 하는가를 다투고 있다.

the Constitútion : 헌법 political party : 정당 not long before : 오래가지 않아서, 얼마 안가서 run [rʌn] v. 운영하다, 경영하다 take sides : 당파를 갖다 oppóse [əpóuz] v. 반대하다, 맞서다 the Féderalists : (미) 연방주의자들 head [hed] v. 이끌다, 거느리다 (= lead) the Anti-Federalists : 反연방주의자들 the nation as a whole : 전체로서의 국가 interfére [intərfíər] v. 간섭하다 the Repúblican : (미) 공화당 the Democrátic : 민주당

주제문 : 1~4행, … however …
핵심어 : political parties

1. 문제의 핵심어 : topic
   본문의 정답찾기 : 1~4행. 이 글의 핵심어가 정당 (political parties)이다.
2. 문제의 핵심어 : Anti-Federalists
   본문의 정답찾기 : 8~9행
3. 문제의 핵심어 : government running, arguement
   본문의 정답찾기 : 8~10행(Even today …)
4. 문제의 핵심어 : Federalist, Anti-Federalist
   본문의 정답찾기 : 본문의 내용을 바탕으로 4개의 답을 하나씩 읽어가면서 오답을 솎아내는 방법이 효과적이다.

【정답】 1. B 2. D 3. D 4. D

[19] 흙을 만져보고 공기를 냄새 맞는 것 외에, 농부들은 이제 총모양의 적외선 계량기를 농작물에 겨냥하여 작물이 언제 급수가 필요한지를 알아낼 수 있게 되었다. 이 휴대용 계량기는 작물의 온도와 대기온도 사이의 차이를 나타내주는 디지털 판독정보를 제공한다. 물이 부족할 때 냉각방식으로 흔히 증발을 이용하는 식물은 햇볕으로부터 흡수하는 열이나 스스로 신진대사로부터 만들어 내는 열을 제거할 수가 없다. 그러므로 만일 그 계량기가 작물이 공기보다 더 덥다고 나타낸다면, 바로 급수를 할 때임을 의미한다.

feel [fi:l] v. 만지다 soil [sɔil] n. 흙 sniff [snif] v. (코로) 냄새 맡다 point A out B : A를 B에 겨누다 gun-shaped ínfrared méters : 총 모양의 적외선 계량기 watering : 급수 pórtable [pɔ́ːrtəbəl] adj. 휴대용의, 이동식의 dígital réadouts : 디지털 판독정보 índicate [índikeit] v. 나타내다, 적시하다 that(= temperature) of the surróunding air be short of ~ : ~이 부족한 evaporátion [ivæpəréiʃən] n. 증발, 기화 rid A of B : A에서 B를 제거하다 absórb[æbsɔ́ːrb] v. 흡수하다 metábolism [mətǽbəlizəm] n. 신진대사 írrigate [írəgeit] v. 급수하다, 관개하다, 물을 대다

주제문 : 첫 문장 핵심어 : infrared meters

1. 문제의 핵심어 : title
   본문의 정답찾기 : 주제문인 1~3행
2. 문제의 핵심어 : farmers, feel the soil
   본문의 정답찾기 : 1~3행
3. 문제의 핵심어 : meters, measure
   본문의 정답찾기 : 3~5행
4. 문제의 핵심어 : plant's cooling
   본문의 정답찾기 : 5~6행(a plant, which normally uses evaporation as a means of cooling)
5. 문제의 핵심어 : plant, cool
   본문의 정답찾기 : 5~8행

【정답】 1. A 2. D 3. B 4. A 5. D

[20] 대부분의 인구가 영세한 자족농민으로 들에 남아 있는 한, 현대산업사회는 발전할 수가 없다. 농부들은 비농업분야의 추구에 필요한 근로자들을 먹일 수 있는 충분한 여분의 식량을 생산하지 못한다. 또한 전통적인 경작방식에는 아주 많은 일손이 필요하기 때문에 근로자들이

농장에서 풀려나 공장으로 갈 수가 없다. 그리고 시장에 내놓을 어떤 것도 생산하지 않는 농민들은 스스로 구매자로서 시장에 갈 수 없다. 소비재에 대한 그 지역의 수요가 확대되지 않는다. 그렇듯이 지역 산업생산에 자극도 없다. 그러므로 현대경제가 성취되려면, 농업은 근로자와 저축을 새로이 산업화·도시화된 분야에 양보해야 한다.

so long as : ~하는 한 the bulk of~ : 대부분의~ subsístence [səbsístəns] n. 생계 nonagricúltural pursúits : 비농업분야 추구 not … nor … : … 도 아니고 … 역시 아니다 while = because hands : 일손 cultivátion [kʌltəvéiʃən] n. 경작, 재배 púrchaser [pə́:rtʃəsər] n. 구매자 consúmer goods : 소비재상품 stímulus [stímjələs] n. 자극 yield [ji:ld] v. 양도하다 úrbanized séctors : 도시화된 부분 achíeve [ətʃí:v] v. 성취하다

주제문 : 첫 문장
결론문 : 마지막 문장(… therefore …)
핵심어 : farmers, modern industrial society, a modern economy, agriculture

1. 문제의 핵심어 : main point
   본문의 정답찾기 : 주제문과 결론문
2. 문제의 핵심어 : subsistence, food production
   본문의 정답찾기 : 1~4행
3. 문제의 핵심어 : a disadvantage of traditional farming methods
   본문의 정답찾기 : 4~6행
4. 문제의 핵심어 : following the passage
   본문의 정답찾기 : 결론문인 마지막 문장을 읽고 유추한다.

【정답】 1. B 2. D 3. C 4. B

Step 3

[1] 청개구리는 1인치도 안되지만, 그 크고 맑은 울음소리는 거의 1마일 밖에서도 들린다. 비록 그놈이 가까이 앉아 있을 지라도 이 소리는 위치를 찾기가 힘들다. 아마 그 작은 놈을 보는 사람보다는 듣는 사람이 더 많을 것이다. 다 자란 숫놈만이 울음소리를 낼 수 있으며, 그 연주를 보는 것은 장관이다. 청개구리는 뒷다리를 걸치고 앉아, 뒤로 기대고서 노래를 한다. 그 하얀 목은 계속 부풀어올라서 막 터질 것 같은 반짝이는 물거품처럼 보인다. 입은 다문 채, 개구리는 2가지 음색의 4마디 가락의 소리를 낸다. 그 다음, 턱

밑의 낭은 늘어진 가죽 주머니가 된다. 다시 울음소리를 내기 위해, 그 놈은 다시 숨을 들이쉰다. 서늘한 날씨가 이어지는 기간이 잠시 개구리를 침묵시키겠지만, 다음에 또 찾아오는 따뜻한 봄밤이면 다시 노래를 부를 것이다.

a tree frog : 청개구리 call : 울음소리(= singing) lócate [lóukeit] v. 위치를 알아내다, 찾아내다 the creature = the tree frog = the tiny animal hind leg : 뒷다리 lean [li:n] v. 기대다 swell up : 부풀어 오르다 a shiny bubble : 반짝이는 거품주머니 be about to (burst) : 막 (터질)것 같은 burst-burst-burst (터지다) with its mouth closed : 입을 다문 채 sac [sæk] n. 낭, 주머니 chin [tʃin] n. 턱 to call again : 다시 노래를 부르기 위하여 (call = sing) take another breath : 숨을 다시 쉬다 spell [spel] n. 일정기간 (= season)

주제문 : 첫 문장(청개구리가 노래하는 모습을 그린 글)
핵심어 : a tree frog, its loud clear call

1. 문제의 핵심어 : meaning of the first sentence
2. 문제의 핵심어 : creature
   본문의 정답찾기 : the creature = the tree frog = the tiny animal
3. 문제의 핵심어 : the frog sings
   본문의 정답찾기 : 5~8행
4. 문제의 핵심어 : tree frog
   본문의 정답찾기 : 1~4행, 9~11행

【정답】 1. C 2. D 3. C 4. A

[2] 역사가들은 영어의 알파벳이 5,000여 년 전 성직자들에 의해 최초로 쓰여진 고대 이집트의 상형문자 또는 '성스러운 글'에서 유래되었다는 것을 대체로 인정한다. 상형문자는 돌에 새겨졌거나 파피루스에 그려진 그림들이다. 이집트가 쇠퇴한 뒤 수세기 동안 이집트에서 상형문자 조각들을 발견한 탐험가들은 그 의미에 관해서 신비감에 빠졌다. 그런데 1799년 나폴레옹 군대의 한 장교가 로제타라는 이집트 마을 근처에서 표면이 세 부분으로 나뉘어 조각된, 매끈하고 두꺼운 검은 돌을 발견하였다. 한 부분은 그리스어로, 한 부분은 상형문자로, 또 한 부분은 민중문자 또는 상형문자 간체로 쓰여진 역사적인 서술이었다. 그 그리스어 서술은 그것이 이집트 글과 꼭 같다고 말하고 있어서, 이 발견이 학자들에게 신비한 고대 조각물들의 판독을 가능케 하였다.

descénd [disénd] v. 내려오다, 유래하다 hieroglýphics [haiərəglífiks] n. 상형문자 sácred [séikrid] adj. 신성한 priest [priːst] n. 성직자, 제사장 carve [kaːrv] v. 새기다, 쪼다 cárvings n. 조각물 inscríbe [inskráib] v. 쓰다, 새기다 papýrus [pəpáiərəs] n. 종이 (paper의 어원) declíne [dikláin] v. 쇠퇴하다 explórer [iksplɔ́ːrer] n. 탐험가 mýstify [místəfai] v. 신비화하다 mystérióus adj. 신비로운 divíde into ~ : ~로 나뉘다 accóunt [əkáunt] n. 이야기, 서술 demótics [dimátiks] n. (고대이집트의) 민중문자, 상형문자의 간체(= símplified hieroglýphics) exáctly the same as ~ : ~와 꼭같이 enáble A to do : A가 ~하는 것을 가능케 하다 decipher [disáifər] v. (암호문을) 판독하다

주제문 : 첫 문장
결론문 : 마지막 문장(…this finding enabled scholars to decipher the mysterious ancient carvings.). 1799년 Rosetta stone의 발견으로 고대 이집트 상형문자의 해독이 가능하게 되었다.
핵심어 : ancient Egyptian, hieroglyphics, Rosetta stone

1. 문제의 핵심어 : facts about hieroglyphics
   본문의 정답찾기 : 3~4행. 이런 문제는 답을 먼저 읽고 난 다음, 본문의 상형문자에 관한 서술문들을 차례로 읽어가며 오답을 솎아낸다.
2. 문제의 핵심어 : Rosetta stone
   본문의 정답찾기 : 6~9행
3. 문제의 핵심어 : Rosetta stone, important
   본문의 정답찾기 : 마지막 행
4. 문제의 핵심어 : Hieroglyphics, mystery
   본문의 정답찾기 : 4~6행

【정답】 1. C 2. B 3. D 4. B

[3] 훌라멩코 무용수처럼 탭댄서도 기본적으로 즉흥연기자이다. 탭댄스를 지켜보면서 사람들은 그 개인의 개성이나 창의성을 음미하려 한다. 영화에서 빌 로빈슨이 춤을 출 때, 그의 기교와 현란한 리듬은 보이는 것과 같이 들린다. 니콜라스 형제들은 극장의 무대 앞 아치나 벽을 타고 뛰어올라가거나, 아니면 플랫폼을 뛰어내려 무대바닥에 두 다리를 나란히하여 내려앉는다. 한쪽 다리를 잃은 페 그레그 베이츠는 의족으로 춤을 추어서 장기를 펼쳤다. 샌드맨 심스는 (프레드 애스테어가 자신의 영화에서 그랬듯이) 모래를 무대바닥에 흩뿌리고도 아주 부드럽게 탭댄스를 추었고, 자장가처럼 고요한 춤을 추며 미끄러지듯 돌아 들어왔다.

tap dance : 탭댄스 flaménco : 플라멩코(스페인 Andalusia 지방 집시들의 춤이나 그 노래의 이름) ímproviser [ímprəvaizər] n. 즉흥시인, 연주가 (= impróvisator) sávor [séivər] v. 맛보다, 음미하다 invéntiveness [invéntivnes] n. 창의성 sophísticated [səfístəkeitid] adj. 복잡한, 어려운 land in splits : 두 다리를 일직선으로 벌려 바닥에 앉다 make a spécialty : 장기를 펼치다 scátter [skǽtər] v. 흩뿌리다 film : 영화 slide-slid-slid (미끄러지다) as soothing as lúllabies : 자장가처럼 고요한

주제문 : 첫 문장 핵심어 : tap dancer

1. 문제의 핵심어 : mainly discuss
   본문의 정답찾기 : 1~3행
2. 문제의 핵심어 : flamenco dancer, tap dancer, similar
   본문의 정답찾기 : 1~3행
3. 문제의 핵심어 : An acrobatic style of dancing
   본문의 정답찾기 : 5~7행
4. 문제의 핵심어 : sand
   본문의 정답찾기 : 8~10행
5. 문제의 핵심어 : tap dancing
   본문의 정답찾기 : 4~5행

【정답】 1. A 2. B 3. C 4. D 5. B

[4] 그러나 과학의 성공인 지적인 흥분이나 실용적인 응용 모두 과학의 자기수정 성격에 의존하고 있다. 어떤 타당한 생각도 시험하는 길이 있게 마련이다. 어떤 타당한 실험도 재생할 수가 있다. 과학자들의 성격이나 믿음은 타당성이 없다. 그 모든 문제는 증거가 그들의 논지를 뒷받침하느냐 하는 것이다. 당국으로부터의 단순한 논쟁은 믿을 게 못된다. 너무도 많은 당국자들이 너무 자주 실수를 저질러왔다. 나는 학교나 미디어에 의해 전달받은 매우 효과적이고 과학적인 사고방식을 보고싶다. 그것들이 정치학으로 소개되는 것을 보게 되면, 분명 놀랍고도 기쁠 것이다. 새로운 증거나 새로운 주장이 소개될 때, 과학자들은 완전히 그리고 공개적으로 자신들의 마음을 바꿀 줄 알고 있다. 나는 정치가가 변화에 대해 마지막으로 열린 마음과 기꺼운 마음을 보인 적이 언제인지 기억할 수가 없다.

intelléctual [intəléktʃuəl] adj. 지적인, 지성의 excítement [iksáitmənt] n. 흥분 applicátion [æplikéiʃən] n. 적용, 응용 self-corrécting cháracter of scíence : 과학의 자기수정 성격 válid idéa/expériment : 타당한 생각/실험 irrélevant [iréləvənt] adj. 관련이 없는, 타당하지 않은 conténtion [kənténʃən] n. 주장, 논지, 다툼 authórity [əθɔ́ːriti] n. 관청, 당국 count [kaunt] v. 신뢰하다

efféctive scientífic modes of thought : 효과적이고 과학적인 사고
방식 astónishment [əstániʃmənt] n. 놀라움 delight [diláit] n.
기쁨 recáll [rikɔ́:l] v. 회상하다, 기억하다 the last time : (접속사)

주제문 : 첫 문장
핵심어 : the self-correcting character of science

1. 문제의 핵심어 : mainly discuss
   본문의 정답찾기 : 주제문인 1~3행
2. 문제의 핵심어 : preceding the passage
   본문의 정답찾기 : 앞 단락의 내용은 첫 문장을 보면 유추가
   가능하다. But the success of science …
3. 문제의 핵심어 : not produce similar
   본문의 정답찾기 : 문제와 4가지 답만 보아도 답이 나올 수
   있다. 같은 결과를 얻지 못하는 실험 (= invalid
   experiment)
4. 문제의 핵심어 : essential to scientists' work
   본문의 정답찾기 : 5~6행(all that matters is whether
   the evidence supports their contentions.)
5. 문제의 핵심어 : arguments from authority
   본문의 정답찾기 : 7행

   【정답】 1. C 2. A 3. C 4. D 5. A

수 없는 líghtweight métal : 경금속 desíre [dizáiər] v. 원하다, 희
망하다 lóngstanding utílity : 지속적인 용도 ínsulate [ínsəleit]
v. ~을 절연하다, 단절하다 médicine [médəsən] n. 의약품

주제문 : 첫 문장 핵심어 : magnesium

1. 문제의 핵심어 : topic
   본문의 정답찾기 : 단락의 전반부는 마그네슘의 추출을, 후
   반부는 마그네슘의 이용을 서술
2. 문제의 핵심어 : magnesium, first, obtain
   본문의 정답찾기 : 첫 문장의 3~5행
3. 문제의 핵심어 : new method of obtaining
   magnesium, direct consequense
   본문의 정답찾기 : 6~11행(Since the direct extraction
   method was developed about 1941 …)
4. 문제의 핵심어 : important to industry
   본문의 정답찾기 : 11~14행(it has innumerable uses
   in other industries where a lightweight metal is
   desired)
5. 문제의 핵심어 : the past fifty years, magnesium
   본문의 정답찾기 : 6~7행

   【정답】 1. D 2. A 3. B 4. C 5. D

[5] 마그네슘은 우리가 엄청난 양의 바닷물을 화학약품
으로 처리하여 얻는 또 다른 광물인데, 본래는 염수(간수)
나 산(山) 전체를 구성하는 백운암 같은 마그네슘 함유 암
석을 처리하여서만 추출되었다. 바닷물 1입방 마일 속에
는 약 4백만 톤의 마그네슘이 있다. 1941년에 직접추출방
법이 개발된 이후에 생산이 엄청나게 증가하였다. 전쟁
때 항공산업의 발달을 가능하게 한 것은 바다에서 나온
마그네슘 덕택이었다. 왜냐하면 미국에서 만들어진 (다른
대부분의 나라에서도 마찬가지인) 모든 비행기는 약
500kg의 마그네슘 금속을 함유하고 있다. 경금속이 요구
되는 다른 많은 산업분야에서 셀 수도 없이 많이 사용되
고 있다. 게다가 장기적인 용도의 절연재료로서 뿐만 아
니라, 인쇄용 잉크, 의약품, 치약 등에도 사용되고 있다.

míneral [mínərəl] n. 광물 obtáin [əbtéin] v. 얻다 vólume
[váljuːm] n. 체적, 용량 huge vólumes of ocean water : 엄청난
양의 바닷물 chémical [kémikəl] n. 화학약품 deríve[diráiv] v. 얻
다, 추출해 내다(= extráct) be compósed of : ~로 구성되어 있다
whole mountain rages : 전 산악지대 a cúbic mile of séawater
: 바닷물 1입방마일 diréct extráction méthod : 직접추출방법
enórmously [inɔ́:rməsli] adv. 엄청나게 aviátion índustry : 항
공산업 half a ton : 500kg innúmerable [injúːmərəbəl] adj. 셀

[6] 옛날에는 부(富)가 식량이나 도구, 귀금속, 보석 등
손으로 만져지는 것들로 측정되고 교환되었다. 그후 물물
교환방식은 동전으로 대체되었는데, 그 동전들은 귀금속
으로 된 것이었기 때문에 아직도 실질적인 가치를 가지고
있다. 뒤에 법률적인 돈, 즉 모든 사람이 인정할 때만 가
치를 지니는 지폐가 동전의 뒤를 잇는다.

오늘날 빛의 속도로 기계들이 윙윙 소리를 내면서 돈
을 '비트'나 '바이트' 배열로 또는 컴퓨터 정보단위로 축
소시켜 만져지지 않는 형태로 바꾸는 전자화폐제도가 점
차 소개되고 있다. 전자식 자금이동수단은 벌써 서로 다
른 은행, 기업, 국가들이 컴퓨터나 원격 통신장치를 통해
돈을 순식간에 보내고 받도록 하고 있다.

méasure [méʒər] v. 측정하다 tángibly [tǽndʒəbli] adv. 만질 수
있게(=in things that could be touched) bárter sýstem : 물물교
환 방식 since = because fíat [fíːət] n. 법령, 재가 fiat money :
법률적인 돈 paper note : 지폐 electrónic mónetary sýstem : 전
자화폐 제도 redúce [ridjúːs] v. 감소시키다 arráy [əréi] n. 배열, 정
렬 whiz [hwiz] v. 윙윙 소리내다 electrónic fúnd transfér : 전자
식 자금이동수단 telecommunicátion devíce : 원격통신 장치

주제문 : 부(wealth)를 나타내는 화폐제도의 변화과정을 순서

대로 나열한 글이다.
핵심어 : 첫 단락(wealth, barter system, coins, paper notes), 둘째 단락(electronic monetary system)

1. 문제의 핵심어 : title
   본문의 정답찾기 : 각 단락의 첫 행을 참고로 한다.
2. 문제의 핵심어 : kind of exchange of wealth
   본문의 정답찾기 : 첫 문장(…exchanged tangibly, in things that …)
3. 문제의 핵심어 : food, tools, precious metals, stones
   본문의 정답찾기 : 첫 문장(…exchanged tangibly, in things that could be touched: food, tools, and precious metals and stones)
4. 문제의 핵심어 : coins
   본문의 정답찾기 : 4~6행
5. 문제의 핵심어 : computerized monetary systems
   본문의 정답찾기 : 10~13행

【정답】 1. B 2. A 3. A 4. D 5. C

[7] 20세기의 가장 작품활동을 많이 한 사진작가 중의 한 사람인 마가렛 버크와이트는 1920년대에서 1950년대까지 세계사의 중인이었다. 학창시절 그녀는 학교생활을 사진으로 기록하였다. 미국 미술계가 모더니즘을 껴안고 기술에서 새로운 미를 찾았을 때 그녀의 경력이 꽃피었다. 미학적 원칙들이 용광로나 세탁기 같은 아주 평범한 대상에 적용되었고, 버크와이트는 그 시기의 최고 산업사진작가 중의 한 사람이 되었다. 그녀의 경력 가운데 1930년대 미국 중서부 지방의 심각한 가뭄이나 제2차 세계대전 같이 아주 중요한 주제들을 역시 촬영하였고, 자신의 작품이 세계에서 가장 유명한 잡지에 실리는 것을 보게되었다.

prolífic [proulífik] *adj.* 다작의, 작품활동이 많은 wítness [wítnis] *n.* 중인 blóssom [blásəm] *v.* 꽃피다 at a time : 한 때 embráce [embréis] *v.* 껴안다 aesthétic [esθétik] *adj.* 미학적인 banál [bənǽl] *adj.* 평범한, 진부한 banál óbject : 평범한 사물 fúrnace [fə́:rnis] *n.* 용광로 wáshing machíne : 세탁기 such (important subjects) as :~와 같은 (아주 중요한 주제들) drought [draut] *n.* 가뭄, 한발

주제문 : 첫 문장
핵심어 : Margaret Bourke-White, photojournalist, witness to world events, her career

1. 문제의 핵심어 : subject

본문의 정답찾기 : 주제문인 첫 문장과 글의 핵심어들에서 추론
2. 문제의 핵심어 : Margaret Bourke-White
   본문의 정답찾기 : 1행(photojournalist), 3~4행(made a photographic record of), 8행(best industrial photographer), 9행(photographed)
3. 문제의 핵심어 : how many years
   본문의 정답찾기 : 2~3행(a witness to world events from the 1920's through the 1950's)
4. 문제의 핵심어 : Modernism
   본문의 정답찾기 : 4~8행
5. 문제의 핵심어 : subject
   본문의 정답찾기 : 8~12행

【정답】 1. C 2. A 3. C 4. A 5. D

[8] 자력은 자석이라고 하는 물체들 사이에서 작용하는 자연의 중요한 힘이다. 자석은 흔히 금속성 물질을 끌어당기는 힘으로 잘 알려져 있다. 지구 자체는 마치 커다란 자석이 중심부를 흐르는 것처럼 작용한다. 자력이 가장 강한 지역이 남북 양극이다. 놀랍게도 지구를 에워싸고 있는 자기장이 원자 주위의 자기장보다 100만 배나 더 약하고, 우리 은하계 주위의 자기장보다는 100만 배나 더 강하다. 자력은 어느 복잡한 산업기술도 실행 불가능한 것이 없는 대량의 전기를 생산하는 데 필수적인 역할을 한다.

mágnetism [mǽgnətizəm] *n.* 자력 mágnet [mǽgnit] *n.* 자석, 자철광 of nature (which is) acting between be known for ~ : ~로 알려져 있다 attract [ətrǽkt] *v.* 끌어당기다 metállic súbstances : 금속물질 behave [bihéiv] *v.* 작용하다, 행동하다(= act) its center = the center of the Earth surprísingly [sərpráiziŋli] *adv.* 놀랍게도 magnétic field : 자기장(場) surróund [səráund] *v.* 에워싸다 atom [ǽtəm] *n.* 원자 it = the magnetic field surrounding the Earth gálaxy [gǽləksi] *n.* 은하계 play an (essential) role in -ing :~하는데 (필수적인) 역할을 하다 inféasible [infí:zəbəl] *adj.* 실현 불가능한, 실천할 수 없는 (= imprácticable)

주제문 : 첫 문장 핵심어 : magnetism, magnet

1. 문제의 핵심어 : title
   본문의 정답찾기 : 주제문 1행 참고
2. 문제의 핵심어 : magnets, be known for
   본문의 정답찾기 : 둘째 문장
3. 문제의 핵심어 : Earth

본문의 정답찾기 : 3~5행
4. 문제의 핵심어 : it
  본문의 정답찾기 : 앞 절의 주어(the magnetic field surrounding the Earth)
5. 답문장들의 핵심어 : objects, magnetic field
  본문의 정답찾기 : 5~7행. 이처럼 본문내용의 서술에 관한 문제는 4개의 답문장을 보고 공통된 핵심어를 찾은 다음, 본문에서 그 핵심어의 위치를 찾는다.

  【정답】 1. C 2. D 3. C 4. C 5. A

[9] 사업상 또는 놀러 자주 여행을 가는 사람들은 흔히 여러 유형의 건강문제로 고통을 받는다. 그런데, 그 고통의 절반 이상은 쉽게 예방할 수 있다. 가장 흔한 질환인 두통은 아스피린이나 진통제를 다량 챙겨 가면 피할 수 있다. 또 다른 흔한 질환은 탈것을 계속해서 이용하다 생기는 멀미이다. 대부분의 건강식품 가게에서 파는 생강캡슐이 치료제로서 효과적인 것으로 알려져 있다. 다른 흔한 질환들로는 효과적인 햇볕화상 방지제를 사용하면 예방할 수 있는 햇볕에 탄 화상, 방충제나 연고를 사용하면 관리되는 벌레물림이 있다. 칼에 밴 상처나 긁힘 등 일상적인 상처에는 밴드나 살균크림 등이 들어 있는 구급함을 권장한다.

on búsiness : 사업상 용무로 for pléasure : 놀러 áilment [éilmənt] n. (가벼운) 질환 take along : 챙겨가다 ámple [ǽmpl] adj. 풍부한 afflíction [əflíkʃən] n. 고통 ginger [dʒíndʒər] n. 생강 rémedy [rémədi] n. 치료 súnburn [sʌ́nbə:rn] n. 햇볕에 탄 화상 súnscreen [sʌ́nskri:n] n. 햇볕 화상 방지제 ínsect bite : 벌레물림 óintment [ɔ́intmənt] n. 연고 cut : 칼에 베인 자리 scratch [skrǽtʃ] n. 긁힌 자리 first-aid kit : 구급함 bandage : 밴드 antiséptic [æntəséptik] adj. 살균 의, 방부 의, 소독하는 recomménd [rekəménd] v. 권하다

주제문 : 첫 문장
핵심어 : travel, health problems, can be prevented

1. 문제의 핵심어 : title
  본문의 정답찾기 : 첫 문장 참조
2. 문제의 핵심어 : travelers
  본문의 정답찾기 : 3~5행(The most common ailment, a headache …)
3. 문제의 핵심어 : motion sickness, remedy
  본문의 정답찾기 : 5~7행
4. 문제의 핵심어 : a solution to a health problem
  본문의 정답찾기 : 3행부터 시작되는 설명문장들을 차례로 읽으며, 각각의 치료제를 찾는다.
5. 문제의 핵심어 : travelers
  답문장들의 핵심어 : health
  본문의 정답찾기 : 주제론적인 문제이므로 주제문에서 유추한다.

  【정답】 1. B 2. D 3. C 4. B 5. A

[10] 치타는 엄청난 질주속도로 잘 알려진 커다란 고양이 같은 동물이다. 단거리에 가장 빠른 동물인 치타는 시속 70마일까지 질주할 수 있다. 한때는 활동반경이 중동지방과 중앙아시아, 인도의 일부지방까지 포함되었으나, 그러나 오늘날, 사냥과 농업의 영향으로 치타는 주로 아프리카 중·동부지역으로 국한되었다.

성숙한 치타는 흔히 명확한 지역 안에서 혼자 살아간다. 치타 암수는 짝짓기를 위해서 잠시만 만난다. 치타는 다른 고양이들의 발톱과는 달리 완전히 감춰지지 않는 날카로운 발톱으로 적을 멀리 쫓아낸다. 치타는 또 포효뿐 아니라 가르랑거림도 할 수 있는 몇 안되는 큰 고양이 중의 하나이다.

Chéetah [tʃíːtə] n. 치타(표범 비슷함) sprint [sprint] v. 질주하다, 역주하다 (sprint) up to (70 miles per hour) : (시속 70마일) 까지 (달리다) at one time : 한때는 restríct A to B : A를 B(지역으)로 제한(국한)하다 well-defined territory : 명확히 지정된 영역 briefly : 잠시 for the purpose of ~ : ~때문에 mate [meit] v. 짝짓다, 교미하다 keep (enemies) away with ~ : ~로 (적들을) 쫓아내다 claw [klɔː] n. 발톱 those = claws retráct [ritrǽkt] v. 움츠리다, 감추다 purr [pəːr] v. (고양이처럼) 목구멍을 가르랑거리다 roar [rɔːr] v. 포효하다

주제문 : 각 단락의 첫 문장
핵심어 : cheetah, speed (첫 단락), live alone (둘째 단락)

1. 문제의 핵심어 : cheetah, known for
  본문의 정답찾기 : 1~3행
2. 문제의 핵심어 : found today
  본문의 정답찾기 : 4~6행
3. 문제의 핵심어 : number of cheetah
  본문의 정답찾기 : 4~6행
4. 문제의 핵심어 : adult cheetah
  본문의 정답찾기 : 7~8행
5. 문제의 핵심어 : most big cats
  본문의 정답찾기 : 마지막 문장

  【정답】 1. D 2. C 3. D 4. A 5. C

[11] 세계 자연의 경이 중에서 나이아가라 폭포만큼 장관은 거의 없다. 미국과 캐나다 국경을 따라 흐르는 나이아가라 강에 위치한 나이아가라 폭포는 실제로 아메리카 폭포와 말굽폭포 두 개로 이루어져 있다. 전자는 국경의 미국 쪽인 뉴욕주에 있고, 후자는 캐나다 쪽에 있다. 나이아가라 강물의 85%는 말굽폭포로 흐르는데, 두 폭포 중에서 더 인상적이다.

매년 약 1천만 명이 폭포를 찾는데, 대부분 여름 관광철 동안이다. 관광객들은 기선을 타고 폭포의 소용돌이 가까이까지 올라가거나, 강 양안에 있는 공원에서 폭포를 구경한다. 나이아가라 폭포는 오랫동안 신혼부부들의 가장 인기 있는 신혼여행지다.

nátural wónders : 자연의 경이 spectácular [spektǽkjələr] *adj.* 장관의, 장대한 as~as … : … 만큼 ~한 lócate [loukeit] *v.* 위치시키다, 두다 bórder[bɔ́:rdər] *n.* 국경 consist of ~ : ~로 구성되어 있다 hórseshoe[hɔ́:rʃu:] *n.* 말굽 the former : 전자 the later : 후자 while : 반면에 impréssive [imprésiv] *adj.* 인상적인 síghtseer [sáitsi:ər] *n.* 관광객 stéamer [stí:mər] *n.* 기선 up close to ~ : ~에 가까이까지 올라가다 bóiling water : 떨어진 폭포수의 소용돌이 view them : watch the water falls destinátion [destənéiʃən] *n.* 목적지 néwlyweds : 신혼부부

주제문 : 각 단락의 첫 문장
핵심어 : Niagara Falls, sightseers

1. 문제의 핵심어 : title
   본문의 정답찾기 : 첫 문장에서 핵심어를 유추해낸다.
2. 문제의 핵심어 : entirely U.S. side of the border
   본문의 정답찾기 : 4~6행
3. 문제의 핵심어 : Horseshoe Falls
   본문의 정답찾기 : 4~7행
4. 문제의 핵심어 : watch the falls
   본문의 정답찾기 : 9~11행
5. 문제의 핵심어 : Niagara Falls
   본문의 정답찾기 : 둘째 단락을 읽고, 일치하는 것을 찾는다.

【정답】1. C 2. B 3. A 4. C 5. A

[12] 1915년까지 영화는 짧았고, 프로그램은 여러 작업으로 구성되었다. 그때, D.W. 그리피스를 비롯한 몇몇 사람들은 완전한 길이의 영화를 만들기 시작하였는데, 멜로드라마와 꼭같은 강렬한 감동을 주었고, 연극이 주는 것 이상의 훌륭한 볼거리를 제공하였다. 결국, 제1차 세계대전이 끝난 뒤, 점점 더 많은 관객들이 영화를 위해 연극을 버렸다. 이런 경향은 2가지 새로운 요소의 결과로 1920년대 후반에는 가속되었다. 1929년에는 이전의 무성영화에 음향이 가미되었고, 그리하여 연극이 주장하던 몇 가지 우월성의 하나는 사라졌다. 1929년에는 심각한 경제공황이 시작되었다. 연극관람의 비용이라는 작은 부분 때문에 청중들이 영화를 보러갈 수가 있었기에, 특히 공황이 깊어짐에 따라 연극관람은 소수만이 볼 수 있는 사치가 되었다.

2차 세계대전이 끝날 때까지, 미국의 연극은 뉴욕시에 약 30개의 극장과, 그곳에서 비롯되는 소수의 유랑극단으로 줄어들었다.

up to ~ : ~(언제)까지 be made up of ~ : ~로 구성되다 full-length film : 완전한 길이의 영화 emotional appeal : ·감정적인 매력, 정서적인 감동 mélodrama [mélədra:mə] *n.* 18,9세기에 걸쳐 유행한 음악을 곁들인 통속극 presént [prizént] *v.* 제공하다 (= províde, óffer, give) spéctacle [spéktəkəl] *n.* 장관, 훌륭한 볼거리 spéctator [spékteitər] *n.* 구경꾼, 관객 spectácular [spektǽkjələr] *adj.* 장관의, 화려한, 볼거리 많은 théater [θí:ətər] *n.* 연극 (= play, drama) desért [dizə́:rt] *v.* 버리다, 포기하다 trend [trend] *n.* 경향, 추세 accélerate [ækséləreit] *v.* 가속화하다, 증가하다 príncipal [prínsəpəl] *adj.* 중요한 claim [kleim] *n.* 주장 superiórity[səpiəriɔ́:reti] *n.* 우월성 vánish [vǽniʃ] *v.* 사라지다 económic depréssion : 경제공황 fráction [frǽkʃən] *n.* 작은 부분 théatregoing [θí:ətərgóuiŋ] *n.* 연극관람(*cf.* théatregoer [θí:ətərgóuər] *n.* 연극(영화)관람객, 관객, 청중 (= spéctator, áudience)) lúxury[lʌ́kʃəri] *n.* 사치, 호사 afford [əfɔ́:rd] *v.* 할 수 있다 déepen [dí:pn] *v.* 깊게 하다, 심화하다 redúce [ridjú:s] *v.* 줄이다, 감소시키다 cómpany : 극단 tóuring cómpanies : 유랑극단 oríginate [ərídʒəneit] *v.* 비롯하다

주제문 : 핵심어인 movie, theatre 등의 역사를 연대별로 서술한 나열식의 글이다.

핵심어 : movie, theatre

1. 문제의 핵심어 : movies could do better than the theatre
   본문의 정답찾기 : 3~5행
2. 문제의 핵심어 : 1920's, objection to films
   본문의 정답찾기 : 6~9행
3. 문제의 핵심어 : people choose the movies over the theatre
   본문의 정답찾기 : 9~12행
4. 문제의 핵심어 : by the end of World War II
   본문의 정답찾기 : 둘째 단락
5. 문제의 핵심어 : 재 진술에 관한 문제이다.
   본문의 정답찾기 : this trend가 지칭하는 말을 찾으면 된다. 바로 앞 문장이다.(5~6행)

making …)
3. 문제의 핵심어 : others
   본문의 정답찾기 : 8~12행
4. 문제의 핵심어 : many mainstream historians
   본문의 정답찾기 : 8~12행

【정답】 1. D 2. A 3. B 4. C

[13] 바바라 터치맨은 미국의 퓰리처상을 수상한 역사가로 대중들 사이에서 돋보이는 방법을 알고 있었다. 미국 독립전쟁 이야기로 베스트셀러 *The First Salute*(첫 인사)의 저자인 터치맨은 역사가 보통사람들에게 받아들여지도록 만드는 특별한 재능을 가졌었다. 책을 출간한 다른 역사가들과는 달리, 터치맨은 사실의 무미건조한 개작에 스스로를 제한하지 않았다. 그녀의 산문은 학문적인 처리를 순수드라마와 노련하게 연결하였다.

터치맨은 박사학위 따기를 거절함으로써 스스로 또 한 번 돋보였다. 그것은 많은 주류 동료들의 비난을 얻기도 했다. 그들에게서 고등교육의 결핍은 그녀의 책을 문학작품이나 학습교재로서 의심을 하도록 만들었다. 그러나 다른 소수파들은 그녀가 박사학위를 받았더라면, 그녀의 역사조사 방식은 실제로 어려움을 겪었을 것이라고 주장하였다. 그들은 역사가들의 작업이 대부분 도서관의 서가 위에 묻혀있는 것은 그들의 따분한 노력이라고 지적하였다. 반면에, 터치맨은 역사를 대중의 관심 쪽으로 가져오는 데 성공하였다.

Púlitzer-wínning histórian : 퓰리처상 수상 역사가 stand out (from) : 돋보이다, 뛰어나다 (= be distínguished) accóunt [əkáunt] *n.* 이야기, 서술, 담화(= story) make (history) appéaling to~ : (역사를)~에게 받아들이게 하다, 설득력 있게 하다 common people : 보통사람들 (= ordinary people, average people) dry retélling : 무미건조한 개작 prose [prouz] *n.* 산문 (*cf.* verse [vəːrs] *n.* 운문) combíne A with B : A를 B와 연결하다, 묶다 schólarly [skálərli] *adj.* 학문적인, 학자적인 schólarly tréatment : 학문적인 처리 high drama : 순수드라마 declíne to do :~하기를 거절하다 pursúe [pursú:] *v.* 추구하다 dóctorate degrée : 박사학위 disrespéct [disrispékt] *n.* 무례, 실례 máinstream cólleagues : 주류 동료들 ↔ a few others : 소수의 다른 동료들 advanced training : 고등교육 suspéct [səspékt] *v.* 의심하다 líterary works : 문학작품 lie buried : 묻혀있다 shelves : 서가

주제문 : 각 단락의 첫 문장
핵심어 : Barbara Tuchman, stand out, declining to pursue a doctorate degree

1. 문제의 핵심어 : title
   본문의 정답찾기 : 주제문인 각 단락의 첫 문장에서 유추
2. 문제의 핵심어 : Barbara Tuchman, a special ability
   본문의 정답찾기 : 4~5행(…a special talent for

making …)
3. 문제의 핵심어 : others
   본문의 정답찾기 : 8~12행
4. 문제의 핵심어 : many mainstream historians
   본문의 정답찾기 : 8~12행

【정답】 1. D 2. A 3. B 4. C

[14] 턱슨 대학의 한 인류학 교수가 '쓰레기처리학'이라고 하는 완전히 새로운 학문분야를 창안해냈다. 윌리엄 라체와 그의 학생들은 1973년부터 턱슨의 주택들 앞에 수거를 기다리는 쓰레기를 연구하였다. 그 지역 위생회사의 도움으로, 그들은 약 120톤의 쓰레기를 검사하고 분류하여 흥미로운 결론에 도달하였다.

한 가지 결론은 중간소득 가정이 저소득 가정이나 고소득 가정보다 음식물을 더 많이 소비한다는 것이다. 또 다른 사실은 가난한 가정들이 한꺼번에 대량으로 구입할 수가 없기에, 부유한 가정들보다 음식물이나 가정용품에 돈을 더 많이 지불한다는 것이다. 결국, 전체 쓰레기량은 금세기 초반의 약 절반에 해당되는 15%까지 내려간다. 이것은 현대적인 냉장방식, 교통, 처리과정과 포장방식 덕분이다.

anthropólogy [ænθrəpáladʒi] *n.* 인류학 sanitátion [sænətéiʃən] *n.* 위생 inspéct [inspékt] *v.* 검사하다 cátegorize [kǽtigəraiz] *v.* 분류하다 middle(low/upper)-income family : 중간(저/고)소득가정 hóusehold ítems : 가정용품 cannot afford to (buy) : (살) 수가 없다 in bulk : 대량으로, 한꺼번에 overall waste figure : 전체적인 쓰레기량 be attríbuted to~ : ~의 원인(탓)으로 돌리는, ~때문에, ~의 덕분인 refrigerátion [rifridʒəréiʃən] *n.* 냉장

주제문 : 각 단락의 첫 문장
핵심어 : garbology, one result

1. 문제의 핵심어 : mainly discuss
   본문의 정답찾기 : 두 단락의 주제문에서 요지를 압축한다.
2. 문제의 핵심어 : William Rathje
   본문의 정답찾기 : 1~4행(첫 단락의 첫 두 문장)
3. 문제의 핵심어 : William Rathje, his students, examine
   본문의 정답찾기 : 2~5행
4. 문제의 핵심어 : a reason for the decrease in waste since the first quarter of this century
   본문의 정답찾기 : 10~13행
5. 문제의 핵심어 : the poor, the rich

본문의 정답찾기 : 7~10행

【정답】 1. C 2. D 3. C 4. A 5. B

[15] 사람들은 흔히 일을 완수할 시간이 결코 충분하지 않다고 불평한다. 계획된 많은 일상적인 일들이 완수되기 전에 시간이 지나가 버리는 것 같다. 시간관리 전문가들에 따르면, 이에 대한 주된 이유는 대부분의 사람들이 무엇을 먼저 해야 할 것인가에 관한 우선순위를 세우지 못한다는 것이다. 사소하고 시간만 잡아먹는 일들을 하다가 지쳐버려서, 중요한 일들은 결코 완수하지 못한다.

성공한 사람들이 흔히 사용하는 한 가지 간단한 해결방안은 매일 완수해야 할 일의 목록을 작성하는 것이다. 이 목록은 가장 중요한 일에서부터 가장 덜 중요한 일까지 순서를 매겨서, 매일 규칙적으로 점검하여 과정을 평가하는 것이다. 이것은 시간을 관리하는 효과적인 방법일 뿐만 아니라, 개인에게 자신의 일을 완수했다는 응분의 만족감을 주기도 한다. 목록을 작성하지 않는 사람들은 임무완수의 중요성에 비해 하루일과의 끝을 불확실하게 맞이하고, 그 초과시간은 정신적·육체적 건강에 심각한 문제들을 야기할 수 있다.

slip away : 놓치다, 지나가다 chore [tʃɔːr] *n.* 일상적인 일, 잡일 get done : 완수하다, 수행하다 according to ~ : ~에 따르면 time mánagement éxpert : 시간관리 전문가 priority [praiɔ́rəti] *n.* 우선 순위 get tired down : 지쳐 떨어지다 trívial [tríviəl] *adj.* 사소한 time-consúming mátters : 시간만 소비하는 일들 solútion [səlúːʃən] *n.* 해결(책) those at the top : 꼭대기에 있는 사람들, 성공한 사람들 keep lists of tasks : 작업 목록을 만들다 order [ɔ́ːrdər] *v.* 순서를 정하다 asséss [əsés] *v.* 판단하다, 평가하다 a much-desérved sense of satisfáction : 응분의 만족감 uncértainty [ʌnsɔ́ːrtnti] *n.* 불확실성 signíficance [signífikəns] *n.* 중요성(= impórtance) contríbute to ~ : ~에 이바지하다

주제문 : 각 단락의 첫 문장
핵심어 : time management, keep lists of tasks

1. 문제의 핵심어 : title
   본문의 정답찾기 : 둘째 문장(… time management …)
2. 문제의 핵심어 : never seem to have enough time
   본문의 정답찾기 : 4~5행(the main reason for this is that most people fail to set priorities about what to do first.)
3. 문제의 핵심어 : those
   본문의 정답찾기 : 7행, those at the top(성공한 사람들)

4. 문제의 핵심어 : time management problem, one solution
   본문의 정답찾기 : 7~8행
5. 문제의 핵심어 : following the passage
   본문의 정답찾기 : 둘째 단락의 시작이 'One solution …' 이므로, 다음 단락을 추론할 수 있다.

【정답】 1. D 2. A 3. D 4. C 5. B

[16] 대부분의 교육전문가들은 조기교육이 어린이들에게 자기능력을 깨닫게 하고, 이 능력을 이용할 수 있는 자신감을 부여해야 한다고 믿고 있다. 이런 점들을 증진시키는 것으로 많은 전문가들이 알고 있는 한 가지 접근방법이 1900년대초에 이탈리아인 마리아 몬테소리가 처음 실시한 몬테소리 학습법이다. 낸시 맥코믹 램부시는 오늘날 400개가 넘는 몬테소리 학교가 있는 미국에 이 학습법을 유행시키는 데 성공한다. 이 학습법은 발견과 조작 행동을 조성해주는 교육자료와 과제 등으로 어린이들이 스스로 학습하는 것을 도와준다. 그러한 탐구를 통해서 어린이들은 촉감을 발달시키고, 어른의 도움 없이 매일의 과제를 어떻게 하는지를 배운다. 다른 이점들로는 언어기술의 향상이나 과학, 음악, 미술 등의 요소들과의 친숙함이 포함된다.

éarly schóoling : 조기교육 awáreness [əwéərnis] *n.* 인식, 깨달음 self-cónfidence : 자신감, 자기신뢰 promóte [prəmóut] *v.* 증진시키다 be crédited with ~ : ~로 신뢰를 얻다, ~에 성공하다 for themsélves : 스스로 instrúctional matérials : 교육자료 facílitate [fəsíləteit] *v.* 조성하다, 촉진하다 discóvery [diskʌ́vəri] *n.* 발견 manipulátion [mənipjəléiʃən] *n.* 조작 explorátion [ekspləréiʃən] *n.* 탐구 sense of touch : 촉감 assístance [əsístəns] *n.* 도움 acquáintance with ~ : ~에 친숙

주제문 : 1~6행(첫 두 문장)   핵심어 : Montessori method

1. 문제의 핵심어 : main purpose
   본문의 정답찾기 : 둘째 문장에 핵심어 'Montessori method' 가 있다.
2. 문제의 핵심어 : Montessori method, first spreading
   본문의 정답찾기 : 5~7행
3. 문제의 핵심어 : a benefit of the Montessori method
   본문의 정답찾기 : 7~13행(The method helps … Other benefits …)
4. 문제의 핵심어 : following passage
   본문의 정답찾기 : 주제문 둘째 문장에 One approach …

가 있음을 참고한다.

【정답】 1. B 2. A 3. C 4. A

[17] 통조림은 오랜 기간 식품을 보존하는 한 가지 방법
이다. 그 공정은 용기에 음식물을 밀봉하고, 궁극적으로
부패를 야기할 수 있는 박테리아를 죽이기 위해 가열하는
것을 포함한다. 대부분의 통조림 식품이 기업에서 생산되
는 반면에, 어떤 것은 가정에서 만들어진다.

집에서 기른 사과, 토마토 같은 과일이나 채소들은 통
조림 하기에 가장 흔한 식품이다. 심지어 어떤 고기류도
통조림에 적절하다. 그러나 아보카도 같은 농산물은 가열
을 권장할 게 못된다. 왜냐하면, 맛이나 조직에 변화가 생
길 수도 있기 때문이다. 오이나 고추를 포함한 다른 식품
들은 처음 식초에 절여 보관되어 아주 저온에서 요리된
경우에만 통조림이 될 수 있다.

잘 통조림된 식품은 3년 이상도 보관될 수 있다. 만일
적절하게 밀봉되지 않았다면, 그 식품은 유기체의 성장으
로 부패될 수 있다. 심한 경우에, 박테리아는 보툴리누스
중독이라는 치명적인 형태의 중독을 일으킬 수 있다. 이
런 이유 때문에, 항아리나 병의 밀봉을 정기적으로 점검
하여, 이상 없이 잘 있는지 확인하는 것이 매우 중요하다.

can [kæn] *v.* 통조림하다 presérve [prizə́:rv] *v.* 보존(보관)하다
exténded [iksténdid] *adj.* 연장된, 오랜 seal [si:l] *v.* 밀봉하다
n. 도장 contáiner[kəntéinər] *n.* 용기, 그릇 evéntually
[ivéntʃuəli] *adv.* 궁극적으로 spóilage [spɔ́ilidʒ] *n.* 부패
homegrówn [hóumgróun] *adj.* 집에서 기른 be (not) advísable
to do :~하기를 권할 만 한(하지 않은) heat próduce : 농산물을 가열
하다 pickle [píkəl] *v.* 식초에 절여 보존하다, 피클로 하다 as long
as ~ : ~한도 까지 (= up to) órganism [ɔ́:rgənizəm] *n.* 조직체, 유
기체 fátal [féitl] *adj.* 치명적인 póisoning [pɔ́izəniŋ] *n.* 중독
régularly : 규칙적으로, 정기적으로 undistúrbed : 이상 없는, 동요
없는

주제문 : 첫 단락의 첫 문장   핵심어 : canning the food

1. 문제의 핵심어 : title
   본문의 정답찾기 : 주제문에 함축되어 있다.
2. 문제의 핵심어 : kill bacteria
   본문의 정답찾기 : 2~3행
3. 문제의 핵심어 : not suitable for canning
   본문의 정답찾기 : 7~9행
4. 문제의 핵심어 : bacteria
   본문의 정답찾기 : 12~15행

5. 문제의 핵심어 : botulism, avoid
   본문의 정답찾기 : 15~16행(For this reason…)

【정답】 1. D 2. B 3. D 4. C 5. B